BOBS
KIPLING'S GENERAL

Lord Roberts at the War Office, 1914, shortly before his death.
(*Mansell Collection*)

Bobs
Kipling's General

THE LIFE OF FIELD-MARSHAL
EARL ROBERTS OF KANDAHAR, VC

by
W. H. Hannah

'He is as full of valour as of kindness; Princely in both.'
HENRY V, IV, iii

LEO COOPER, LONDON

First published in Great Britain, 1972, by
LEO COOPER LTD
196 Shaftesbury Avenue, London WC2 H8JL
Copyright © *1972, Mrs W. H. Hannah*

ISBN 0 85052 038 X

Printed in Great Britain
by Ebenezer Baylis & Son Ltd
The Trinity Press, Worcester, and London

CONTENTS

ILLUSTRATIONS

MAPS

PREFACE

The story of Frederick Sleigh Roberts (Bobs to his generation) is essentially simple, for it is the life of a soldier of brilliance and renown in an Imperial age. He was immensely brave, and his soldiers, British and Indian alike, worshipped him. This was a commonplace in the Victorian age, only the degree of his distinction was unique.

Yet there were deeper undertones, for Roberts began his career in 1852, as orthodox a subaltern as ever set foot on a parade ground. In the last two years of his life, however, when an earl and a field-marshal, he became, in the service of a cause he loved, virtually a rebel. Roberts was a man of unflinching patriotism, and though his domicile was Irish, he was, as Queen Bess would have said 'mere English' to his marrow. It may be that he has something to teach the western world today.

CHAPTER I

Victorian Mosaic

To most people who lived through the year 1837, there may have seemed little momentous in its passage, yet in retrospect we know that that quiet year marked the opening of Britain's greatest era. Few can question that the Victorian age, ugly and marred as it often was, constituted one of the highest pinnacles of material and spiritual achievement that Britain has ever attained.

The girl who gave the age its name came to the throne as the youthful monarch of the most powerful nation in the world, and when she died in 1901, an ancient woman, Britain was still supreme. Yet in those same years, years during which General Frederick Sleigh Roberts was to achieve his fame, energies and powers came into being which were to change for ever the political, geographical, and social order of Europe. Europe—and Britain—would never again be the same. Though the nation had been immeasurably enriched in striking power and industrial wealth, the funeral cortège which set forth from Osborne to carry the aged Queen to her last resting place marked the term already set upon Britain's greatness. Few then recognized it, but the shadows were already closing, and the *Pax Britannica* was in pale decline.

Above all, the Victorian age was for Britain a time of peace; yet, paradoxically, her army was almost perpetually in action. Few would dispute that in Wellington and his Peninsular War generals, Britain had possessed a splendid officer corps, but by 1837 the laurels of Waterloo and Spain were a trifle faded, and the victors themselves already old. Nonetheless the spirit of the aged but formidable Duke still brooded over Horse Guards, and his influence lay heavy upon the army as a whole, even as far afield as India.

The result was stagnation, as became amply apparent when the Crimean War broke out after forty years of comparative peace. The army still used the methods of the Peninsula, but the military genius who had administered them was gone. Raglan, a pathetic shadow of the useful and heroic young officer he had been in Spain and at Waterloo, had only one basic rule with which to solve a conundrum—what would Wellington have done? But the Duke's incisive tones by then were stilled beyond recall, and there was no help to be gained from Raglan's associates.

When *The Times*, not yet its modern and respectable self, daringly quoted Chatham's acid comment that, 'I do not know what effect these names have on the enemy, but I confess they make me tremble' to describe the British military leaders of the day, there were few people to contradict.* Certainly no one could deny the courage of these men. At Waterloo, Raglan, then Lord Fitzroy Somerset, had endured the amputation of his right arm, unanaesthetized, without so much as a groan, and had then called out as they bore off the severed limb, 'Hallo! Don't you take away that arm till I have taken off my ring.' Nor could it be said that Raglan was in any way unique, for courage was common to them all. The fault lay not in the fibre of these men, nor even always in their intelligence, but in that instinctive resistance to technical change which at some stage of almost every nation's history seems to afflict its leaders. Yet, as soldiers before them and since have found, time waits for no man, and to fight the next war with methods culled from the last inevitably proves disastrous.

Nevertheless, it would not be just to regard the British armies in the Crimea as wholly antediluvian. Archaic though staff work, tactics, and administration often were, technical innovations *were* breaking through. The British Army was the first in the world to use telegraph communications on active service, and their construction of a light railway to link the Crimean front with the base was almost daring by the standards of 1854. Even those regiments who stormed the Alma in all the glory of shako and scarlet tunic were for the most part armed with the French Minié rifle or a later Enfield of even more revolutionary design.

* *The Reason Why*, Cecil Woodham-Smith, p. 136.

Nor could British military effort be judged solely on the basis of the Queen's Regiments at home. There had grown up overseas, mostly disregarded and invariably disdained, a rival army composed of European as well as sepoy troops, under the control of the East India Company. The origins and existence of 'John Company's' army stretched far back beyond either the birth or the coronation of Queen Victoria, but it was to achieve its zenith in her reign. Though John Company's senior commissioned ranks were often senile, in an age when antiquity was no bar to service, the army as a whole had seen plenty of action and the best of its units were very good indeed. It was, in every respect, an army apart, for in the Queen's Service, soldiering in India was cordially detested by those officers with enough money and influence to be particular (though to those who had neither, it sometimes offered useful opportunities for promotion). That it also had grave disadvantages for some on their return to England, was especially obvious when they had the ill-luck to serve such officers as the splenetic Lord Cardigan.* Yet Wellington himself had once been called a 'Sepoy General'.

There were many able men in the British Army at home, yet it was India which proved the crucible of military genius in the 1850s. Smouldering animosities amongst the native populations provided continual chances of action in an age when warfare in the colonies still resembled its European counterpart in essentials. Men such as Wolseley and Roberts learned their trade as subalterns in the reeking swamps of Burma and among the arid hills of the Frontier, and it was experience destined to stand them—and Britain—in good stead in years to come.

Inevitably, John Company's officers were influenced in military matters by their so-called social superiors in the Queen's Army, but as time went on they proved themselves remarkably independent. New traditions were forged and, under the stress of experience, new systems in India created a corps of officers who had little to learn from and much to teach their British Army counterparts. Unlike the Queen's Army, purchase of commissions formed no part of regimental tradition in the sepoy armies and, especially on the fierce frontiers, merit often came to the fore. Though rigid seniority held many able officers back, talent survived in a manner usually impossible at home.

* *The Reason Why.*

The shortcomings of the Queen's Army could be traced to a number of sources. Wellington's antipathy to any social or political change in the army was notorious, but it would be unjust to assume that his prejudices in these fields were translated into a resistance to technical change. Indeed, there is evidence to the contrary, for in the years immediately before his death, he was distressed by the state of Britain's defences, reputedly suffering insomnia over our undefended coast-line. *Punch* published a cartoon of the Duke, faced with a French invasion, trying to wake a comatose British Lion which merely replied, 'All right, old boy, I shall be ready when I'm wanted.'*

The real danger was that Wellington, like every masterful genius, had so dominated his subordinates, that his death left them barely capable of thinking for themselves. He himself had never found any difficulty in improving and adapting, especially in the field, but his highly conservative political responses had, in the case of certain of his senior subordinates, been translated into opposition to improved techniques, and the results were disastrous.

Beyond the resistance of the Duke, moreover, lay the inertia of Parliament and the British people, with all their traditional anti-military sentiment. Most vociferous of all in their opposition to the army were those Whig and Radical elements which had been gaining ground since the time of the controversy which led to the Reform Bill. In all, it was hardly surprising that the army needed an urgent overhaul. (None of these difficulties applied in the same measure to the sepoy armies, though they had peculiar problems of their own.)

Change, however, could not be stayed. The Duke proved mortal and with the passage of time the worst anachronisms and iniquities in the Queen's Army (such as the purchase of commissions) were swept away. Imperceptibly too, under the influence of such changes, the nature of the British corps of officers altered. Though the 'Gentleman' remained a social and sporting prototype, under the influence of world affairs their metamorphosis into professional military men proceeded, though not as steadily as in India. The squire, especially from Ireland, remained the backbone of the commissioned ranks, but now that ability rather than cash for purchase became the yard-stick of

* *Punch*, XIV, 33.

14

promotion, British Army officers began to study their business. In contrast to the Indian Army, career officers remained a minority in Britain for decades but their numbers began to swell sharply after 1870. Of such men, Kitchener was merely the personification; he was not unique. In reverse proportion, the dandified young subalterns with whom Disraeli had exchanged epigrams in his youth at Gibraltar, began to dwindle in an army increasingly preoccupied with the serious and sometimes bloody business of Imperial adventure. Dilettantes had existed but rarely in John Company's army, for life was too short and perilous for frivolity, and soldiers had to know their business if they were to stay alive.

Nonetheless, the commissioned ranks of the British and Indian Armies were steadily drawing closer. In the time of Clive, there had been able Company men, but the slur of mercenary traditions tainted them. 'Military adventurers' seemed an adequate description for many who had risen in a hard school and, in some cases, seen service under native princes. But by Roberts' time all this was changing. There were not many, perhaps, who had been to Eton with him (or before him) but there were many who shared his outlook and upbringing. Imperceptibly but steadily, the Company's service had become respectable, and its officer corps was becoming identical in social outlook with its equivalent in England. In military ability and experience they were often far in advance, as men such as John Nicholson were soon to show.

Meanwhile, several thousand miles away, in matters of equipment and tactics, the military world of Britain was also changing slowly. Die-hards, and there were many of them, still clung to the idea of infantry marching to battle in close-fitting scarlet tunics, thus forgetting the ideas with which Sir John Moore had imbued his riflemen on the heights above Sandgate in the dawn of the century. 'Brown Bess', the ancient musket, had been long since discarded. Yet change was not swift enough, as keen young officers were not slow to complain, especially during the tenure of the Duke of Cambridge as Commander-in-Chief, who, until his resignation in 1895, did all he could to block progress. There was, however, a limit to the obstructions that even royal dukes could raise, and military reform continued with slowly increasing momentum. Even the Square, beloved of traditionalists, was conceded to be unsuitable against such enemies as the Afghans, although British officers of the Indian Army had long since learned this in the hard school of experience. Further, the old and brutal disciplinary methods were gradually abandoned, and with them something of the stupefying drill routine by which redcoats had in the past been trained. Cardwell's army reforms of 1868–71 were only the first of a series of steps designed to raise the status and expectation of men who, till then, had been largely recruited from the ranks of unemployables and criminals. In India, especially, there was a harshness and horror attendant upon the lives of British soldiers which lives on, largely unread, in the lesser-known of Kipling's works; indeed something of these conditions still survived up to 1939. But again, this was a lesson which the officers of the Indian Army had already learned. If anything, the Indian Army before the Mutiny had tended to the other extreme, and the sepoys had been pampered to a degree unheard of amongst British regulars.

There were logical reasons for the differences in attitude between the officers of the British and Indian services. Whereas through the exigencies of 'Purchase', the commissioned ranks of British regiments were continually changing, those of the Indian units remained relatively stable. The age of retirement was also high and elderly colonels who had spent a lifetime of service with the same regiment, tended to sentimentalize over the brown and (in the case of Bengalis at least) meek soldiers they commanded. What they failed to realize until too late was that the gentle appearance of the Bengali sepoy concealed a sharp ferocity which, under the spur of religion and politics, was deadly. The British Army officers for their part, taking little trouble in getting to know their men, needed battle to teach them what their grandfathers of Peninsular days had learned— that in courage and loyalty, essential attributes for a first-class soldier, the 'Tommy' had few equals.

Little by little, the conditions of service improved as Cardwell's reforms, and the efforts of men like Roberts, lightened the burden of the British soldier during the closing years of the nineteenth century. It was long overdue. No one could doubt that the old British Army had been game, for every page of British history is studded with proof of its heroism. Bravery alone, however, had ceased to be sufficient. As von Clausewitz had expounded, the object of war was to defeat and destroy your enemy, and not to be killed yourself. With new schools of scientific warfare arising on the Continent, and above all in Prussia, a vast increase in tactical and technical skill was imperative if British heroism was not to be swept aside in massacre. As Moore had discovered over half a century earlier, something more than the old drill-sergeant's methods were required to produce a thinking as well as a brave and disciplined soldier.

Such was the context of Frederick Sleigh Roberts' life. It was a story of extraordinary adventure and courage. In the emerging school of professional 'Career' officers, he and Wolseley were foremost, and it is for their part in the transition that they must be judged. The metamorphosis was, for British arms, often painful, as attested by a number of minor but bloody colonial reverses in the days before Bobs had risen to fame. Yet it is not the least of these two officers' achievements that, when the real test came in 1914, the 'Old Contemptibles' were the equal of the best that either their allies or their enemies could put into the field. That this should have been so was the work of many men, some unjustly forgotten, but especially of Roberts and Wolseley. Where equipment was lacking, as it so often was, this was often the fault of political cheeseparing rather than of the prejudice, inactivity, or stupidity of military leaders, as is today often popularly believed.

Certainly there were nostalgic side-eddies, such as the mystical reverence accorded to horsed cavalry by its exponents, and few can doubt that a serious study of the potential of air and armoured warfare was grossly deferred by all nations, including Germany. Neither Bobs nor Wolseley would ever have claimed infallibility, but they did their best, rarely spared themselves in the process, and their achievements were great. Certainly, as a whole, the British General Staff were at least competent strategists and permitted themselves no such luxuries as the fallacious doctrine of *offensive à outrance*, which was to cost the French so dearly. In the later years of the First World War, the new leaders of the army which Roberts and Wolseley had done so much to build, found that the improvements in weapons of defence had cast a heavy disadvantage on the attacker: but then that was a burden which all armies endured in the First World War. It is against the background of their problems as well as of their successes and failures, that the greatest Victorian soldiers must be judged, and few impartial observers can doubt that they emerge with distinction.

To Wolseley must go the primary credit for forging the new British Army, not least because he was himself a British Service man. Yet Bobs, the Indian Army officer, came a close second. Wolseley was at his best amid the heights, battling for innovations, whilst Bobs, the greater field commander and a man of magnetic leadership, kept his feet firmly on the ground. It was Bobs who re-created the romantic legend of *la vie militaire*, long after it had been extinguished in a prosaic and industrialized Britain. His march from Kabul to Kandahar is an epic that will be remembered for as long as British traditions survive. In his final years in India he also transformed the life of the British soldier, and he shares with Kitchener the credit for modernizing the Indian Army. Later still, at an age when most men wear carpet slippers, he was to snatch victory from defeat in South Africa and lead his men to triumph over Kruger's commandos. As the last Commander-in-Chief of the British Army, he was then to find himself in an impossible position, yet even here he persevered against all odds. As the closing years of his life showed, Bobs was as unafraid of public abuse as he was of the enemy's bullets. He failed in his battle for conscription, but he saved Ulster at a time when Liberal politicians were prepared to barter her for a short-term political advantage.

It was inevitable that rival 'Wolseley' and 'Roberts' schools of thought should have grown up, principally among their staffs, for they were the two foremost European military figures of their age. Neither man desired this rivalry, though Wolseley's attitude helped to create it, for he disliked Bobs and regarded him with uninhibited jealousy. In fact, the rivalry was probably inescapable, for Wolseley was the more learned and Roberts the more compelling; but both had genius, and the Victorian land forces were of insufficient size to contain two such ducks in the same pond. The tragedy was that, after two men of their stamp, genius skipped a generation in the British armies and was absent when most needed—in the years immediately before and during the first half of the Great War. It was not until 1918 that the star of Allenby shone in full if belated splendour and it is significant that he, of all British generals, stood in the direct line of the Roberts tactical tradition.

Not the least of the Victorian soldier's difficulties lay in the immense diversity of his tasks. An army which is engaged in police actions as different as the Red River Rebellion, the Indian Mutiny, the First Zulu War, and the several Afghan campaigns is always bound to be at a disadvantage when trying to formulate a general policy for formation, tactics, and equipment—particularly in an age when communications were rudimentary. Colonial warfare created tough, courageous troops and brave, resolute, junior leaders but it did little or nothing to prepare higher commanders for campaign warfare on a national scale against European adversaries. The defenders of Rorke's Drift were immortal soldiers, but it is doubtful whether their experience could have contributed anything to the army's ability to cope with such problems as faced them at Mons. Twenty years earlier the answer might have been different, for then the gulf that separated 'savage' and conventional warfare was not so great. After 1870, however, the last lingering distinctions disappeared, in theory at least, for few discerning military commentators could question that the way to win European wars economically lay in the scientific approach.

The German Army, in contrast, had no Algeria or India to divert its energies and, in common with most potential aggressors, it knew exactly what it hoped to do. As a result, the best brains of the German General Staff were engaged in ceaseless preparation for 'The Great Day'. In contrast to the French and (still more) the British military leaders, the German Generals had strong political—and financial—support. Even the German colonies were of minor importance, prestigious rather than tangible assets, and punitive expeditions against them tended often to resemble manœuvres with live ammunition against living targets. It is impossible to imagine von Lettow-Vorbeck and his predecessors in Africa being criticized with the same venom as were Bobs and Kitchener over their Imperial campaigns.

The life of Frederick Sleigh Roberts that follows makes no claim to establish milestones of military history. It tells straightforwardly how a young man, sailing for the East at a time when

Britain was at the height of her power, won honour for himself and glory for his country. We shall learn something of his life, of the conditions in which he worked and fought, and of the armies in which he served.

It was a brave and splendid age. Though peril and disease abounded, and a few weeks' campaigning reduced bright uniforms to rags, there was a magic in the scarlet and green of the marching troops which the few still alive who saw them will never forget. It was a bold and spirited age, in which simple codes of honour were acknowledged and largely followed. The commanders led from the front and were often men of high intelligence and chivalry, and almost always of surpassing courage. Moreover, once fusion between the scientific and the traditional had been achieved, their foresight was often penetrating. In particular, men of the stamp of Napier,* Wolseley, and Roberts meticulously planned their campaigns down to the last detail. The changed conditions of war meant inevitably that the splendid uniforms and the brave music of drum and fife became more and more the exception, as the army changed its vocation and became units of soberly clad craftsmen.

It has been said that Roberts and the other great Victorian generals remain famous long after their deaths because of their environment rather than their gifts, but it is probably generally true that the times tend to produce the leaders suited to them. Who can deny that but for the age of Empire few today would have heard of Roberts? Plainly he owes much of his fame to the fact that his career coincided with the Imperial noon-day, creating valuable openings for his talents and flattering consequences for himself.

His gifts were nonetheless dramatic, and the results considerable, not least in the Indian Army where, by the end of his service, Roberts had achieved a degree of operational efficiency far in advance of the British Service. This was especially so in marksmanship, for the limited supply of ammunition and the unrealistic nature of the range work at home produced a standard so poor among British troops that, during the South African War, Boer commandos openly boasted that they could approach infantry units with relative impunity.

Yet it was basically the same army, though re-equipped and

* Lord Napier of Magdala, an Indian Army officer.

retrained, which marched into battle in 1914 and their rifle-fire was then so accurate and rapid as to be mistaken by querulous German prisoners for machine-gun fire. They were clad in khaki, armed with breech-loading Lee-Enfield rifles, and fought for almost the first time in close support of the *Pantalons Rouges* of France, instead of against them. Spiritually, nonetheless, the British Expeditionary Forces were the heirs of those immortal Fusiliers who at Albuera in 1811 had stormed the French positions, undeterred by loss until at last, in Napier's historic words, '1,500 unwounded men, the remnant of 6,000 unconquerable British soldiers, stood triumphant on the fatal hill.' For their courage, they had to thank their discipline and their tradition; but for the innovations which had brought them, technically and professionally, into the twentieth century the 'Old Contemptibles' could thank a small number of politicians, a handful of military writers, and a much larger and more energetic group of officers, of whom Wolseley, Roberts, and Kitchener were the most prominent. The same was true of the Indian Army which, though it showed less tenacity than the British Army in France, performed dauntless service in the Middle East. Without sepoy troops, where would the British in Mesopotamia have been, and in the Second World War what division excelled the record of the 4th Indian (Red Eagle) Division?

By 1939, Bobs had been dead for a quarter of a century, but his tradition lived on for, more than any other man, he had come before his death to personify the best of what men still mean when they speak of the 'Indian Army'. He was not, nor would he claim to be, the sole fount of military wisdom of his age, but he and Wolseley were undoubtedly the two greatest—perhaps the only really great—British generals between Wellington and Wavell. The consequences of their work were momentous for England since, in the First World War, without such a regular British force imbued with the courage of the past and the skills of the present, Britain must inevitably have gone down to ruin before the citizen armies organized by Kitchener could take the field. As it was, the professionals sacrificed themselves, buying time for their incurably civilian countrymen to organize into new battalions. The fact that the force commander, Sir John French, was unsuited to his task is no valid criticism of the

British Army, or of its architects, since in this as in all its principal defects (such as size and the shortage of equipment) the remedies lay outside the soldiers' control. The same was true of the Indian regular formations that supported them throughout the early months in France.

By the time that peace was restored, the old brave ideal of an Empire on which the sun would never set was fading, for something of the soul of Britain had been buried with her myriad soldiers in the mud of the Somme, and at Passchendaele. In India, nationalist movements had gathered fresh momentum and the new Britain lacked either the strength or the resolution to deal with them. Decades were to pass before the last Imperial finale in Africa, but after 1936 few discerning men could doubt whither the trend led. It was upon the Indian Empire that most of Bob's energy and skill had been lavished, together with the blood and courage of the troops he had led, and yet, in retrospect, we can see that their efforts were not wholly wasted. For the military machine built up by Wolseley, Roberts, Kitchener, and a handful of others survived, in the same essential fabric, to win victory with England's allies, in 1918 and again in 1945, all over the world. Though the weapons changed, the spirit and framework did not, and the Britons who fought and died so tenaciously before Monte Cassino were often the sons of fathers who had gone 'over the top' less than thirty years before in France, sometimes in the same regiments.

The Indian soldiers also proved themselves in World War II as they had in the First War, a quarter of a century before. Often bitterly reviled by their political fellow-countrymen, the sepoys remained overwhelmingly true to their allegiance. At Keren, in Egypt and Libya, in Burma and the Arakan, they fought resolutely under British and Indian officers and won high honour for their courage. Steeped in a tradition which the British had long begun to spurn, most men of military family in the Punjab would as late as 1945 have been able to describe Bobs with passable accuracy. How many in London could have done the same? In short, though the British and Imperial-Indian military machines often faltered, they never failed, and in their very tenacity they went far to redeem all other faults.

It is in an attempt to describe this man, who personified so much of the old British tradition now dead, that the following pages were written. Most of the material fruits of his work have withered with the Empire he served. But gallantry, humour, and, sometimes, honour survive, and these were all virtues in which he excelled. There is a fairy-tale quality in his life and spirit, a magnetism in his character which can never be excelled. 'As full of valour as of kindness', he was, 'princely in both'.

CHAPTER II

The Jewel in the Crown

To the Great Britain of the 1850s, India was as remote as is Antarctica to us; perhaps more so. Sea travel was slow, precarious, and uncomfortable. Moreover, there were important distractions at home. The Industrial Revolution was reaching new pitches of intensity, national prosperity was achieving new zeniths, and each brought fresh problems in its train. Above all, the media of news dissemination were slow and, judged by the standards of today, extremely amateur. Journalism was ponderous, newspapers expensive, and the news that filtered through from the fringes of Empire was often weeks out of date (though for all that not necessarily more inaccurate than similar items today).

It is hardly surprising that to the man in the street, India and, still more, such countries as Burma and Malaya were as insubstantial shadows. India was far from being the brightest jewel of the Imperial diadem which she later became. There was a vague popular awareness of Clive, who had won great battles, and perhaps even of Hastings, who had fought a seven-year legal action to clear his name, but little more.

Among the upper classes, knowledge of India was little more precise, and antipathy correspondingly more pronounced. Stylish military men abhorred service in India. Aristocrats remembered with distaste the graceless 'Nabobs'—as the plutocrats of John Company were called—who had descended on Britain towards the end of the eighteenth century, their pockets filled with illicitly acquired gold. As for the rich industrialists of the 'Black Country', they were too busy making money to bother about such remote places. India was unknown to most men, but to the upper classes India was indelibly bourgeois;

and it was not even, in their view, an attractive middle class. No Kipling had yet arisen to paint the romance, the perils, and the mystery of Imperial service. There was nothing to recommend life in faraway India to mid-Victorian England.

It is hardly surprising in these circumstances that the British in India tended to emerge as a tribe apart, born of and returning to the home isles, but maturing their own traditions, living in their own special ways, and even speaking a language which though emphatically English, was full of strange terms that were both incomprehensible and irritating to those who had never lived in the East. Patriots to a man, gallant to a degree, the British Indians tended to find themselves out of touch with England and Englishmen when (if they were lucky enough to survive that long) they returned home on pension, in the fullness of years, to die.

The servants of John Company soldiered and administered, fought and died, uncomplainingly and for a pittance, with the minimum of control from the directors. In an age when communications were poor and haphazard, a close and inhibiting control from the centre was impossible. Subordinate commanders and even civil commissioners, if they could not be controlled, had to be trusted instead and the results were, on the whole, good. Political life in England had also much to do with this state of affairs. MPs were not professionals; by and large, amongst the Tories at least, they were usually country gentry and, disliking controls themselves, they were not eager to impose them on their fellow-countrymen. Although the British Indians came from all types of home, they were in the main middle class, though once out in India, they tended to form themselves into castes, as the Indians also did, until in the end 'Poonah' became a music hall joke. Some were drunkards, of course, some were lechers, some were drug addicts. A few practised extortion and took bribes. But in the main they were men of high integrity, who faced death without complaint, endured years of separation from their children, and enforced a rigid standard of honour among their own kind. In a land where bribery had been taken for granted, they became famed for integrity. Taxes were just, landlords were controlled, and social diseases such as *Thuggee* were crushed.

Among such men, the name of Roberts deservedly stands

high. A Tom Thumb in size, he had by the end of his life become a giant of legend. The little field-marshal, whiskered, stern, and yet somehow conveying an impression of kindliness, held in the hearts of the late Victorians a position nowadays reserved for cinema actors. A lord of the far frontiers, Bobs, on his Arab charger 'Vonolel', brought a whiff of romance to pallid London and the industrial masses of England. Vicariously they enjoyed the heroism and agony of a score of desperate battles in distant passes and, through the medium of the painters of the Imperial noonday, a vision of the British square, always outnumbered and ultimately always triumphant, locked in mortal combat with swarming heathen tribes.

All this lay in the far and undreamt future when on 20 February, 1852, Bobs set sail for India as a newly commissioned officer, freshly passed out of the Honourable East India Company's military academy at Addiscombe. Puny after a delicate childhood, he would never today have been considered for army service. As the son of a serving general in the Company's employment, he started off with a built-in advantage, but so had dozens before him. India, the land of promise, was also the land of tragedy, as a multitude of scattered and forgotten graves recorded. Even the distinction of being an old Etonian, unusual as it was in the Company's service, had little meaning in a sub-continent where survival of the fittest was the iron rule.

Character, coupled with an extraordinary zeal for his profession, were the two factors which took Bobs in the end to the heights, and his love of soldiering was certainly no accident, for service in the armed forces of the Crown had become a tradition among the Anglo-Irish squirearchy. A garrison race, their genius lay in battle, and long before Wellington had raised their standard to immortal heights, no campaign had been complete without its quota of Protestant subalterns from Ireland, as often as not leading Southern Catholic troops.

The voyage proved uneventful, if slow, and Bobs took time off to enjoy Cairo where, inevitably, he stayed at Shepheard's Hotel. Another Anglo-Irish passenger who journeyed with him bore a name without which no British or Indian force was ever complete; the Goughs stud almost every chapter of Victorian military history, and usually with glory. Years later Bobs was to befriend Sir John Gough's nephew, Hubert, and the Roberts family were to stand by him at the time of his unjustified dismissal from the Fifth Army in 1918.

On 1 April Bobs landed at Calcutta, and received his posting to the Bengal Artillery Headquarters at Dum-Dum. Few youngsters of his generation had much good to say of Fort William, and Bobs was no exception. But, despite a dismal reception, since most of the garrison was away on service, India remained for him the land of adventure. Throughout his life, peril was to act as a stimulant, and this was fortunate since only the very brave or the very undiscerning knew peace of mind in mid-Victorian India. Whatever his station in life, death and disease in many and terrible forms were constantly at the white man's elbow. For the non-commissioned and their families, life was a brutal and often unsuccessful struggle to survive, and even for the officers and their wives, luxury was merely a comparative term. The Colonel's lady and Judy O'Grady were sisters in courage, endurance, and a profound knowledge of tragedy.

The India to which Bobs was now introduced stood on the eve of The Mutiny; an India on which the palsied grip of John Company had already begun to loosen; above all, an India in which, deferring to the sacred rule of seniority, old and rigid men sought to govern vast territories still incompletely pacified, and peopled by fierce and warlike tribes. There was ability in plenty, courage unlimited, but promotion depended less on ability than on dead men's shoes. At a time when a major-general of sixty-nine was a relative youngster, the prospects for quick advancement were grim. The great figures of the past were gone, and those of the future still to come. Only on the lawless borders, free from the paralysis of government, did the great spirit still survive amongst men such as Nicholson and the Lawrences.

To young Roberts, however, India was still a world of promise and he took to the life with alacrity. As a Company's officer, he had seemingly little to expect except years of poor pay, slow promotion and the constant derision of his social superiors—the officers of the British Army who held the coveted Queen's Commission. Even supernumerary second-lieutenants of Bengal Artillery, however, could still dream, and extroverted Bobs rarely wasted time in melancholy. His four months at Dum-Dum seemed, as he afterwards wrote, 'like four years', but by the end of July they were over, and early August saw him on the road to Peshawar.

An age accustomed to jet aircraft and space flight is inclined to take travel for granted, but in the India of the 1850s there were few Europeans disposed to a similar view. Though *Thuggee* was to all intents and purposes dead, slain by the genius of Col Sleeman, ordinary *dacoits* were still an ever-present reality, and there were other and equal perils attendant upon long travels across the countryside. All this young Bobs now discovered as he set out for the north-west, a journey which was to take him three months. The first stages passed easily enough; by barge as far as Benares and from there by the Indian equivalent of stage coach to Allahabad.

Thence he went to Meerut, where his fancies were much taken by the *élan* and efficiency of the Bengal Horse Artillery, a *corps d'élite*, whose uniform included such military extravagances as brass helmets, red plumes, and white breeches. To Bobs, as romantic as he was ambitious, only one solution seemed possible, and from then on he was, as he wrote, fired by a 'fixed resolve to leave no stone unturned in the endeavour to become a horse gunner'. At Meerut the roadway ended, and the rest of the journey had to be made by *doolie*. At first sight the *doolie* seemed picturesque enough and Bobs has left a dramatic word-picture of the coolies shuffling through the night, bearing his litter behind the torch-bearer, who held his stinking, smoking beacon continually aloft. But the picturesque tended to pall after 600 miles, and there were other uses for the torch, such as scaring off wild animals, as Wolseley found six years later, when a Bengal tiger sprang among his bullocks on their way north-west to action in the Mutiny.

It was an exhausting method of travel, largely by night, when the coolies kept up an incessant chatter, and the *dak* bungalows where travellers spent the heat of the day left much to be desired. Kipling's short stories are filled with references to these isolated wayside halts, the scene of much that was tragic and grim in the forgotten passages of nineteenth-century British India. Frederick Roberts was, however, tough in sinew and spirit for all his sickly childhood, and it was in high heart that he reached Peshawar, focal centre of the Frontier.

This first posting proved the key to his subsequent career,

for the North-West Frontier was even then the legendary rim of Empire, scene of some of the greatest triumphs and disasters ever experienced by British arms in Asia. Once a 'Frontier' man, there was no escape from its thrall, and Bobs succumbed immediately. To those who liked to live dangerously, the gaunt and indomitable Pathans had an irresistible appeal and, among their savage mountains, they were always spoiling for a fight. It was on the Frontier that Bobs had his first taste of 'service', and, fittingly, it was upon the Frontier that his most memorable service was achieved.

All this, however, lay far in the future, and for the present Bobs had the dual duties of acting as ADC to his father and learning his trade. Aged nearly sixty-nine, Sir Abraham Roberts had only now succeeded to command of a division, and such was the competition that he considered himself lucky to have achieved it so early. Father and son were virtual strangers to one another, after years of enforced separation, but they seem to have agreed very well. An engraving of the old man in *Forty-One Years in India* shows him in civilian clothes, nearing his dotage but still proudly upright. Unfortunately, their service together was destined to be short-lived. Decades of service in a cruel climate had undermined the old general's health, and in a matter of months he was compelled to retire.

Garrison life continued to absorb Bobs for the next year. As ADC to his father he held something of a privileged position, but he was conscientious at his battery duties, and the CO of the artillery battalion* to which he belonged was not a man in any event inclined to allow subalterns, however well connected, to shirk regimental routine. Popular, and a vigorous sportsman, Bobs entered into the social life of Peshawar enthusiastically and made many friends among the young officers of his own seniority who were to endure for the rest of his life. It was in Peshawar too that he developed the extraordinary sympathy and love for British troops which were to distinguish him throughout his service in an age when the European rank-and-file were too often treated, even by their own regimental officers, as expendable ne'er-do-wells. It was an affection that Kipling shared to the full.

The East India Company included in its armies European

* East India Company Gunners referred to battalions rather than regiments.

units, often of very high calibre, and amongst these the discipline tended to be almost as rigid as in the Queen's force. In contrast, control amongst many of the sepoy regiments was often lax with the Indian troops, themselves immune from corporal punishment, permitted to watch the flogging of white soldiers. Bobs himself could never bear to watch flogging, which he rightly regarded as brutal and degrading. When the need arose, he could exact vengeance and restore discipline with ruthless precision, but, especially with European troops, he preferred to rely upon his own peerless magnetism and powers of leadership, and they rarely failed.

By September 1853, trouble, perennially present on the Frontier, frothed over afresh, this time with the murder of Col Mackeson, the Commissioner of Peshawar. The British of the mid-Victorian age were rarely slow to act, and the Pathan murderer was promptly seized and as summarily hanged and his body burned. Nowadays such action would have attracted the attention of the world but the world of 1853 had other matters to consider. Only the tribes, already spoiling for a fight, chose to regard the cremation as an insult to be avenged in blood, and the first action took place, to Bobs' dismay, while he was away, escorting his father to Nowshera on the first stage of the old man's journey home to retirement. Sorry as he was to see his father go, Bobs' regret at missing action seems to have overshadowed all else.

After two years' service in India, it is indicative of the risks he and his countrymen had to face that Bobs should have been seriously weakened by persistent bouts of fever. The prescription, as so often when doctors do not know what else to offer, was a holiday in Kashmir. Whether his health improved as a result records do not reveal, but his reaction to that beautiful and tragic country was never in doubt. A Spartan in a land that appealed unequivocally to the senses, Bobs (unlike many other young officers) found no pale hands beside the Shalimar, but he was never to forget the haunting beauty of the Kashmiri scene.

On his return to Peshawar, he found to his delight that he had, as he put it, 'Been given my jacket',* and if his pleasure was somewhat lessened by the prospect of a posting to Ambala, that could always be contrived away—as indeed it was. The truth

* Accepted into the Horse Artillery.

was that Bobs usually managed, in a very honourable fashion, to get what he wanted. Luck and a courtly presence were to favour him until the end of his life.

The unit he now joined was composed, as befitted a crack corps, entirely of Europeans, the bulk of them Irish. Of magnificent physique, most, as he remarked, 'could have lifted me up with one hand.' Like all good officers, he was immediately enthusiastic and fiercely loyal to their interests, whilst their initial amusement at this Tom Thumb of a subaltern changed speedily to admiration of his horsemanship and courage, for neither mount nor competition defeated Bobs for long. A pleasant existence, it was well suited to his temperament, and by the usual rules of the East India Company's military forces, there it should have ended some forty years later with a colonel's or—at most—a major-general's pension and a retirement passage to England, if he was fortunate enough, let it be repeated, to have survived that long.

That this was not the ending was due to many circumstances, amongst them Bobs' own transcendent genius. The first step in the right direction was when, again on sick leave, he lunched with another Anglo-Irishman, Col Becher. Becher seems to have taken a liking to this fever-wasted but indomitable stripling who also happened to be the son of a general. Bobs, moreover, though never slow to challenge what he believed wrong, was assiduous in his attentions to the 'top brass', and the results throughout his career proved fruitful. Now, as thereafter, his magic touch proved true. As Quartermaster-General, Becher headed a department of incomparably more scope and importance than its name suggests today. He also held interesting appointments within his patronage, appointments vital to a young officer if he was not to spend a lifetime on the barrack square, rising by tedious steps to command of a regiment when he was too old to enjoy it.

Aware of all these factors, Bobs would have been mad to turn down a chance of staff employment for, despite his pride in the Horse Artillery, promotion lay through the staff. Regimental service would also greatly have reduced his opportunity for active soldiering since, whilst every expedition had its quota of staff officers, a regiment stationed far from troubled theatres could spend many years without operational experience. When

therefore he was offered the chance of officiating as DAQMG*
early in 1856, he grasped it avidly. Paradoxically, though he was
henceforth to see virtually no regimental service, his career
proved to be one long vista of the action for which he craved.
Appetite quickened, he set himself to learn Hindustani and, after
passing the test with flying colours, he was confirmed as a
substantive officer on the staff. His feet were now firmly set on
the ladder of success.

The next year was uneventful, with short spells of regimental
duty interspersed with staff duties. Trouble on the Frontier had
been followed by relative tranquillity, with the Amir of
Afghanistan leaning towards the British for help against a
belligerent Persia. Though the Shah's drums beat loudly for a
time, British arms carried with them a heavy prestige, and
British soldiers had the reputation for shooting straight. The
trouble came to nothing, and the real significance lay in the fact
that the Amir of Afghanistan, Dost Mahomed, did not forget
Britain's help. When, a few months later, the Indian Mutiny
burst like a cyclone over Northern India, Dost Mahomed, with a
gratitude as unusual as it was unexpected, never wavered. In the
darkest hours of the British Raj, when the Company's troops
were fighting for their lives, their north-west frontier remained
secure—it was a debt of honour not altogether generously
redeemed.

By April, 1857, the dark clouds that presaged the Mutiny
were piling high, and towards the end of that month an event,
insignificant on the surface but of extraordinary influence on
Bobs' career occurred when, as a staff officer surveying Cherat,
he unexpectedly found his tent pitched beside that of the Deputy
Commissioner, Lt-Col John Nicholson. That meeting between
the future Commander-in-Chief and the tall, black-bearded
Nicholson was to prove one of the great formative influences of
Bobs' life.

Among all the great names and personalities with which the
history of British India is studded, few can match that of
Nicholson for sheer force of character, vigour, and achievement.
In strength and courage, he was already a legend in his middle
thirties, and his magnetism and powers of leadership would have
set him apart in any age and nation. Strengthened as these great

* Deputy Assistant Quartermaster-General.

gifts were by his patriotic fervour, Nicholson was a man to whom others instinctively looked in times of crisis and, as the Mutiny was soon tragically to reveal, they did not look in vain. It was no accident or quirk of the Oriental mind that at this time a sect of Indians existed who called themselves the 'Nicholseyns', worshipping their hero as a minor deity. His own reaction to the cult was equally characteristic for, being neither conceited nor patient, he invariably lost his temper and beat them.

This was the man upon whose company young Roberts was now briefly thrown—a man who loved children, yet never married; a man who could threaten to shoot a dithering superior in times of crisis, but exacted an iron obedience from those who served under him; a man for whom his soldiers would gladly have died, yet who blew mutineers, as often as not without trial, from the mouths of cannon. It was with this man that Bobs was destined to serve, after the interval of a few short weeks, in the bloody passages of the Indian Mutiny.

Theirs was to be a short friendship, for if it was forged in peace, it was tested in battle and ended with Nicholson's heroic death on the eve of victory beside the Kabul Gate in Delhi, but it was an experience which Bobs, even at the pinnacle of his fame, never forgot. As he wrote, many years later, when an old man, 'John Nicholson was a name to conjure with in the Punjab. . . . Nicholson impressed me more profoundly than any man I had ever met before or have ever met since. I have never seen anyone like him. He was the beau-ideal of a soldier and a gentleman.' High praise from the pen of Victorian England's most dashing general. It is also a description that sketches Bobs himself to a nicety.

CHAPTER III

The Great Mutiny

THE story of the Indian Mutiny is a well worn path, and nowadays it is fashionable to ascribe its causes to the brutality of white sadists upon brown innocents, though the truth was far from this. Not cruelty, but neglect; not ferocity but idleness; not the excesses of youth, but the supine complacency of old age were the real causes of the Mutiny. The Government's sins were those of omission rather than commission. It was a desire to profit by the palsy of their rulers that provided the plotters with their fundamental inspiration, even though immediate grievances amongst certain classes made their path the easier.

There could be no denying that the sepoy army had degenerated of recent years. The best of John Company's units, white and brown, were, as we have said, very good indeed but the best were too few. Between the crack corps, vigorously officered, and the second-rate or nondescript, lay a vast gulf. In general, the commissioned ranks were a great deal more experienced than their opposite numbers in the Queen's Regiments, but even this was not enough, for whilst the inefficient officer in Victoria's service had the sturdy echelons of British NCOs to fall back on, sepoy units stood or fell by the leadership of their officers. The signs of this slow degeneration had not passed unnoticed by an observant native populace. Bobs' beloved Horse Gunners might manœuvre endlessly, their accoutrements gleaming in the bright sun, but there were other regiments—and too many of them—where the officers were dirty and drunken, and the sepoys, relieved of the discipline that had held them together, lounged insolently, refusing to salute and spitting covertly in the dust after their superiors had passed. Nor was the degeneration confined to the army. If anything, it was less marked amongst the soldiers than amongst the populace at large, for the soldiers at least had periodic bouts of action to keep them up to the mark.

The truth was that John Company had fallen on evil days. Even the directors at home, once far-sighted, had relapsed into apathy, and as secretariats multiplied, field-control waned. Gambling, fashionable amongst the upper classes in the England of Regency days, had imperceptibly become *démodé* under Victoria's stricter régime, but in India its popularity remained to blight the worth of too many of the official classes, for men in debt rarely make good commissioners or colonels.

It would be wrong to suggest that any of these shortcomings was universal, but there was sufficient decay to smear the Company in the eyes of a native population that admired strength but was always critical and always ready to take advantage of weakness. Like the Curate's Egg, John Company's rule was good in parts; the trouble was that too much of it had recently become bad. All this had been noted by the best of the Company's servants, but the defects in organization were too deep-seated for individuals, in most cases, to alter. Even the structure of the Company's forces created a grave disadvantage, for the armies were divided into presidential commands. Geography and poor communications made it necessary that Bengal, Madras, and Bombay should each be organized into independent military entities, but it was suicidal to regard them as wholly separate organizations, each with its own traditions, training procedures, and regulations. Even more dangerous was the tendency to rely overwhelmingly in certain areas on one class or one race for recruiting. The Bengal Army provided a prime example of this, for its sepoy strength included sixty per cent of high caste Hindus, a fair proportion being Brahmin. In Madras, the proportion of Hindu sepoys was even higher, despite the availability of a tough and valiant Muslim race—the Moplahs.

All these shortcomings appear self-evident in retrospect, but it took the catastrophe of 1857 to open the eyes of the high command to the necessity for mixed-composition regiments, and even then years passed before the idea was implemented. Yet there can be no doubt that, had regiments from Tamil-speaking, Maharatti, and Sikh areas been included in the Bengal Army, the flow of information to the authorities in the months before the outbreak would have been far greater, and the Mutiny would have been more spasmodic when it did come. Even then, so fatuous was the attitude of some of the officers and rather more of the civilian administrators, that they would still in all probability have buried their heads in the sand. In their eyes the sepoy could do no wrong.

Military intelligence apart, the Government of India had excellent reasons for expecting trouble, even if the extent of it was a general surprise, for there were several fertile causes of genuine discontent already existing. The Native State of Oudh, in particular, had long since been the scene of disgraceful oppression by its own dynasty, and it was inevitable that sooner or later the Company should intervene in the name of justice and sound administration, as in fact it had done in so many other parts of India. Nonetheless, Company innovations had often been harsh and tactless, exciting fear amongst the *Zamindars*** throughout the north that they were to be dispossessed.

Inevitably, those with a genuine grievance did not stand alone, for India was the home of intrigue, and plotters were not wanting to fish in troubled waters. Local Indian newspapers, allowed full rein by a Government steeped in the tradition of freedom for the press, poured out a steady stream of sedition into the receptive minds of the semi-educated. Some Indian noblemen, incensed by real or imagined grievances, and others who saw additional power for themselves as the prize, were quick to lend their support to such incipient discontents. Even a few Frenchmen, still resentful of their exclusion by British arms three-quarters of a century earlier, were not above dabbling in the muddy waters of intrigue. Above all, and infinitely powerful amongst a superstitious peasantry, an old tradition throve that British rule would topple a century after Plassey—and Clive had won Plassey in 1757.

All these factors had combined with a hundred others to mark 1857 as the year of destiny. *Suttee*, the practice of burning Hindu widows alive, might not always commend itself to the widows themselves but it certainly yielded attractive dividends to the Brahmin priests, and when the moment of vengeance came they were not to forget that the British had abolished it.

* Land owners.

The most publicized cause, however, was a blunder for which the British rulers had little excuse. Though it was only the immediate cause of the Mutiny, the decision of the Director-General of Ordnance to supply grease which included elements of the fat of pigs and cattle to ease the loading of the Enfield rifle was a gaffe of the first order. If the cow was sacred to the Hindu, the pig was anathema to the Muslim. Such an innovation would probably have caused trouble at the best of times, but in an army as run down as the Bengal Army, and as oppressed by grievance and ill-discipline, it pushed matters over the edge.

By mid-April the tension was mounting fast and sinister omens increasing. The magistrate of the Goorgaon District had reported in March that *chupattis** were being passed from village to village as a signal and the despatches were multiplying. 'From the north to the south; from the east to the west' went the message, whose meaning none admitted to knowing. Already, too, the rumours without which no bazaar was complete were spreading. 'All sepoys are to be baptized.' 'The children of Princes are to be reared as Christians.' But this time it was gossip with a difference, for the rumours were believed. Matters soon took a form familiar to the colonial administrator of the mid-twentieth century, but then still novel to the British, as shadowy figures slipped from door to door. Cantonment houses also caught fire with unaccountable regularity—too unaccountable and too regular for their British occupants' comfort. A few old and trusted servants (and sometimes even sepoys) slipped into an admired sahib's study to warn in whispers of the peril, but in the main there was only a sinister silence.

Nowadays such information would have brought the Special Branch down to investigate, thick as flies on honey, but in 1857 there was no Special Branch, and what existed of the Indian police was embryonic and no more reliable than the sepoy army. Above all, senior officers, relaxed over their evening port in such comfort as the climate would allow, were not prepared to listen to those of their subordinates who did discern the true state of affairs. At Government House, Canning writhed and fretted in the Calcutta heat but his subordinates, despite their experience, lacked his intuition. Warnings to General Anson, the Commander-in-Chief, India (though a Queen's Army man),

* Flat cakes of unleaven bread.

went unheeded. An Anglo-Irish cavalry subaltern, inevitably named Gough, was warned by an Indian officer of the exact time planned for the Mutiny, but when he sought to relay the message to his Commanding Officer, Col George Smyth of the 3rd Light Cavalry at Meerut, Smyth insulted him.

In such an atmosphere the days dragged on with omens multiplying and official ineptitude supreme. Sepoys refused orders to load, and were court-martialled. It was weeks now since Mangal Pande, a sepoy of the 34th, had murdered his adjutant and sergeant-major at Barrackpore, a few weeks less since he had been hanged, but still the whisper went round, 'Remember Mangal Pande.' Not all the British were blind. Here and there officers were taking precautions on their own responsibility. The British rank and file were disinclined to trust their sepoy comrades-in-arms. In Lucknow Sir Henry Lawrence, doyen of the great administrators of the north, had long since made his dispositions. Similarly, in the Frontier area, centred on Peshawar where Bobs was stationed, little was left to chance, for the men in charge were experienced, tough, and courageous. They were, above all, young. Edwardes, the Commissioner, was thirty-seven, Nicholson was thirty-five, and Chamberlain, commanding the Punjab Frontier Force, thirty-seven. Untrammelled by the lethargy of age, they were firm in their refusal to prejudice security by sloth. Above all, when the moment came, by striking hard they were to prove that decisive and timely action meant more than any concentration of armed men under irresolute commanders.

In Meerut, contrastingly, few men were to prove resolute. While Brigadier Archdale Wilson dithered and Col Smyth scoffed, a very few junior officers discerned the shape of things to come, only to have their opinions contemptuously brushed aside. In the barrack rooms the reverse held true, with white soldiers and junior NCOs turning over plans to disarm the sepoy regiments. British troops had little cause to love their Indian counterparts, and they held the fighting qualities of the Bengal Army in low esteem. The tragedy was that when battle opened, paralysis at the top prevented British troops from being effectively used. No plans existed; no dispositions had been made at Meerut, and so the 60th Rifles were marched back to quarters to change into campaign uniform after Church Parade whilst, a few hundred yards away, British women were dying under the impact of countless violations or, disembowelled, lay spread and naked, their bodies gleaming under the smoky flare of a hundred fires.

It was indeed only from the north-west, where youth and courage ruled supreme, that salvation was to come.

*　　　*　　　*

So the opening salvoes of the Mutiny thundered through the evening shadows of the 10 May, and by next sunset the trail of slaughter had sent Delhi into blazing revolt. At Lahore, Deputy-Commissioner Montgomery and Brigadier-General Corbett proved the equal of the native troops and, parading them, ordered that they throw down their arms. When the sepoys hesitated, an 'About Turn' revealed the 81st (British) Regiment, grimly ready, and beside them Irish gunners standing by their cannon, linstocks aflame in their hands.

In the Punjab generally, all went according to plan, for the quality of its administration was high, its military commanders decisive, and the rural population true. It was no accident that, thereafter, the Punjab should have become the core of the British Raj. Meanwhile, at Cawnpore, Lucknow and a dozen other places the flames of Mutiny burned high with, too often, administrative officers actively impeding the military command. Some soldiers in high places were to fail in the hour of their test, but others were to find the path to victory hedged with every conceivable obstacle. 'The sepoys are loyal.' 'We must not show alarm.' 'It would be an insult to the Indians.' So ran the arguments against positive action, arguments pressed in the teeth of all evidence. The refusal of the administration to countenance resolute steps in the hour of crisis proved fatal.

But in Peshawar there was no mistake. Hardly had the news of calamity come in from Delhi before John Nicholson, who feared no man, was busy plundering the mails for intelligence. With an Empire falling about his ears, was this the time to pause for the sake of legality? The fruits justified his actions, for all the eight native regiments stationed there, and totalling 5,000 men, were shown to be planning mutiny. There were just 2,000 British regulars and a handful of civilians to oppose them.

The sequel came swiftly, with Bobs, a muted and junior observer, attending a conference at General Reed's house on 13 May. Unlike the interminable meetings held by the nervous General Wheeler at Cawnpore, its proceedings were swift and to the point for all those present knew their minds. Edwardes and Nicholson, men of legendary stature in the Punjab, undertook to recruit the wild tribes of the north-west into British service. No one else had quite their influence, and the tribesmen would march under no other leader than Nicholson. Using their names alone, these two were to bring thousands into the balance on the side of the hard-pressed British troops, and the reinforcement proved decisive. Another and equally important decision was to form a mobile column—Victorian India's equivalent of a commando—under the leadership of Brigadier Neville Chamberlain. It was a unit which promised much in the way of hard fighting and swift manœuvre, and to his inexpressible delight, Bobs was appointed to it as staff officer.

These were decisive steps, taken none too soon, for it was already clear by 14 May that, far from facing a sprinkling of disaffected regiments, they had a vast military conspiracy to combat, a conspiracy affecting the bulk of the regular units of the Bengal Army in Northern India, and especially at Oudh.

It was to prove a cruel war, fought out against a treacherous enemy with no quarter and under a pitiless sky. Incredible odds faced the British—often odds of twenty to one—and yet in the end they always triumphed. Bobs was in his element. Brave as a lion and tough as rawhide, he revelled in the hand-to-hand combat which was a feature of the campaign. More important for his future, he was thrown among the brightest and best that the British in India could produce, a gallant company in which names such as Probyn, Hodson, and Tombes featured. It was an age of patriotism and courage in which men such as Battye of the Guides Cavalry, falling in action, could utter as his last words 'Dulce et decorum est pro patria mori' without fear of derision. It was spirit such as this that enabled men to storm forward, time and again, against fearful odds, and to bear the desperate loneliness of the night watches. It was a spirit personified in Frederick Roberts. By 14 July he had been under fire many times and, that day, in action on the Grand Trunk Road,

he received his first wound, though he was able to drag himself back to camp.

Back in Simla, and then in Ambala, General Anson, the Commander-in-Chief, wrestled with a problem as awkward as any with which a campaign commander might have to deal. All the best officers were agreed that the first target must be Delhi, for every week that passed with the rebel garrison there unvanquished added to sepoy prestige as surely as it reduced that of the British—and British prestige in India was in short supply in the spring of 1857. This Anson saw as clearly as any man, but he also saw how few and, too often, how young and untrained his British soldiers were. In contrast, the mutineers, richly supplied with British arms, were sheltered confidently behind strong fortifications. Anson may have been slow to heed warnings before the outbreak, but it is hard not to sympathize with him once the alarm had sounded. With the Frontier officials (men such as rough, tough, capable John Lawrence) pressing for an immediate advance to save what remained of

Britain's reputation and, consequentially, of tribal support, Anson was in an unenviable position, for at the same time a sizeable military school (comprised of men such as Sir Henry Barnard) was preaching caution. In the end the Frontiersmen's pleas proved decisive, and on 19 May Anson prepared to march on Delhi. By the 26th, General Anson was dead.

The men in command at Peshawar, however, wasted no time. By 18 May, Bobs, escorting his general, had reached Rawal Pindi. From there they hurried on to Wazirabad and, driving along the Grand Trunk Road, found their vehicle suddenly turned turtle when the ponies' reins broke. History does not record whether Chamberlain, like another general almost a century later, remarked, 'When you've all quite finished walking over your Commander [. . .]'* but it is clear that, though bruised, they finished the journey intact. Soon afterwards they reached Wazirabad and Bobs, detailed by his superior to report their arrival to the station commander, awoke a very grumpy colonel of the Queen's Army who cursed him roundly, disputed Chamberlain's seniority as a Company officer, and generally made himself objectionable. It was not Bobs' lucky day.

By now the mobile column was fully operational, and the British amongst them were anxious to move, but a snag remained over the sepoy regiments still attached to the column. If there was as yet no outward sign of mutiny amongst them, there was also no comfort either in the sight of the sullen brown faces or the sloped muskets of the 35th Native Infantry at Lahore. The news coming in from all sides had in fact deprived even their own officers of any faith in the *Pandies*,† as they were already coming to be called, and a few nights later there was striking confirmation of British suspicions when a spy reported that the 35th was scheduled to mutiny at day-break. Fortunately Chamberlain, who had not commanded the Punjab Frontier Force for nothing, acted promptly. The regiment was paraded, and two sepoys whose muskets were found already loaded were tried and condemned to death by court-martial.

Two hours later, as a muffled drum played, the regiment marched out to form three sides of a square. On the fourth side

---

* Wavell to Fergusson. (B. Fergusson, *Wavell, Portrait of a Soldier*.)
† After Mangal Pande.

stood two cannon, and to the mouths of these the would-be mutineers were bound. Then, as 600 men watched, tensely at attention, 'the word of command was given; the guns went off simultaneously, and the two mutineers were launched into eternity.' It was harsh justice, but so were the times, and the lesson was not without its effect. Lady Canning, secure inside Government House at Calcutta, might continue to inveigh against any who counselled strong measures, but the stark truth was that the British in Northern India were fighting for their lives.

CHAPTER IV

The Siege of Delhi

THE speed with which Nicholson and Edwardes had disarmed
the native troops at Peshawar, no less than the executions at
Lahore, were already having a powerful effect along the
Frontier, where the Pathan worshipped strength. Edwardes
remarked that, 'As we rode down to the disarming a very few
Chiefs and yeomen attended us.' But when they rode back, it was
a different story, for then 'friends were as thick as summer flies'.

Elsewhere, the story had been less happy. At Ferozepore a
blind belief in sepoy loyalty had all but cost the British the most
powerful arsenal in Northern India, and in the end it was the
little man—the private soldier, the clerk, and the subaltern—
who, by his courage, won what his superior's complacency had
all but forsworn. Matters at Multan were better, but only just,
for there it was the will and personality of only one man—the
commanding officer of the 1st Irregular Cavalry—that held the
situation in check.

Meanwhile the mobile column was at last on the march.
Chamberlain had gone on to Delhi, and Nicholson had not yet
arrived, so Bobs, as staff officer to the amiable nonentity who
had succeeded Chamberlain, found himself for all practical purposes in charge of the column. As he wrote, 'It was a somewhat
trying position for almost the youngest officer in the force', and
only the sudden benignity of Campbell, the colonel whom he had
awakened at Wazirabad, made things at all tolerable. Campbell
indeed was to prove more and more helpful. Experienced and
efficient, he had, after the first burst of anger, accepted Chamberlain as commander on the grounds of his greater Indian
experience. Now, tolerating the feckless Col Denniss on the
basis of his seniority, he took Bobs under his wing, prompting

44

him to give all the orders that Denniss should have given. Later still, when John Nicholson took over on the 20th, the elder man bowed yet again, accepting the young brigadier's directions and proving a loyal, zealous subordinate.

The first stop for the mobile column was Jullundur, where British control had come within an ace of being toppled through the ineptitude of Brigadier Johnstone, and here Bobs received a lesson in Indian psychology when Nicholson scolded a Sikh general in peremptory tones for breaching etiquette by wearing his shoes in the house. The breach had seemed insignificant and the other officers present, fearing to offend the Kapurthala hierarchy at this critical time, would have let it pass. The proof of the pudding was, however, swiftly shown to be in the eating, for Bobs noted the immediate change in the attitude of the Rajah's entourage after 'Nikal Seyn' had spoken. Before Nicholson's outburst the little party of Britons had been suppliants on the verge of defeat, in Kapurthalan eyes, pleading for aid. Now, there was no doubt of the Rajah's loyalty, and impertinence was immediately replaced by courtesy. It was a timely lesson, not lost on Bobs.

From then, until his death, the mobile column was to be Nicholson, and Nicholson the column. Rarely in the history of war can a tough body of professionals have been so dominated by the personality of one man and he, in theory at least, a civilian. Now sweeping east, now west, his goal ever Delhi, the spell of his iron will lay upon friend and foe alike. His tall figure, questing far, struck terror into the enemy. His trumpets, pealing in the dawn, personified Nemesis to the mutineer and deliverance to the besieged. This was the man, disliked by officers he had surpassed and worshipped by his soldiers, British and Indian alike, that strode the stage with masterful step. Not since Rupert of the Rhine had such a dramatic figure dominated the British military scene.

There was, of course, much more to Nicholson than the mere trappings of a *beau sabreur*. The magic of his personality was to entrance Bobs for the rest of his life, surviving all that was earthly of Nicholson by fifty-seven years. He was a devoted professional and a military craftsman of high order. Abrupt and dictatorial, loving danger for its own sake, he was also a reflective commander, tactically ingenious, daring but never reckless

45

of his men's lives. Behind Nicholson's broad high forehead dwelt a wealth of calculation and intelligence. Here was a fitting leader for desperate ventures and forlorn hopes. Risk was merely an added spice—his pastime in less troubled days had been hunting the tiger on horseback with a lance. He had no respect for rank unallied to merit, which in itself stamped him as original in an age obsessed by precedence and seniority. Sentimentality he rejected with contempt, especially when the interests of his country demanded ruthlessness. Yet he delighted in children, would weep for a friend slain, and give money to a beggar he deemed deserving. His mind dwelt naturally in the rarefied atmosphere of a great commander, yet he never failed to apply an inherent common sense to the problem at hand. A military innovator, in a ponderous age that had forgotten the lessons of the Peninsula, he organized his flying columns into cavalry units followed by infantry in light wheeled vehicles (*ekkas*), the equivalent, in the days before discovery of the internal combustion engine, of Guderian's *Panzergrenadiers*. Wrote Bobs many years later, himself by then the greatest British field general since Wellington had toppled Napoleon, 'Nicholson was a born commander.'

By mid-June, Bobs' own share of the mobile column's exploits was a thing of the past, for he was on his way to Delhi, where gunner officers were in urgent demand. On the 28th he arrived, and nothing could have been more depressing than the sight which met his eyes. Though the British were the besieging force, only the mutineers' lack of courage had made this possible, for in personnel, artillery, and equipment the royal forces were hopelessly outnumbered. With Anson already dead, Barnard was now Commander-in-Chief, but his days were also numbered, and by 5 July he would be gone too, blue with cholera, brave but indecisive to the end. Nonetheless, such were the odds ranged against them that Barnard wrote no more than the truth when he predicted, 'The whole thing is too gigantic for the force brought against it.' With even spades at a premium in 'Delhiforce', and loyal Hindus as scarce as rubies, there were few to query the material accuracy of his remarks.

The gravest omen of all was a partial but serious collapse in morale. Not merely were sepoys deserting, but British soldiers were refusing to obey orders. When the mutineer hordes had attacked on 23 June (before Bobs arrived at Delhi), officers and NCOs had been forced to drive them back almost unsupported, serving even the guns whilst the regular crews lay sullenly watching. Yet there was much to be said for the troops, distasteful as the scene was, for conditions were unbearable. With the noon temperature frequently at 130 degrees, life in any circumstances would have been uncomfortable. On the bare ridge or, at best, under the canvas tents that offered the only cover available, mere existence had become a torment. Flies, bloated with human flesh, clustered everywhere in black greedy clouds. Mosquitoes swarmed voraciously, jackals abounded, and the unseen perils of dysentery and cholera struck incessantly. The stench of decomposition hung over everything, tainting the food, poisoning the nostrils, emanating continuously from the piled rotting mounds of unburied mutineer dead.

Such were the circumstances in which Bobs entered the siege, and on 30 June he was under fire once again, at first in the morning, when treacherous Hindustani troops fired into the backs of their officers, and again in the afternoon when he was on reconnaissance with Brigadier Showers. From then on, action came his way thick and fast for, though the assault on Delhi itself had to be postponed due to the planned treachery of Hindu troops, offensive patrols and minor engagements were continuous. Such an action occurred on 3 July, near the Western Jumna Canal, with Bobs taking part as a staff officer, and again on the 14th, when an attack was launched by the mutineers against Hindu Rao's House, a landmark as famous to 'Delhiforce' veterans as 'Mouquet Farm' was to prove to their great-grandchildren on the Somme over half a century later. It was on this occasion that Bobs received his first serious wound.

It is hard to comprehend the full torment a casualty had to face in 1857. Those fortunate enough to escape the castration and disembowelling reserved by the enemy for his prisoners, had still to run the gauntlet of gangrene, tetanus, and a score of other hazards prevailing in a climate where even a simple cut became a major risk. Without anaesthetics or, usually, even disinfectant, the surgeons could do little more than hope, and hope was a fragile staff on which to lean in July 1857. Even the very stretchers were often useless for lack of men to bear them. As for field hygiene, it did not exist. Latrines, as modern armies know them, were wholly absent, and water supplies were invariably contaminated. The wonder was that any British personnel survived.

Fortunately, Bobs' wound was not very deep, for the bullet that entered him had first to drive through a leather cartridge case attached to his belt. Even so, though Bobs euphemistically described himself as merely feeling 'faint and sick', the injury was enough to keep him on the sick-list for two weeks and off his horse for a month. It was not until late in August that he was operational again.

By 17 July, supreme command had changed once more. This time it was General Reed, in whose house Bobs had attended the Peshawar meeting, who relinquished command due to ill-health, and the results were potentially grave. No one could have accused Anson, Barnard, or Reed of brilliance, but they had at least been competent soldiers, if a little out of their depth in the extraordinary conditions of the Mutiny. Now, however, the choice, such as it was, devolved upon no less a person than Brigadier Archdale Wilson, the former commander at Meerut. Tall, gangling, tormented in spirit and weak in resolution it is impossible not to feel sympathy for him, faced as he was with such a momentous task. Not in intellect but in character was he weak. His intentions were good, but he did not possess the capacities of even a mediocre field general. Thus lacking in drive, determination, and the electric powers of leadership, he had the misfortune to be faced with as searching a test of military skill as any Victorian officer had yet encountered. Probably the only person who could have infused the necessary confidence in him was his wife, and she was away in the hills. Few officers before Delhi expected great things of him.

But events now showed that though few men have genius, given conscience and patriotism, even the mediocre can accomplish much. Archdale Wilson had never sought glory. Now, faced with the appalling problem so suddenly thrust upon him, he was to act with wholly unexpected decision. No field commander, he was a shrewd administrator with a clear and penetrating mind and within hours his reforms had begun, as lines were cleaned, sanitation improved, and regular reliefs arranged for the troops in the fighting line. Economical of his men's lives, he also stopped the wasteful business of hunting the enemy up to the city walls whenever an attack was repelled, for the barricades were lined with sepoy sharp-shooters whose fusillades, at such close quarters, had already cost the British dear.

So Wilson worked on, throughout the summer heat, as the temperature rose ever higher and the casualty and sickness rate soared. It was a sacrificial task too as, tortured by an ulcer, he contrived to survive on arrowroot alone, but his work was to bear fruit in the end. Though, as Bobs wrote of him, he was 'a soldier of moderate capacity', he was also the best immediately available and his selection had only been achieved by passing him over the heads of three others. It is true that at the moment of supreme decision his nerve was destined to fail, but by then a kindly Providence had placed at his elbow a man whom nothing and no one would ever daunt. The moment was the storming of Delhi, and by then John Nicholson would be there.

From July until the end of August, though the royal troops were continuously engaged in action, Bobs was uncommitted, for he was still recovering from his wound. Reinforcements had been steadily, though all too slowly, filtering through. One of the most significant of the new arrivals, on 3 July, had been a brilliant engineer. A Scotsman, Col Richard Baird-Smith was destined to occupy one of the principal positions in the whole campaign and, after Nicholson, no man did more to ensure a British victory than he. A man who would almost certainly have been described contemptuously by reactionaries like the Duke of Cambridge as 'a military intellectual', Baird-Smith's zeal for victory burned as brightly as any, and at the darkest hour of the assault, when all hung in the balance, he was to provide Nicholson with priceless support. His was the will to win that kept Wilson constant before Nicholson's arrival. Heavy, brooding, ever devising schemes for destroying the rebels' capacity to fight, he dismissed all suggestions of retreat with dour contempt.

Another marked improvement lay in the field of intelligence. Once the weakest point in the British armoury, it was by now fully organized as, night after night, Indian spies crept in and out of the rebel stronghold, spurred by hopes of rich reward. The main-spring and inspiration of this work was one of the most remarkable personalities produced by the Company's army. Of dark and evil reputation, William Hodson shared with the devout Nicholson three primary attributes. He feared no man, his patriotism burned high, and he had an extraordinary capacity for inspiring the wild Sikh horsemen who rode under his command. Here the resemblance ended, for Nicholson was a man of exemplary character, whilst the taint of fraud had for years been associated with Hodson's name. Among other things, he had used the general break-down of law and order resulting from the Mutiny to murder at least one of his Indian creditors. Already a byword for corruption and debt, he and his Scarlet Flamingoes (as Hodson's Horse were called) spurred far and wide in search of mutineers and loot. Quarter was rarely asked and never given by such men. Fouché* could have taught William Hodson little in the art of espionage, nor Murat† in the art of battle. A man from whose side of the road honest soldiers were wont to cross in times of peace, he was now at once a moral liability and a military necessity to the forces of the Crown. These were the men who led the army of the Queen, the great personalities whose fame was supported by the heroism of a few thousand white and brown soldiers, nameless but true to their salt. As Bobs was to write, the infantry corps in early September were 'mere skeletons'. Battle and the toll of disease had reduced strong men to staggering spectres, and it was upon such a force, ragged, short of ammunition, dying on its feet but indomitable, that John Nicholson now descended.

By the time of his arrival Wilson had begun to show unmistakable symptoms of panic. Physically as brave as any man, ill-health and the weight of responsibility had broken his will to win. There was logic in his viewpoint, for it was—on the surface—madness to try and carry Delhi by storm with the forces at his disposal. A natural procrastinator, he dwelt heavily upon the need for reinforcements before he could march to the assault. He loved guns and a comprehensive artillery preparation was necessary, but the limbers were empty of shot, and where were the required cannon? Reserves of manpower were important, yet the very assault troops looked as if they could hardly drag themselves out of the forward positions. 'For God's sake don't drive me so,' groaned Wilson to the pitiless Baird-Smith.

What Wilson was in danger of forgetting is that wars are

* Napoleon's Chief of Police.
† Imperial Marshal and commander of the Napoleonic Cavalry.

not won by logistics alone, and only rarely by playing safe. Campaigns are lost more often by delay than by commitment. Bobs wrote, 'Fortunately for the continuance of our rule in India, Wilson had about him men who understood, as he was unable to do, the impossibility of our remaining any longer as we were. They knew that Delhi must either be taken or the Army before it withdrawn.' There were others who said the same more openly. Rumbled Sir John Lawrence angrily from the Punjab, 'Every day's delay is fraught with danger.' Nicholson and Chamberlain were hammering ceaselessly at the tired old general, and their theme could be summed up in one word— 'Assault!' Without it, they knew, the tribes would rise and that would spell the end. The wild Multanis who worshipped Nicholson followed the standard of his invincibility. But let him fail. . . .

In such circumstances, Nicholson began to plot. Let Wilson refuse to attack and they would remove him, he propounded to his friend and confidant Bobs. Only thus could British India be saved. And so that no one should accuse him of being prompted by personal motives, he was prepared to stand down himself and serve under Campbell, the crusty but able commander of the 52nd, if Wilson had to go. Bobs 'was greatly startled', as well he might have been, for what Nicholson had suggested to him amounted, if carried through with the aid of others, to mutiny— and mutiny was punishable by death. Not that this would have deterred Nicholson, for he was ever impatient of technicalities when his country's interests were at stake. It says a great deal for Bobs' confidence in his friend that, though appalled by the first impact of the idea, he never doubted Nicholson's purity of purpose. Years later, when himself a field-marshal and a peer, he was to write, 'Whether his action would have been right or wrong is another question [. . .] at the time it seemed to me that he was right [. . .] after having often thought over Nicholson's intended action and discussed the subject with other men, I have not changed my opinion.' It was a thesis designed to have profound effects on Bobs himself when, later still and as the final act of his career, he felt obliged to challenge the British Government's intended betrayal of Ulster.

In the end it was never necessary for Nicholson to go to these extremes for, faced with an angry array of senior officers,

Archdale Wilson querulously capitulated. At Army Headquarters and, no less, along the rebel lines, Nicholson's
personality now reigned supreme, for as news of his arrival
spread morale rose to a new peak. Already, in the enemy lines,
mutineers looked furtively over their shoulders as the whisper
spread, 'Nikal Seyn is here'; with his arrival all hope seemed to
have fled from the rebel camp.

By 11 September, indecisiveness lay in the past as Wilson and
rebels alike were brought to bay. With such guns as were
available pounding day and night at the great walls, all men
knew that assault was imminent. Conditions were indescribable.
The bombardment continued without respite, until the air was
thick with smoke. Gunners, ravaged by the sun and stained
black with powder, dropped like stones from heat stroke.
Soldiers, dragging themselves from sick-bays, pallid with fever,
often with bandaged wounds still oozing blood, clustered
moodily, watching with expert eyes as the masonry fell in great
masses from the beleaguered walls. Even the dying on occasion
sought to crawl to the assault, so great was the desire for
vengeance. That day Bobs, serving the guns in forward
batteries, was knocked over by an enemy round-shot. Not
inaccurately was Kipling, years later, to write of him,

> If you stood 'im on 'is head, Father Bobs,
> You could spill a quart of lead outer Bobs.

Luckily, apart from bruises, no harm was done by the round-
shot, though the young gunner beside him lost an arm.
Elsewhere the losses were appalling as rebel counter-fire
reached a crescendo. Mutineer morale was dropping fast, but
they could still fight. Indeed they had no option, for the rebels
knew there would be no quarter. With Nikal Seyn blowing
sepoys from the guns, it was better to die in battle.

The 14th dawned fitfully, after a night of tension and
spasmodic fire. Reconnaissance parties had been out during the
darkness and returned to report the breaches practical. Wilson,
haggard and near to break-down, would once more have drawn
back, but he was given no chance, for Baird-Smith grimly cut his
pleas away—they had long since ceased to be orders—with
pithy Scottish logic. Every hour that passed, as Bobs wrote,
'was a loss to us and a gain to the enemy'. As an argument it

weighed little with Wilson, whose mental condition had by now reached a stage of almost continual hysteria, but few took any note of what he had to say, for the whole army, from Nicholson down to the youngest drummer boy, was determined to attack.

A few hours later, Bobs, standing on the 'crenellated wall which separated Ludlow Castle from the road', saw 'Nicholson at the head of his column and wondered what was passing through his mind'. 'Was he,' speculated the tough little red-haired soldier, 'thinking of the future, or of the wonderful part he had played during the last four months?' Though Bobs could not know it, there was to be no future for Nicholson. The Company's officer who, through sheer strength of character, held the whole force in thrall, was already marching into history at the head of his regiments. Edwardes' words, recalled by Bobs so many years later, and spoken of the man he so idealized, were a fitting epitaph. 'You may rely upon this, that if ever there is a desperate deed to be done in India, John Nicholson is the man to do it.'

Events now moved swiftly for, among the column commanders at least, there was no doubt of how Nicholson's well-laid plans should work. The great man himself had made his last rounds, shaking hands with private and field officer alike, final letters had been written, and in Her Majesty's 75th Foot old Father Bertrand, the Catholic Priest, had come forward with the colonel's assent to bless all denominations. 'We may differ some of us in matters of religion, but the blessing of an old man and a clergyman can do nothing but good.' Columns were concentrated, muskets loaded, and prayers offered.

Now, under the fierce Indian sun, the clamour of the guns fell suddenly still. Five thousand troops, white and brown, were poised for the charge. Then, Nicholson raised his hand at the head of the first column and the 60th Rifles swept forward with a cheer, skirmishing towards the walls, their musketry smashing into the battlements at the top. The rebels' reply was immediate. Cannon and small arms alike poured a storm of fire on the assaulting columns. Already outnumbered many times, the British force was now to be exposed to an additional peril as they stood isolated and in full view on the edge of the glacis, halted for lack of the storming ladders whose carriers lay dead or wounded to the rear. Scores of the assaulters died within minutes, and then they were into the breach and over, the ditch and approaches piled with dead and dying, the remnant swarming up ladders that rested on the bodies of their comrades. British, Gurkhas, and Sikhs of the first column were on the rampart now, clubbing, bayoneting, hurling such enemy as remained to their deaths below.

In the sectors allocated to other columns, success was variable, but by noon a small band of dedicated sappers had blown in the Kashmir Gate, and avenging formations were smashing their way into the city along lanes that sparkled with fire. Casualties soared, and under them Wilson's nerve once more gave way, for Nicholson, the mainspring of the assault, was already mortally wounded. Consternation spread amongst the senior officers as Wilson, with all a weak man's emphasis, propounded retreat, for every Indian Service officer knew only too well the effect that such an order would have on the wavering tribes of the Punjab. Equally characteristic was Nicholson's comment when told of the suggestion—'Thank God I have strength yet to shoot him, if necessary.' That it was not in the end necessary was due almost entirely to the senior staff, for Nicholson's determination was widely shared. So the troops remained in Delhi, inching their way along the blood-soaked streets against bitter resistance and enormous odds.

During all this time Bobs, to his chagrin, was a mere spectator, for once his work with the guns had been completed, orders came for him to return to staff. Deputy-Quartermaster-Generalships had their advantages but also their drawbacks, as he was now to find, since for most of the day, whilst the storming columns battled their way forward, he and Edwin Johnson, the AAG*, had to dance attendance on an Archdale Wilson by now wholly distraught. In the end Bobs was able to escape, purportedly to gather information, and it was while on this mission that he found Nicholson lying near the Kashmir Gate, his *doolie* abandoned by bearers avid for loot. His wound was plainly mortal; as Bobs wrote, 'Death [was] written on his face.' Nicholson himself was aware of the fact, for in reply to Bobs' query he replied simply, 'I am dying; there is no chance for me.'

Inside the city matters were far from satisfactory, as Bobs

* Assistant Adjutant-General.

found. Leaderless men were clustered in many places, without knowledge, and often gripped by panic. Their officers dead or wounded, there was no one to whom they could turn, and it was in fact whilst rallying Her Majesty's 8th Foot that Nicholson himself had been shot down. Scourged by the fire of rebels who had no longer any hope of escape and were accordingly ready to sell their lives at the highest price, some units ground to a halt. Morale in other regiments began to waver, and a few of the men, worn to breaking point by the rigours of the campaign, took refuge in looted drink. Such incidents were, however, the natural by-product of battle and, despite reports suggesting the contrary, they were few. Bobs, who covered almost every part of the city recaptured by the British that day, wrote, 'I did not see a single drunken man throughout the day of the assault.' If fault there was, it lay in the exhaustion of the soldiers, the enormous odds that faced them, and the weakness of the high command.

The truth was that, with Nicholson mortally wounded, the mainspring of the assault had wound down. Baird-Smith and Chamberlain, the two men who could have replaced him, were both *hors-de-combat*, the one through illness, the other through wounds, and only their iron determination had kept them in the field at all. Archdale Wilson, the nominal commander, was reduced to babbling incoherence, capable of neither constructive tactics nor of inspiration, keeping in touch with the ebb and flow of battle only through his aides. Perhaps the only man who was present and who might have been able to take up in some measure where Nicholson had left off was Hodson, but he was too junior and too discredited. In any event he was a Company officer, and only Nicholson had been accepted unreservedly by the Queen's men.

This was a day in which Bobs ran rather more risks than was usual even in his adventurous career for, though he had taken no part in the assault, he and the other aides were continually under fire. Archdale Wilson, whatever his faults as a commander, was no coward and he did not hesitate to expose himself to risk. With sniping from every roof and vantage point that could offer cover, few men were to find safety in Delhi that day, and as streets changed and rechanged hands moreover, it was often difficult to know on which side of the 'Line' one stood. Bobs early discovered the truth of this when, riding through a narrow alley with two other staff officers,* he was attacked by a large party of mutineers, his horse was shot from under him, and he was lucky to escape with his life.

Conditions worsened sharply in the ensuing days as soldiers, frequently in a semi-coma from fatigue, carried the attack forward against a defence garrison ten times their number. The insubordination, which had virtually disappeared under Nicholson's iron leadership, was again becoming widespread. 'For the first time in my life I have had to see English soldiers refuse to follow their officers,' wrote William Hodson, appalled by cowardice where murder and armed robbery left him cold. Yet there was a great deal of excuse for young and exhausted private soldiers, often untrained, and unnerved by what was for many their first glimpse of war. Casualties had been enormous, even though by sunset on the day of the assault, as Bobs wrote, 'Only a very small portion of the walls of Delhi was in our possession.' For that, out of an initial attacking force of 5,000, three out of four column commanders, sixty-six other officers, and over 1,100 men had fallen, killed or wounded. When one considers that a high proportion of the loyal troops, white and brown alike, were almost untrained recruits, they had not done badly.

Meanwhile the advance continued remorselessly as small parties edged their way continually forward in the face of ferocious opposition. Neither the weakness of Wilson nor the occasional breakdown in the morale of individual units were enough to interfere with the steady overall discipline of the British line. Demoralization was spreading fast in the rebel lines, and sepoys were now sliding away into the darkness in small groups or singly, whenever opportunity offered. Nonetheless, the opportunities for a major mutineer break-away were sufficiently limited to ensure that odds against the British remained fantastically high.

By now, as progress slowed, the tactics of attack had altered. Wild assault was abandoned. In those bullet-swept streets few men could survive, let alone fight. In the dingier alleys, the upper windows of the houses were often only five feet apart, and from these the sepoy musketeers poured out a remorseless fire. Cannon too, loaded with jagged, rusty fragments of iron,

* Norman and Johnson.

played their part with horrible results. In such circumstances, frontal assault was not to be thought of, for the British had no men to spare. Sapping from house to house, an interminable process, provided the solution as mole strove desperately against mole. In such a pattern, Bobs was to distinguish himself as he and the others with him worked towards the Lahore Gate under command of a young sapper officer, and on the 19th they broke straight through to the Burn Bastion and captured it without loss.

Next day Bobs was in at the kill as, still sapping their way towards the Lahore Gate, his party unexpectedly smashed into a courtyard among a cluster of terrified money-lenders. A few pointed threats and the glitter of steel quickly overcame their reluctance to act as guides, and in no time the British had charged into action, scattering and killing large numbers of astonished sepoys without loss to themselves. The way ahead lay clear and, as Home, already hero of the Kashmir Gate episode, blew in the entrance to the Mogul Fort, the 60th Rifles —with Bobs voluntarily 'attached'—burst through the gap.

The last lap had now been reached in Delhi as mutineer morale finally plummeted and resistance collapsed. That evening the Union Jack flew once more over a scarred and bloody capital. By midnight victory was theirs. Next morning, his troubled spirit happy at last in the knowledge of success, Nicholson died. Only a triumph of will-power had enabled him to survive so long, and now the need for it was gone. Only one more scene remained to be played, and this by the most dramatic actor of them all. However unwilling and timorous a part in the Mutiny he had himself played, the old and deposed King of Oudh was throughout the focal rallying point of mutineers and civilian rebels alike. Now, with the collapse of all their hopes he, the last of the Mogul Emperors, fled with his two sons to the tomb of Humayon, his ancestor, and it was here that Hodson found them on the 21st.

For Hodson, it was a final chance to win honour as the clouds which had long since gathered above him darkened once more. He had filched the documentary evidence which proved him guilty of fraud, but there were others who knew too much— others, unlike the Muslim money-lender, who could not be cut down at will. Now, however, as he rode up to the tomb with his

Scarlet Flamingoes—red-sashed, black-bearded, predatory Sikhs —the seizure of the King seemed to Hodson to offer the last opportunity of redeeming his name. With the whole army feverishly seeking the aged monarch, his would be the scoop of the campaign. It was a matter of minutes to secure the old man, and of hours to return to Delhi, announcing the fact with a nonchalant 'only the King' to the astonished guard commander who challenged him. So far so good, but in Hodson's eyes there was a forfeit to be paid, and within twenty-four hours he was back at Humayon's tomb. The exact details will never be known with certainty, but the outline seems clear. Capturing the King's sons in a bullock cart, he stripped and shot them in cold blood. It was a deed wholly typical of William Hodson, the sometime Jekyll who was more often a Hyde.

CHAPTER V

Pipers to Lucknow

ONCE Delhi had fallen, the issue was never again in doubt. Though, intermittently, the mutineers were to fight hard, the supremacy of royal arms was established. There were to be perils in plenty, violent engagements, lively skirmishes, and lonely reconnaissances—all nerve-racking enough for anyone who lacked Bobs' extraordinary fascination for danger—but the nature of the warfare had now wholly changed. The concentrated columns, the heavy bombardments, the huge casualty list packed into a few short hours—all these were things of the past after Delhi. Save in a few places, the rebels' ardour was noticeably lessened. With vengeance in the air—and British and Indian loyalists had old scores in plenty to settle—there were mutineers who were still prepared to fight to the death rather than surrender, but some also who tended to melt into the countryside whenever opportunity offered and, if possible, before combat was joined.

It often follows that what is essentially 'mopping up' proves a great deal more protracted than the decisive battle itself, and this was true of the campaign that followed the fall of Delhi. Much remained to be done, for though the immediate enemy was in recoil, Sikhs, Punjabi Mussulmans, and Afghans were still watching from the wings, and any major reverse would have undone all the good Nicholson had died to achieve. Now, with Cawnpore calling urgently for aid, Bobs had not even time to attend his friend's funeral, for as the drums beat sadly behind the cortège, he was riding out south-east along the dusty road that led to Cawnpore, as DAQMG of the scratch force detailed for its relief. Commanded by Greathed of the 8th Foot, it was only 2,800 strong, yet so weakened were the survivors of the siege of Delhi that Wilson had difficulty in finding even this number.

As Bobs rode out that early morning of 24 September, 1857, he was as depressed as it was in his nature to be. All that was mortal of Nicholson lay behind him, and in front lay the dingy street that ran from the Lahore Gate by the Chandni Chauk. Hardened soldiers though they were, the column found themselves hard-pressed by what Bobs called the 'unimaginably disgusting' atmosphere, 'laden as it was with the most noxious and sickening odours.' For the area through which they now marched was 'a veritable city of the dead' in which, besides themselves, only the dogs and vultures moved. Corpses were strewn and piled in every direction, and the flies rose in black clouds as the columns passed. Bobs was glad to leave Delhi behind him.

By the 28th they were in action again, at Bulandshah, and Bobs had another horse shot from under him. However, no harm was done, the rebels were cleared away, and after a few days the scratch force reached Khurja, where they found the skeleton of a mutilated European woman laid out against the bridge. In the end they marched on, after hanging the few mutineers they found there, but for a time the officers had a hard task to control the soldiers, who wanted to put the town to the sword. A great deal is written today of the vengeance Britons exacted during and after the Mutiny, but the other side of the coin is also apparent. Officers did control their troops, and rebel atrocities were of a kind most calculated to anger British soldiers.

At Khurja the force received its first intelligence of Lucknow, brought to them in a false-bottomed plate by a fakir, and on 5 October Bobs thoroughly enjoyed himself pursuing rebels from Aligarh as they scampered off through the high corn. The real highlight came, however, when they changed course and marched to Agra in response to urgent appeals which indicated that the city was in a state of siege. Instead the garrison turned out, immaculately attired, to greet them, whilst pretty girls, fresh and clean in their starched dresses, sneered (to Bobs' indignation) at the ragged, dirty rescue column. 'We were not then aware of what soon became painfully apparent,' he wrote acidly, 'that neither the information nor the opinions of the heads of the civil and military administration of Agra were to be relied on.'

He had good grounds for his remarks, since the 'information' of the Agra authorities was nearly to cost him his life. Told on arrival by the elegant personages who greeted him that the enemy had fled, and that a search by 'thoroughly trustworthy men' had confirmed this, the rescue column sat down to breakfast. It was a breakfast fated not to be eaten, for firing broke out and Bobs, hurrying to the parade ground, sword in hand, found himself caught up in the vortex of a surprise rebel attack. With musketry volleying, elephants trumpeting, and a motley crowd of Indian civilians shrieking in terror, the din was appalling and, to add to all, the Horse Gunners opened up supporting fire from the nearby park.

Bobs was quickly involved in a hand-to-hand struggle with a rebel cavalryman, who had so frightened the little Irishman's mount by waving his turban that it refused to budge. With his revolver jammed and the *sowar** manœuvring for position out of sword's reach, the outlook would have been grim for Bobs, had not a friendly lancer despatched his enemy with a well-aimed thrust. Soon afterwards the mutineers retreated and the royal troops took up the pursuit, and it is an interesting commentary on Victorian reverence for precedence that when an officer senior to the column commander (Greathed) appeared on the scene, the whole pursuit had to be delayed whilst he learned the details and took over command. Having spent the whole Mutiny in relatively comfortable Agra, the new man, Col Cotton, was immaculately clad and not over-zealous in the advance. In the end, however, despite Col Cotton, the action finished well, for they overran and captured the mutineer camp, taking thirteen guns and a great deal of ammunition. By ten o'clock the troops from the column, all Delhi veterans, were back in Agra, indignant as ever with the Agra Command and contemptuous of the Agra troops' inability to march. History does not record whether Bobs ever finished his breakfast.

By 14 October the troops were on the march once more, glad to leave Agra, with its smart soft parade-ground troops and its inadequate leadership, behind them. The road lay through Mainpuri, where they paused only long enough to destroy the

* Indian Cavalry soldier.

rebel Rajah's fort before marching relentlessly on. With their torn, faded equipment and faces burnt mahogany by the sun, the column had long since ceased to resemble the pipe-clayed armies of tradition. Yet the men, despite their fatigue, carried themselves bravely and well. Many had been in action almost continuously since May without leave and with hardly any respite.

On the 23rd Bobs was again engaged in hand-to-hand combat at Miran-ki-Serai, where over 800 mutineers were preparing to retreat. Rebel morale was no longer equal to even the semblance of a stand against less than half their numbers, and the whole action took the form of a pursuit rather than an engagement. Nonetheless Bobs, as usual, contrived to be in the thick of whatever fighting there was, and his charger emerged with its rump laid open by a sabre. Reading the tally of horses shot and sabred under Bobs, it is hard not to sympathize with them.

The city towards which Greathed's column now marched was the scene of one of the most brutal tragedies in a mutiny distinguished for both brutality and tragedy. In times of peace Cawnpore had been gay—too gay perhaps for the serious study of realities. Amateur theatricals had boomed, dances and balls flourished, and even the despised British soldier had found as agreeable a niche there as he was ever likely to find in the India that preceded the Mutiny.

The trouble lay, as almost always, not in the fibre of the troops, but in the capacity of the men at the top. Trust is a pleasing virtue, but blind trust continued in the teeth of evidence may be a perilous vice. It was an outlook which General Sir Hugh Wheeler, the Anglo-Irish Divisional Commander, was to maintain to the end, ignoring his duty to the hundreds of souls under his charge. In fairness, it must be stated that even a competent soldier would have found the difficulties almost overwhelming, since 3,000 Indian troops, both cavalry and infantry, were there to measure against only 300 British soldiers allied to such talent as the commander might be able to skim from the European civilians. The fact remains, however, that Sir Hugh did not try. With a total lack of realism he preferred to trust the sepoys. Later, when even he could no longer ignore the evidence of their mutinous intentions, he had recourse to the grossest forms of appeasement.

May 1857 had seen Cawnpore prepared for the worst. As a first step the general had forbidden any celebration of the Queen's Birthday, lest it offend sepoy susceptibilities, and then even attendance at church was forbidden, for the same reason. With a stupidity impossible to credit, he rejected the suggestions of the station commander, Brigadier Jack, that they build a fortress at the magazine, choosing instead, for quite inadequate reasons, an indefensible site near the sepoy lines. As the European population panicked—and well they might—crowding into two squalid buildings, irrespective of age or sex, Wheeler, indecisive as ever, conferred with his disapproving subordinate, the Brigadier. 'The Nana Sahib will help us,' and, inevitably, 'We must trust the sepoys' were his persistent themes. Messages to the outside world were still more fatuous; 'All is well at Cawnpore.' 'Well for whom?' cast back the walls in mocking echo. And so the tragedy had happened, with the garrison penned like sheep into a tactically indefensible position, the women and children huddled with neither shade nor shelter under the hail of sepoy guns. There had been courage enough, with the cannon, outranged and outnumbered, firing to the last, but the cards were stacked against them, and Wheeler had to capitulate. The remainder of the story is grim enough to horrify even a century later, for it is an account of British blunders certainly, but above all of treachery and sadism.

The facts are simple and incontrovertible. The Nana agreed safe conduct, and it was on such terms that the garrison surrendered. All this was much to the rebels' advantage since, pathetic though the stockade had been, its defenders had fought so sturdily that rebel attacks had secured no foothold within the defences. After the truce, however, it was a different matter, for the troops were out of their entrenchments, their artillery was surrendered, and their deployment was effectively prevented. With Wheeler still blindly trusting to the Nana's integrity, the defenders embarked upon the boats which, they fondly imagined, would take them to Allahabad. It is impossible to imagine John Nicholson so duped; only the second-rate were to fall victim to the Nana's wiles. Now, as the boats set sail, the rowers, by pre-arrangement, dived overboard, the sepoys lining the banks opened fire, and the grim rebel cavalry closed in. To such an unequal contest there could only be one ending and, an hour later, as the cruelly mutilated and the mercifully dead floated down the Ganges, 120 women and children lurched back to the *Bibigarh** under sepoy guard. The first phase was over.

By 15 July the position had changed again, for now Havelock was marching from the east. That day, his pipes skirling defiantly, his men bent on rescue, he had twice fought much larger rebel forces, and each time had laid them low. Now, thirty-odd miles from Cawnpore, a grim Biblical figure, he was poised for the knock-out blow which should, he fondly believed, rescue the women and children from the Nana's hands. What he could not know was that as the Madras Fusiliers, led by Stephenson, crested the hill and charged down to capture the bridge over the Pandu Nuddhi—the last obstacle before Cawnpore—five silent men were entering the *Bibigarh*.

Controversy will rage over the Nana's part for as long as the Mutiny is discussed, with his apologists claiming his innocence, but certain facts unmistakably emerge. Of the five men who entered that night, armed with swords, one, the leader, wore Sepoy Red and was a member of the Nana's bodyguard. His name was Savha Khan. It was at his command that the sepoy guard outside levelled their muskets, and in defiance of this command that, sick with the shame of what was now to happen, they fired high. Thereafter they took no further part.

For the 120 women and children inside, as Savha Khan and his assistants—two Hindu untouchables and two Muslim butchers—entered, it was the moment of truth. First they tied Mrs Jacobi and Mrs Probett to the pillars and *hallaled* them across the throat, as Muslims do to a bullock. Then they swung a three-year-old child above their heads, bringing his chin firmly down over the iron hook embedded in the wall until the point protruded through his mouth. . . .

By midnight, when they left the room at last, no human being remained alive within. Savha Khan had broken three sabres.

The sequence of events in Cawnpore is important, for it did more to embitter the course of the Mutiny than almost any other incident. The rank and file of the Victorian armies were as rough and tough as they could be and the officers, for all their elaborate hierarchy, could generally act with as ruthless a

* The House of Women.

decision as they judged the situation to require, but there was no doubting their chivalry. The old code of the Peninsular armies lingered on. Women and children were sacrosanct in principle and usually in fact, even when positions were taken by storm and the garrison put to the sword. And if, as happened not infrequently in the reaction after battle, the appetites of soldiers maddened by drink and enforced continence spilled over into rape, it was merely an instance of the flesh being weak; it did not modify the general rule. The offenders, moreover, when caught, were usually hanged.

The impact of the atrocity at Cawnpore was all the greater through being premeditated for there was no doubt that neither the massacre on the boats at Sati-Choura Ghat nor the final slaughter of the women and children in the *Bibigarh* were chance affairs. They had been deeds carefully considered and they were as carefully accomplished. Circumstances also implicate the Nana himself in these crimes, and his very rank increased the enormity of the outrage in Victorian eyes, for Victorians were ever ready to accord rank, and especially hereditary rank, its due.

After Cawnpore, all this was changed. Gone was the blind affection that so many British officers had felt for their sepoy troops. Gone too was even a pretence at respect for the Hindustani by the British soldier. The Tommy had never taken much trouble to conceal his distaste, but now even the superficial veneer was abandoned. They were all 'niggers' to him, unworthy of consideration except for the Gurkhas and (perhaps) the Sikhs, Punjabi Mussulmans and Pathans. When Bobs and his men paused to look at the Sati-Choura, he was not exaggerating when he described the 'intense sadness and indignation' that overwhelmed them, for many of those who had died were fellow officers and the wives and children of fellow officers, people whose table they had in the past shared.

From Cawnpore, the new objective of the column became Lucknow, where Havelock's men were beleaguered with the remnant of Sir Henry Lawrence's indomitable garrison and, despite heavy casualties, the column was now in a better position than ever before to carry out its purpose. Still heavily outnumbered, they had acquired incomparable reinforcements in the shape of four companies of the 93rd Highlanders, whose pipes and flaunting kilts enlisted Bobs' admiration almost as much as their gallantry in action. With them also marched those of Havelock's men who had been left in Cawnpore on account of sickness. Nauseated by the atrocities of the Nana Sahib, the whole force was inspired by a single goal—the relief of their countrymen besieged in Lucknow. They were determined to win through or die in the attempt.

On 31 October, Bobs came near to achieving the alternative fate when, riding far ahead of the column on reconnaissance with his assistant, Lt Mayne, he was surprised by a large enemy force and had to ride for his life. Mayne, a youngster of his own age, got away in fine style despite the storm of small arms fire that followed them, but Bobs' horse stumbled and rolled down into a *nullah*,* cutting its rider's hand badly in the process. In the end horse and rider escaped, but only in the nick of time, for as Bobs' charger swam through the current, the enemy appeared on the bank, opening fire afresh with a hail of badly directed musketry.

Such incidents, of daily occurrence in this campaign, must have been unnerving, but it is typical of Bobs that within the hour he was back in action, his zest for combat undiminished. This time the odds were less unequal, and though his force was still heavily outnumbered, it was a matter of seconds before the enemy broke and fled, giving Bobs his chance of revenge as he rode them down at a headlong gallop through the long grass.

By 5 November, all opposition at the approaches to Lucknow had been cleared away, and the relief force was able to prepare for its ultimate rescue of the British garrison at bay in the heart of the city. That day, riding by, Bobs saw what no mutineer had yet been able to achieve, as Light Infantry and Highlanders fled in all directions before the onslaught of a swarm of bees, disturbed by a Lancer subaltern who made his own languid escape on a charger. Wrote Bobs, masking reality with Victorian decorum, 'The Highlanders were heard to remark on the unsuitability of their dress for an encounter with an enemy of that description.'

Whether Hope Grant, now commanding the column, hoped to be given the chance and glory of relieving Lucknow is not clear but, if so, they were ambitions doomed to failure, for on

* Ravine.

66

9 November Sir Colin Campbell took over command. 'Old Khabadar'* was, in his own inimitable fashion, one of the great figures of British military history. Aged sixty-five and a man of the people, he had risen by sheer merit from the ranks of the Peninsular Army to generalship, knighthood and, later still, a peerage in the service of his Queen. Men questioned humorously whether he was more careful of his money or of his men's lives (he was notoriously parsimonious of both) but always affectionately and always *sotto voce*, for Sir Colin when roused had the temper of a fiend incarnate. What men never questioned was that he knew his job, for there were no two opinions on that. 'Old Khabadar' was a soldier of high quality. Thin, crabbed, and inclined to favour the kilted Highlanders from whom he had risen, he had the confidence of all troops and the devotion of his fellow-countrymen.

Now, as the troops massed and Sir Colin pored over the maps so dear to his meticulous soul, the whole force was thrilled by an exploit as gallant as any yet performed. Henry Kavanagh was a square-jawed, Irish, Company's clerk, a civilian perennially in debt and the father of a large family. Few men besides his immediate associates and the bailiff had taken much note of him till now, yet when Outram, the commander in Lucknow, sought for a means of carrying a message to Campbell, it was Kavanagh who volunteered. It was a suicidal mission, for it lay through mutineer lines. Worse still, if he was caught, it meant a death of unspeakable agony, for the rebels were expert in the infliction of slow and mortal pain. In such knowledge Kavanagh volunteered and, against all odds, succeeded.

Sir Colin took infinite pains to perfect his plans, but once they were completed he acted decisively. After an unpromising first encounter, he also seems to have taken a liking to Bobs, and on the 13th, when they were out on a feint reconnaissance together, he gave the young staff officer the task of leading the attacking force to the Dilkusha Park. It was typical of Bobs that he wasted no time, for as soon as they returned to base he sought out an Indian prepared to act as guide and immediately reconnoitred a hidden and little-known line of advance.

The morning of the 14th dawned brightly, a day destined to live long in the annals of British India. Long before sunrise the

* 'Old Careful'.

troops were awake, cleaning muskets, checking kit, refilling limbers, and by 0900 hours the advance was well under way. Ahead lay the Dilkusha ('The Park that soothes the Heart'), and beyond its walls, amid lawns that stretched green and inviting towards the Martinière, Bobs could see deer grazing. Then, quite suddenly the scene changed as the first enemy shot crashed among them, and the cavalry trumpets pealed the 'Charge!' Within seconds they were over the wall and into the park, tangling furiously with an enemy anxious only to run. In the end it all went well, with Johnny Watson charging an enemy squadron all by himself, but Bobs found it a disappointing skirmish, for the enemy broke and fled and the Martinière was occupied without further ado. From there they could see, far in the distance, the outlines of the Residency they had come to relieve, and as the 24-pounders of Peel's Naval Brigade swung into action, the whole force knew that they were on the verge of victory.

Two days later Bobs had the unpleasant experience of finding his way back to the Alumbagh (another park—'The Garden of the World') by night, with an escort, to collect ammunition, but this time without his guide who had fled. In the end, however, he managed his task and returned to Sir Colin, whose pleasure at seeing him again was complimentary in the extreme. An even greater pleasure was now in store for, as Bobs wrote, he was able to 'refresh the inner man with a steak cut off a gun bullock which had been killed by a round shot[. . . .]' By such delights are campaigns remembered in later years.

High drama now followed as the advance continued, the pipes skirling, the kilted Highlanders deploying in the relative cool of the morning. Ahead they could see the domes and minarets of Lucknow gleaming in the pale sun, and for a time it seemed as if the feint reconnaissance of the previous day would buy a cheap success, as chance after chance was lost by the enemy, and even the canal crossing was unopposed. Then, quite suddenly, a storm of fire swept the forward elements from a now thoroughly awakened rebel garrison, and for a time 'the greatest confusion ensued'. The truth was that the royal troops had been caught at the gravest disadvantage. 'Don't bunch' is sound tactical doctrine for assault groups in any era, as Moore had been swift to emphasize in the Peninsula, yet here the rebels had caught the cavalry packed at the head of a narrow lane at a time when the guns and infantry were pouring in behind them, making retreat impossible. Only the coolness of a young gunner officer, Blunt, in bringing his troop swiftly into action, saved the leading units.

The check had come from a cluster of garrisoned houses on the right and, above all, from the Sikandarbagh. This stately pleasure park (the 'Garden of Alexander'), where lovers had dallied in kinder days, had now become a fortress. Encircled as it was by walls twenty-four feet high, with bastions at every corner, it would have been a formidable obstacle at any time. Now it had been additionally fortified, and its garrison stood at 2,000 mutineers. For them, surrender was out of the question: it was a fight to the finish and, standing at bay, they opened a decimating fire on the forward British troops.

Without reinforcements the day might have gone disastrously for Greathed's troops since, Bobs included, they were pinned down by a curtain of rebel fire. Help, however, came swiftly as the 53rd doubled forward from Hope's brigade, deployed to the left and swept the enemy from the forward positions he held. After them surged the 93rd Highlanders, not to be outdone, leaping onto the roofs of rebel-held huts, prising open the tile and thatch, and bayoneting the sepoys within. Campbell's trust in kilts was not misplaced.

What had passed so far, however, was a mere curtain-raiser to the battle now about to begin, for the next objective was the Sikandarbagh itself. Within minutes the artillery had opened up, the round-shot and shell scything great fragments from the white walls. The fate of the mutineers standing at bay inside was sealed as British troops cut off the route that led from the main gateway. Henceforth there would be no escape; it must be a fight to the finish.

Ten, then fifteen, then twenty minutes passed, and still the guns fired, the smoke of their discharge staining dark across the summer sky. Campbell himself was hit, struck by a bullet that had already killed the British gunner ahead of him, but the old man still sat his horse, proud and erect. Around him lay the infantry, and Bobs could hear them muttering impatiently, the Highlanders, secure in their position as pampered favourites, more vocal than the rest. And in the end Sir Colin allowed himself to be persuaded. The hero of Balaclava, he had taken many a chance with his own life, though rarely with those of his men. But now he was going to be rash. 'Do you think the breach is wide enough?' he called—it was three feet by three. 'Aye, Sir Colin,' answered two dozen voices. The old man swept his helmet from his head.

What followed is best described in Bobs' own words as one Indian and three British regiments charged into a paralysing fire, their red coats and the bright kilts of the Highlanders gleaming in the sun. Though the breach, Bobs admitted discreetly, 'would have been better had it been larger [. . .] it was a magnificent sight, a sight never to be forgotten—that glorious struggle to be the first to enter the deadly breach, the prize to the winner of the race being certain death!' First came a Highlander, then a Sikh, and both were shot dead. After them swept a flood, impatient, irresistible, ruthless, asking and giving no quarter. A slight check and they were through, cold steel the order of the day, for 'Cawnpore dinner', all nine inches of it, mounted on the end of an Enfield rifle, was the menu served by men who remembered the *Bibigarh*.

Bobs, following hard in the footsteps of the first wave, was himself unscathed, but found the body of a fourteen-year-old British drummer boy lying in the breach which he had been one of the first to storm. Meanwhile, in the corner of the old walls, the remnant of 2,000 mutineers were making their last hopeless stand as, without hope of surrender and with no chance of escape, they fell in great swathes from bayonet and ball. Wrote Bobs of the closing passages of the battle, 'There they lay in a heap as high as my head, a heaving surging mass of dead and dying, inextricably entangled.' Hardened professional soldier though he was, even Bobs was horrified. 'It was a sickening sight, one of those which even in the excitement of battle and the flush of victory make one feel strongly what a horrible side there is to war.' Some of the dead and wounded were burning, their tunics aflame, the bodies of the less fortunate writhing as the fire seared them. The screams of agony were interspersed with less piteous sounds since 'those near the top of this ghastly pile [. . .] vented their rage and disappointment on every British officer who approached by [. . .] abuse of the grossest description.'

Worse was still to come, for ahead of them lay the Shah Najaf Mosque, the great white building whose dome, surrounded by thick jungle, reared into the afternoon sky just half a mile away. This too was to prove a mutineer stronghold, heavily garrisoned by desperate men, whose defence was to cost the British dear. The advance guard had already blundered as, pushing forward clumsily, Barnston's battalion of detachments had attracted a cascade of fire which hurled it back in blood and panic. With their commander dying at the apex of their advance, Barnston's men streamed back towards the little group of mounted staff officers who waited by Sir Colin. Yet the retreat was as swiftly curbed as it had begun for Major Norman spurred out from the staff and led them into the attack once more. It was one of the few occasions when Bobs' reaction in such matters was slower than the next man's.

Nearer the mosque, conditions resembled nothing so much as the medieval idea of Hell, for by late afternoon the fog of war lay so thick across the scene that the Muslim mutineers who garrisoned the walls had to illuminate them with torches. Rebel gunners, engaging in an artillery duel with Peel's Naval Brigade, swiftly found the range of cannon and infantry alike, and the ground was littered with dead and wounded. With dusk already beginning to close in, it was essential to breach the fortress before darkness finally fell, since the British force, always heavily outnumbered, was now too sharply reduced by casualties to risk a night outside the mosque. It was a crucial moment as, from the high walls, the Muslim sepoys kept up a steady fusillade, while others hurled everything imaginable upon the assaulting parties below. Men fled screaming, their uniforms ablaze with the burning oil poured on them, whilst others writhed, desperately scalded by cascading streams of boiling water.

Sir Colin, who had not been the hero of Balaclava without reason, now rode out, sword in hand, towards the walls. Half a century of hard campaigning had weakened neither his nerve nor his will to victory. Overhead, the round-shot from Peel's heavies continued to smash into the masonry, whilst the lighter discharge of grape from Middleton's Field Battery burst over the summit, giving some measure of protection to the advancing troops. Rockets, flaring through the night, also soared over the walls, to burst deep in the enclosure. Nonetheless, losses were mounting dismally as Sir Colin led his cherished 93rd towards the walls. Close at hand, Bobs was watching glumly and, even among the cheering Highlanders themselves, protests at the old general's hardihood flared up. There was, they said, only one Sir Colin, whilst they could look after themselves.

At this stage the picture suddenly changed. First, a rebel bugle call rang out, and then a questing Highlander found a tiny breach in the walls, unsuspected by the rebels. Within minutes a patrol had won it, and within a quarter of an hour the Mosque was theirs, as the enemy fled headlong to the rear. Victory, but no elation, belonged to the royal forces, for outside in the darkness and the jungle, the dead and wounded lay in their heaps. Maria Germon noted in her diary that it had been 'a most exciting day',[2] but she was inside the Residency. In the Mosque, pride was overshadowed by sorrow, and it was to the wail of lamenting pipes that Bobs lay down to sleep. He had been almost sixty hours in the saddle.

Early in the morning they were on the move once more, with another field-marshal of the future, Garnet Wolseley, distinguishing himself at the approaches to the Moti Mahal. Though the fighting was tough and at times fierce, the supremacy of the British was by now almost unchallenged. Rebel troops were unwilling to engage in hand-to-hand conflict any more, though they could still offer spirited musketry opposition, and did so when Bobs raised the Union Jack three times on a turret of the Moti Mahal at Sir Colin's order. Quixotic though it sounds, the gesture had a practical purpose—to show Outram at the Residency how far the relieving force had advanced. 'Old Khabadar' never risked the lives of those under him for mere effect.

Not until the 17th was the relief of the Residency finally effected, for neither Sir Colin nor the commanders in the Residency were men to jeopardize their forces needlessly in that most costly of actions—street fighting. Appropriately enough, when the junction of forces did come, Henry Kavanagh, the civilian clerk who had carried Outram's message in such intrepid fashion, first provided the link between them. A man who basked in peril, he was one of the most striking figures produced by Lucknow during those twilight days of the siege.

By the 19th, Sir Colin was in a fever of impatience to be away once more, and with good reason, for the enemy fire was as strong as ever and enemy morale, which had broken in the initial stages, showed signs of rising once again. The truth was that the British force, splendid though its soldiers were, could never hope to do more than relieve and evacuate the garrison. Its numbers, always puny, were shrinking daily with the inevitable wastage of war, and it is to Sir Colin's credit that he should have so stoutly emphasized this fact, for there were *beau sabreurs* in plenty to point out the advantages of now attacking the Kaisar-bagh, now somewhere else. As it was, 'Old Khabadar' would have none of such fantasies. Evacuation was, he declared, the order of the day, and that meant evacuation *now*. When Outram expostulated at the short notice set, Sir Colin flared up. 'Nothing is impossible, sir,' he snapped, his Scots accent, as ever, the more noticeable for his anger.

Everything was ready on the 22nd, and that day the long lines of civilians, flanked by soldiers, moved out towards Cawnpore. It was a motley procession, with every conceivable class and race involved. Officers' wives, clutching the tattered remains of their finery, *ayahs* carrying babies, camp followers, the wounded in *doolies*, British soldiers, and loyal sepoys—all straggled through a countryside still alive with marauding bands of robbers and, hovering at a discreet distance, organized bodies of mutineers. Amongst the throng struggled Maria Germon, weighed down with half a dozen sets of underclothes, crinolines, jewellery, and other paraphernalia which she resolutely refused to abandon.

Behind them lay Lucknow, the scene of so much gallantry and skill, the graveyard of 350 European defenders and of 140 sepoy auxiliaries who had remained loyal. Though the credit for the foresight and skill which had established the defence remained Sir Henry Lawrence's alone, the courage and tenacity of the garrison on whom he had had to rely could not be faulted. Bobs, taking time off on the 17th for a brief sight-seeing tour, had been struck by the ruins, indicative of the desperate nature of the fighting. The survivors, too, though they said little, showed the strain and hardship of the preceding months in their faces. As he wrote, 'It was a sad little assemblage: all were more or less broken down and out of health.'

There was one last service that the men of Cawnpore were

to perform as a body, for even now it was this garrison that took much of the brunt as rear-guard during the withdrawal. Perhaps it was fitting that they should have been the last to leave the city which had been the scene of their epic. Outram saw them march out, but there was one face significantly absent, for Havelock was dying. Legendary both for courage and piety, he met death as he had faced life, without fear, his son with him to the last.

One of the very last to leave was Bobs, for as staff officer he was ordered to make contact with Col Hale, commanding the left wing of the rear-guard. Unpleasant as the journey was, since it involved the use of tiny winding tracks any one of which could have hidden a party of mutineers, the return was worse, for this he had to make alone. Bobs wrote that, 'I could not help feeling that I was not in at all a pleasant position, for any moment the enemy might discover the force had departed and come out in hot pursuit.' In the end, all went well, as Bobs put spurs to his horse and galloped after the main force. Finding the Chief of Staff, Mansfield, who had given him the original orders, he duly reported, and was neither pleased nor flattered to find that that gallant officer had forgotten all about him. What made it worse was that Mansfield was not even normally forgetful but one who 'exactly remembered the particulars of any order he gave, no matter how long it took to execute it'.

The march back to Cawnpore started in earnest on the 27th after Havelock's funeral, carried out with full military honours. On the morning of the 28th Bobs was ordered to ride on ahead to find out the true position at Cawnpore. It was an assignment which nicely illustrated the perilous nature of staff work on campaign in Victorian Asia, in contrast with the pampered and envied luxury reputedly enjoyed by the staff between 1914 and 1918. On the face of it, a more dangerous mission was hard to conceive, for Windham, the officer in charge at Cawnpore, had sent a series of alarming messages to the Commander-in-Chief. Sir Colin was a man neither easily rattled nor disposed to risk his best staff officers, but in the face of Windham's pleas for help, there was no real alternative, and Bobs rode out with a nominal escort of two *sowars*. Fortunately his star, as always, was in the ascendant and he crossed the bridge to Cawnpore without difficulty, finding his way into the city, where he discovered everything to be in a state of chaos. After a brief interview with the general there, he was about to return, preening himself on the swift discharge of his duties, when the Commander-in-Chief, complete with staff, suddenly arrived. Though forty years in age lay between them, there was little to choose between Sir Colin and Bobs in matters of speed.

The return to Cawnpore marked a new phase in the task of pacification. The first and most important stage had ended with the fall of Delhi, but there had still been much to do. Now, with the close of the Lucknow expedition, the second stage had finished. No more major garrisons remained in peril, and though many of the larger towns were still enemy-occupied, their fall was now merely a question of time. Imperceptibly, too, the character of the fighting was to alter still further. The period of the great battles closed with Delhi; that of major engagements ended in December 1857 before Cawnpore. Thereafter, in increasing measure, the campaign became the junior leader's prerogative, as the mutineer forces split into small, fast-riding bands. Squadrons and sometimes, though more rarely, regiments went into action as composite units, but the day of the larger formations was almost over.

On the night of 5 December, Bobs lay down to sleep in happy anticipation of the offensive which they were to assume on the morrow, for the royal forces had regained the initiative. It was to be the turn of the Gwalior rebels, and especially of the Nana Sahib, to receive a taste of their own medicine.

CHAPTER VI

Victoria's Cross

THE officers grouped round Sir Colin Campbell on 6 December, 1857, were, though they did not know it, privileged to see one of the last attacks carried out by British troops in the full traditional panoply of the 'Thin Red Line'. Thereafter there were to be many engagements in which red coats were worn, but there were few, save perhaps for the First Boer War, in which such numbers were to be involved. When major war came again, as it did in 1899, the glory of full regimentals was already passing into history, and men stormed over the top in effacing khaki. In 1857, however, the soldiers of the Queen still marched to war in all the splendour of the past, whilst the Company's men especially tended to an oriental extravagance all of their own. By 6 December, the gleam of scarlet and gold braid was a trifle dulled by the rigours of campaign, but the regiments were still a splendid sight as they marched out to battle.

The scene was the approach to Cawnpore; the contestants 5,600 British and loyal Indian troops against over 25,000 rebels. The enemy enjoyed a slight superiority in artillery, and though a few of their troops had no great experience, the bulk of them were trained and practised soldiers. They were also the hard core of the rebellion, for they included the Rani of Jhansi's contingent as well as those of the Nana Sahib. As well they knew, there could be no redemption for them. Flight or victory were the only alternatives to death, and victory was by now a distant mirage. In theory at least, the rebel legions, led by Tantia Topi and the Nana himself, could be expected to fight desperately.

At 0900 hours exactly, the guns opened fire, cannonading

across the canal onto the enemy entrenchments, and by 1100 hours a general British advance was under way. The kernel of the plan was a feint on the enemy's left, with the real blow being delivered to his right. From his vantage point, Bobs was able to watch the whole manœuvre evolving, as two infantry brigades pushed forward in line, covered in true Peninsular style by the 4th Punjabis, who had fanned out ahead of them in skirmishing order. 'It was', wrote Bobs, 'a sight to be remembered [. . .], before us stretched a fine open grassy plain; to the right the dark green of the Rifle Brigade [. . .] nearer to us, the 53rd Foot, and the 42nd and 93rd Highlanders in their bonnets and kilts, marched as on parade, although the enemy guns played upon them.'

To a young staff officer, avid for glory but still firmly tied to his general's apron strings as a mere spectator, it was a tantalizing spectacle, for there seemed little prospect of action for him. Then, quite suddenly, the position changed as the rebel right wing swung back into full retreat. To follow up was essential, but where were the cavalry and the guns? Biting his lips with impatience, Sir Colin waited a few minutes more for the missing troops. Then, as he announced his decision, fifty years of hard campaigning were thrown aside and, for the space of a few hours he was again the boy of fifteen who had marched in the Peninsula. He would, he said, lead the pursuit himself, with one battery and his own staff and escort.

Bobs wanted no second bidding. 'What a chase we had! We went at a gallop, only pulling up occasionally for the battery to come into action, "to clear our front and flanks".' In the end they had to halt and wait for old Sir Colin to catch up, for sixty-five years had told after all. And in the middle of everything, the missing horsemen and guns arrived, chagrined at having missed the chase and full of fine fury at the guide who had led them astray. 'So off we started again, and never drew rein until we reached the Pandu Nuddhi, fourteen miles from Cawnpore. The rout was complete.' Nineteen guns fell into British hands, and all over the area rebel formations dissolved as 'sepoys scattered [. . .] throwing away their arms and divesting themselves of their uniforms, that they might pass for harmless peasants'.

For most men it might have seemed excitement enough for a

lifetime but that same evening saw Bobs riding back to Cawnpore, through an area swarming with enemy defectors, to
reconnoitre the night's bivouac. Since 'there was some risk in
going alone', another daring subaltern volunteered to accompany him, and on the way they cantered over the body of Hope
Grant's ADC, Salmond, his throat cut from ear to ear. Later
still, and by now thoroughly exhausted, Bobs thought himself
lucky, as indeed he was, to get a hunk of mutton, some dry
bread, and a bottle of beer from Probyn and his 2nd Cavalry.
Almost as pleasant was the space the cavalryman cleared for
him to sleep beside their bonfire, for wise men did not sleep
alone in the mutineer-infested darkness of the approaches to
Cawnpore in 1857.

For the next fortnight Bobs, like most subalterns in the force,
was kept busy with small expeditions, but it was not until
23 December that they marched away to Fategarh. Their objectives were now more of a police nature, the immediate purpose
being to pacify the Doab and open up communications once
more between the Punjab and Bengal. Nonetheless, there was
action in plenty on a small scale, especially for adventurous
subalterns, and Bobs rarely missed his chance.

One such incident occurred on 2 January, 1858. For a long
time the rest of the infantry had been smouldering with resentment at Sir Colin's favouritism towards the Highlanders, and
this morning rumour was abroad that he intended reserving for
them the honour of assaulting Khudaganj. It was a perilous
distinction, but one which the Irish of the 53rd* coveted fiercely.
As Mansfield's old regiment, they also felt themselves entitled
to some consideration. Now, as the Scotsmen formed up for the
attack, a bugle pealed the charge and the 53rd were off, cheering
lustily, with half a hundred angry Highlanders trying vainly to
catch up. Sir Colin Campbell was furious, 'but the 53rd could
not be brought back, and there was nothing for it but to support
them.' Within seconds 2,000 men had been launched into the
assault, and it only needed seconds more before they could
make out the colourful uniforms of the sepoys escaping from
the village.

It was a battle in which Bobs was, once again, to have his

* Though this regiment became the King's Shropshire Light Infantry, its ranks
were full of Irishmen at this time.

fill of excitement under the orders of Hope Grant (who now placed himself at the head of the cavalry) for almost at once they were away with the general leading the Brigade, Bobs a little to his left, and an adventurous Irish medical officer, Tyrrell Ross, on his right. It was a charge, if not in the classical tradition, at least full of excitement, for those mutineers who were overtaken always fought to the last. As group after group saw their hopes of escape outpaced, they turned and fought it out with volley and bayonet. In such circumstances the charge shortly became a series of miniature battles, and in one such hand-to-hand encounter Bobs in quick succession saved the life of a loyal *sowar*, killed his assailant and then, single-handed, hunted down and slew two mutineers who were escaping with a battle-standard. It was a close-fought struggle, for one of the rebels had placed his musket against Bobs' body and pressed the trigger. Fortunately it misfired, and Bobs, disposing of him, captured the standard. For these acts of extraordinary courage and pugnacity Frederick Sleigh Roberts was awarded the Victoria Cross. It was fitting recognition of a soldier whose bravery and zest for action were, even in those early days, already legendary.

The award came in every sense as a climax, since for Bobs the Mutiny was almost over. Climate and campaign had taken their toll of a constitution fundamentally delicate, and under the stress of those last months his health was swiftly breaking down. A month's enforced idleness in Fategarh did little to help him on the road to recovery. For most of the army, anxious as they were to complete the operations, it was a frustrating experience to spend a month of inactivity whilst the Commander-in-Chief and 'Clemency' Canning, the Governor-General, argued on the priority of objectives. There were also other disputes, some latent and others open, as Queen's officers, sublime in their ignorance of conditions in the Indian sub-continent, arrived by the boat-load, confident of their right to command. The more stylish were also, as those officers unfortunate enough to have served under the Earl of Cardigan had found,* openly contemptuous of those of the Queen's service who had soldiered previously in India.

All this was, indirectly, part of a feud between the newly

* See *The Reason Why* by Cecil Woodham-Smith for a good account of this.

emergent professional officers who studied their calling and the 'society' faction, as personified by the household troops and the cavalry, who claimed the right to preferment by virtue of their superior social status. Serving as he did in India for almost all his career, Bobs was involved in these disputes to only a minor extent, for the issue was largely fought out in London. But it is certainly true, though unadmitted, that during the latter part of his service, his Indian Army origins definitely prejudiced his promotion. The man who emerged as champion of the professional officers in Britain was Wolseley, now a major serving through the Mutiny campaign in the 90th Light Infantry. Himself a man of outstanding military ability, he was later to lead the 'home' school of professional officers in strong if unacknowledged opposition to Bobs' own circle. But this was 1858, and it was as true as any generalization to say that the society faction of the army reigned supreme in England. Only in India did professionalism find favour in high places.

The leader of the court or society faction in the army was already that Duke of Cambridge who, for the next forty years, was to exercise such a baleful influence over military evolution in Britain. Himself a brave soldier, and not wholly devoid of military ability, he held sound ideas on the isolation of the army from politics. He was also the soul of patriotism, and a man who had devoted his whole life to the army. Unfortunately not only was he absolute in his opposition to technical change (military 'intellectuals', which included staff college graduates in his eyes, were anathema to him), but he was unable to divorce his social prejudices from the serious business of selecting the higher commanders. It was this royal and militant reactionary who now sent his nominees to India, confident of their right to command, scornful of the impact of their ignorance, and blissful in his disregard that the burden of the day had till now been borne by the Company's officers and a few of the Queen's Service, largely from the less fashionable line regiments.

It was fortunate for British arms that the Commander-in-Chief was a man of Sir Colin Campbell's mettle. The son of a carpenter, he had risen by sheer merit through the ranks and was as much the soldiers' hero as Bobs was later to become. He was a man of strong and uncompromising character and, at the age of sixty-five, retained the originality of thought that had distinguished him in former years. Morally and physically fearless, Sir Colin had also no intention of being weighed down with a lot of nincompoops as subordinate commanders. He was no radical, for he respected rank and lineage as much as the next man, but he also loved his troops and he was not prepared to sacrifice either their lives or his military reputation on the altar of society. As he explained to the royal duke with wholly uncharacteristic tact, 'An officer unexperienced in war in India cannot act for himself.' Warming to his theme, he became less tactful. 'The state of things at present does not permit of trusting anything to chance, or allowing newcomers to learn, except under the command of others.' As was usual at this time, Sir Colin won his way.

Early in February, 1858, the force marched north-west to Lucknow, Sir Colin (for once) bowing to the dictates of 'Clemency' Canning. On the way they halted to destroy certain walled fortresses, amongst them Mianganj, where rebels had concentrated, but in the main the march lacked incident. The truth was that by now the mutineers had lost all appetite for contesting the passage of loyal troops. If cornered, they would still fight ferociously, but where escape offered, they invariably faded away.

On 25 February Bobs and a friend had what to most people would have been a harrowing experience when chasing a *nilghai*.* Incorrigible hunters both, they thought nothing of questing far ahead of the main force, and on this day they were surprised by what they believed to be a squadron of enemy cavalry. It was a fate not uncommonly suffered by British officers at the time and, with his horse blown after a hunt, Bobs had no illusions as to his probable fate. With the mutineer horsemen opening out and preparing to charge, the two subalterns exchanged last farewells, 'When lo! as suddenly as they had appeared, the horsemen vanished,' wrote Bobs. 'We could hardly believe our eyes, or comprehend at first that what we had seen was simply a mirage.' In the end, however, 'Our relief, on becoming convinced that we had been scared by a phantom enemy was considerable.' It was two chastened and shamefaced hunters who made their way back to bivouac, but the shock had been salutary 'and we determined not to risk it again'.

* A bush cow.

After months of rebel supremacy at Lucknow, the boot was now at last on the other foot, and early in March the British closed in. Though far superior in numbers and even armament, the mutineers' enthusiasm for battle had decreased to vanishing point. Nonetheless, the British took their time, for the urgency had evaporated and in Campbell and his divisional commanders, the force had leaders who only took chances when they had to. Though, as Bobs wrote of his own general, 'It was thought by some that he was unnecessarily anxious and careful', Hope Grant was to prove one of the finest military leaders of the Victorian era and a man of strong and attractive personality.

The usual preliminary skirmishes over, the army got down in earnest to the business of wresting Lucknow from the mutineers on 9 March, when volunteers swam the Gumti to reconnoitre the far bank. On the afternoon of the 11th, bombardment was already well under way, the gunners stripped to the waist in defiance of all medical theses of the time. The dark pall of war hung heavily in the sky, but though the enemy kept up a hail of steady fire, it was clear that their heart was not in the struggle. Their cavalry had already broken and fled, and mutineer corpses littered the approaches to Lucknow. It was a scene well calculated to impress any visiting notable, and the timing of the arrival of the Nepalese general, Jung Bahadur, was felicitous. Nepal had been one of Britain's most loyal allies during the Mutiny, just as her Gurkha tribesmen had provided the Company's most loyal regiments. Looking at Jung Bahadur, Bobs—no mean judge of Oriental character—found it easy to understand why, for the general was a fine figure, 'tall for a Gurkha—with a well-knit wiry figure, a keen dauntless eye, and a firm determined mouth.' The interview was destined to be brief, for Sir Colin swiftly ended it for himself and his staff alike on the plea of important business, but Bobs, hurrying into action yet again, carried with him a renewed impression of Nepalese strength, which he was never to forget.

Across the river, at the Begum Kothi, where the breach had been stormed, Bobs found the ditch piled high with the jetsam of war. Casualties had been heavy, and kilted Highlanders lay intermixed with the bearded and *puggereed* Sikhs who had fought shoulder to shoulder with them in the assault, whilst around them, infinitely more profuse, sprawled the corpses of the mutineers in extravagant Oriental uniforms. A desperate courage alone had enabled the breach to be stormed, for the mutineers had stood at bay, and it was here that William Hodson, so strangely similar to Nicholson of Delhi, had been wounded. Like Nicholson, he had fallen with a bullet through the body; like Nicholson, he had dropped at the head of his men, sword in hand, at the very mouth of the breach; like Nicholson, he had lingered a little, in mortal agony, before he died. They had both loved their parents, these men so strangely similar in their patriotism and power to inspire others, but in so little else. 'Oh my mother!' cried Hodson as he fell. There the likeness ended, for Nicholson's death set a seal upon his immortality, whereas Hodson, already thief and murderer by repute before his death, was proved to be so beyond doubt afterwards, when his effects were searched. The truth was vicious enough without calumny and Bobs, who, like the rest of the Army, admired the soldier but detested the man, was able to dispose of the slander that Hodson died while looting. The best that could be said of him in Victorian parlance was that, if he had lived like a black-guard, he had fought and died like a gentleman. Fortunate to the end, moreover, he had died at the psychologically correct time.

By the 15th, Lucknow was already virtually reconquered, and with few casualties, yet it was one of Sir Colin's less happy victories. Unaccountably lacking in his usual foresight, he had failed to use his cavalry as a cut-off until it was too late, with the result that the defeated enemy had been allowed to stream northwards through the gap. From here they had been able to fan out across the countryside, merging with the peasants and causing, as Bobs remarked, 'The needless death of thousands of British soldiers.' Even when Sir Colin, no laggard in correcting his own errors, sought to plug the gap with Campbell's Cavalry Brigade, that brigadier 'completely failed to do what was expected of him'. Bobs and his own general, separated from the rebels by an unfordable river, could only watch in impotent fury as the mutineers escaped.

In another climate, the consequences of their escape would have been of little moment, for the mutineers' value as fighting soldiers had descended almost to zero, and they could have been mopped up at leisure. The peasantry also, never slow to align themselves with the winning side, were beginning to show marked hostility to the rebels. From their assumed position as the unquestioned heroes of Northern India, the mutineers now found that they had descended to that of common foe. Hunted by the civilian population as by the military, their uniforms had become a badge of shame and a passport to death. Even the arms they carried made them a tempting target for a populace of inveterate musket-thieves. But the real trouble caused by their escape was the effect of the climate on British troops. The death toll had always been appalling, even for the Company's own European troops, but amongst the fresh drafts now arriving daily from England to reinforce the Queen's regiments it was bound to be catastrophic. Apple-cheeked lads from the Shires were a great deal more susceptible to tropical scourges than the leathery veterans of a dozen Indian summers. By May, 1858, deaths from disease were running at the rate of 1,000 a month amongst British troops alone, with those from wounds at only a hundred. When one considers the limited number of European regiments* involved, it was a fearful toll. Even during Kipling's time, the perils were appalling, as Jhansi McKenna's experiences,† fictional only in identity, showed. But Kipling was a quarter of a century later in time and in medical advancement. The British camps of Mutiny days sometimes resembled less a concentration of shock troops than a huge and primitive ward from which the burial parties plied continuously. With the sun beating down on canvas roofs, day seemed an eternity, and night a vigil of tormenting thoughts. Suicide was frequent and murder rare only by comparison. Danny Deever was not alone in his fate. ‡

Despite the climate, the Commander-in-Chief did not stay his plans when he saw the mutineers escape. On the 22nd, Hope Grant marched off to Kursi in pursuit. With him went Bobs and, commanding the cavalry, Capt Sam Browne, the designer of the famous belt. Heavy guns and infantry inevitably slowed the rate of their advance, however, and the enemy had got wind of their approach and fled before their arrival. In consequence, Hope Grant rode on with the cavalry and launched them unsupported

* Less than 100,000 European troops were in India in April, 1858.
† *Daughter of the Regiment*, Rudyard Kipling.
‡ *Danny Deever*, Rudyard Kipling.

against the mutineers. It was a fierce action, and Bobs seems not to have taken part, though he was present as escort to his general. The honours of the day went to Sam Browne, and on the 24th they reached Lucknow once more. For Bobs the Mutiny was over.

The truth was that for months his health had again been breaking down under the incessant strain, and only his determination to continue had enabled him to survive this far. By mid-March the cumulative effects of months of campaign without leave had reached their climax. The Medical Officer was emphatic and, with the major struggle over, there was no longer any reason to delay. Six years to the day after he had landed in India, Bobs handed over as DAQMG to Wolseley and took his leave of the Commander-in-Chief, Sir Colin Campbell. The old man was kind and, still more satisfactorily, was full of practical promises for Bobs' advantage. With the certainty that he would be gazetted brevet major in the not too distant future, Lt Roberts embarked for Britain on 27 April, 1858. It is interesting to speculate as to what his future would have been, had he not been obliged to proceed on sick leave, for Wolseley, replacing him under Hope Grant, laid the foundations of his own greatness in the process. Grant thereafter ensured that Wolseley was his staff officer in other theatres, including China. The probability is that in Bobs' case, his Indian Army Commission would once again have fettered him to India, unlike Wolseley, who was British Service.

*   *   *

Whatever one's interpretation of the mutineers' activities or of the conduct of the British forces so many years ago, other factors help in providing perspective. During the Mutiny the scales were not weighed in Britain's favour in the short term, whatever the long-term prospects. The men who stormed Delhi in what was the fiercest battle of the campaign, were outnumbered several times over in both personnel and arms, and during the whole Mutiny there were never more than 100,000 white troops in the field at any one time. It was the quality of the European and loyalist forces and their leadership which led to victory; in no sense did they enjoy technical or material advantage.

One frequent criticism of the British conduct of the Mutiny campaign is that it caused permanent damage to Indian faith in Britain, but this is quite untrue. Such damage as there was had been occasioned by the slow decay of John Company and not by sharp military reprisals against the mutineers. In fact a subcontinent inured to years of the grossest misrule by its own leaders was disposed to accept that the execution of mutineers was a natural consequence of rebellion. Any less vigorous punishment would have elicited surprise and criticism. The question of whether or not the mutineers had been formally tried was academic to a peasantry little accustomed to judicial process and long acclimatized to the arbitrary processes of their own native overlords.

A century of scientific and mechanical progress has made it difficult to step back across the gulf of years to the almost incredibly primitive conditions in which Bobs as a young man lived and fought in India. With anaesthetics rarely available and with putrefaction and gangrene an ever-present element of life, to be wounded almost always meant unrelieved agony if not a lingering death. *Doolies* were usually in short supply through the desertion of their bearers, and rough-wheeled *ekkas*, jolting along the uneven tracks of India were, for the lucky, the only ambulances available. For the unlucky, and they were many, disablement could mean, as it so often meant in 1914–18, lying untended through burning days and bitter nights, with the additional certainty of castration, torture, and protracted death if found by the rebels. It is hardly surprising, therefore, that British and loyal Indian troops tended to deal summarily with mutineers who fell into their hands. There was a long debit to redeem.

CHAPTER VII

Imperial Staff Officer

To the country gentleman of the mid-Victorian age and, above all, to the Anglo-Irish squire, there was only one sport worthy of the name, and that was hunting. The prints of the day immortalize what was, to Britain's forefathers, an everyday scene—the ruddy faces, the stirrup cup, the pink coats, and the spirited slender-necked horses that they rode. The horn sounding the 'Gone Away' as Reynard broke from covert, and the music of the hounds streaming after him in wild pursuit were all part of a national tradition that has long since died. It was a tradition which exacted tribute as well as conferring privilege on its devotees, for gentlemen were expected to be tough and fearless, taking the good with the bad, and bearing pain without complaint. The hunting field and allied sports set the fashion of the day and, as Lord Kitchener was later to remark, they proved an ideal relaxation for army officers in an age which demanded, above all, courage and endurance from its military men.

Into such a life Bobs, a gay young bachelor on leave, threw himself with enthusiasm. He had always delighted in field sports, and it was a devotion destined to grow with the passage of years. Now, fresh from the parched and ugly scenes of the Mutiny, the green banks of Waterford seemed to him a paradise. 'Every English tree and flower one comes across on first landing is a distinct and lively pleasure.' He might have added that every meet of the Curraghmore Pack was an equal delight. With his parents, against all expectation, not only alive but well, and his invalid sister hanging on his words, life had everything to offer to an ambitious young subaltern in the years '58 and '59. Only one element was missing from his life, and that Ireland was soon to supply.

'There too, I found my fate, in the shape of Nora Bews, a young lady living with a married sister not far from my father's place, who a few months later consented to accompany me on my return to India.' In such stilted terms Bobs in his memoirs introduced as perfect an engagement and marriage as any man has a right to expect, for from then on till 1914 Nora was his constant stand-by and support. If she lacked Bobs' personal magnetism, she was still a splendid character in her own right. Upright and as brave and determined as Bobs himself, Nora held to her principles with an open and sometimes devastating tenacity. Like almost all British women in mid-Victorian India, her life was to be clouded with many sorrows, first as child after child died and later when all the things for which she and her husband had stood seemed thrown into the balance. Yet her faith never wavered. In the dark days of 1918, after Bobs' death, when Hubert Gough, the son and nephew of some of their oldest friends, stood unjustly impugned for the retreat of his Fifth Army during the German offensive, Nora in her old age was to prove one of his stoutest champions. Neither fame on the one hand nor ill-health on the other could move this inflexible Victorian from the path she believed to be right. In some circles, as she grew older, she was (with reason) regarded as a dragon, whilst by others she was as profoundly loved, for her generosity to the young and lonely was unstinted. She was, in almost every respect, the ideal counterpart for the red-headed youngster who later became England's foremost general.

It was therefore with the stamp of professional success upon him—had he not been decorated with the VC by the Queen herself?—and with the prospect of domestic happiness assured, that he set sail with his wife for India late in June, 1859. The time of year was unpropitious, as those who have sailed the Red Sea know, but to have delayed would have cost Bobs his job in the Quartermaster-General's Department, and 'this, we agreed, was not to be thought of, so there was nothing for it but to face the disagreeable necessity as cheerfully as we could'. Neither of them was in the best condition for facing such a voyage, with Bobs himself far from recovered from the Mutiny campaign.

It is an interesting comment on the maritime practices of the day that, when passing a coral reef near Mocha in the Red Sea, they found the officers and men of a wrecked P & O ship, the

Alma, disconsolately heaving at the luggage which remained on board in an effort to salvage it. Farther on still, they themselves were to encounter heavy storms until, on 30 July, rudderless and broken down, their own ship was guided into Calcutta. Under the stress of it all, Bobs' health broke once more, and it was as a fevered invalid that he landed to begin his second tour in India.

A greater shock than 'my old enemy Peshawar fever' turned out to be Bobs' posting, which filled him with alarm. Morar, never a health resort at the best of times, resembled a furnace in August. Far worse, it was commanded by Brigadier Robert Napier. As a subaltern, Bobs was usually at pains to accommodate his superiors, but even the best subordinates are at times misunderstood, and he had been royally snubbed by Napier at Lucknow during the Mutiny. Now, as memories of this unfortunate affair welled up afresh, the Roberts household was cast into gloom. Once again, however, his luck was to hold as, journeying towards Morar, Bobs received fresh orders to report back to Calcutta. It was with unmitigated delight that he obeyed, though mystified by the cause. Was it a summons for China where Britain was once again on the brink of war? Hope Grant, his old commander, was destined to command there, but by now his new DAQMG, Wolseley, was irreplaceable. Could it be Calcutta? But what was on offer in Calcutta? Still puzzled but buoyantly cheerful, Bobs rode back to the great port, dropping his wife *en route* at Hazaribagh.

The job turned out to be one of vital promise for a junior officer, being nothing less than to organize the Viceroy's triumphal march. With the Mutiny crushed and the districts pacified, there were rewards and honours to be conferred on the loyal, and subtle warnings to be issued to those who had wavered. It was a task which required presence, position, and dignity; and who better suited to the task than Lord Canning, Viceroy of Imperial India?

So the entourage moved onward, ponderously magnificent, flanked by the blue and green of the cavalry with, in the centre, the infantry marching in steady scarlet ranks. A battery of Horse Gunners, Bobs' own arm, rode with the column, and behind them elephants, camels, mules, and bullocks. The whole line of march, complete with 20,000 human beings, occupied twenty-four miles from start to finish. And in the centre drove

Lord Canning, the first Viceroy in the Imperial India that Victoria had proclaimed the previous year. About him rode his viceregal escort of lancers, their pennons fluttering in the breeze, and everywhere the livery of countless lackeys and bearers from the palace staff glinted like birds of paradise against the drab background of the Indian landscape. All this was elaborately contrived, for the Victorians were never afraid to impress with ceremonial.

Impress they did. Whilst loyal rajahs and noblemen waited complacently for the rewards rightfully theirs, those not so loyal eyed the lean dark cannon furtively, mindful of the fate of so many mutineers. For in the heyday of the Empire, a law biblical in its simplicity prevailed, and the loyal were rewarded as surely as the traitorous were destroyed. Six months of pageantry and military display were destined to have a salutary effect on those who had doubted and to gladden the hearts of those who had stood firm. The route lay through Cawnpore, Lucknow, Agra, all the great centres of the north at which Bobs had fought or halted, and the romance of it all did much to reinforce Bobs' belief in military life.

There had already been considerable temptation for him to leave the service, for on arrival in Calcutta he had been offered a post in the Revenue Survey Department. It was a chance at which most young married officers would have leapt for the higher pay was a tempting bait. Fortunately for Britain, there were matters more important than pay to Bobs and, as he wrote, 'The recollection of the variety and excitement of the Mutiny was still fresh upon me, and I had no desire to leave the Quartermaster-General's Department.' So in the end he remained a soldier, attending the viceregal camp, planning the pomp and ceremony, even finding time to show a long-suffering Nora the battleground at Lucknow. It was an exciting interlude, blazoned with all the colour and heraldry Victorian India could evoke, and the impact upon the native peoples was powerful.

The whole project involved Bobs in a vast amount of detailed work, with the risk that, if organization went wrong, his reputation would be permanently marred, for with great names in the entourage and general officers commonplace, any slip would surely be noted. The advantages for an officer of calibre were correspondingly high, since he had unmatched opportunities for revealing his ability to the 'top brass'. Though Bobs made full use of such openings, it would be wrong to delineate him as a mere careerist for, though ambitious, he was not inordinately so, and he was never servile nor prepared to compromise on principle. Throughout his career he was careful to cultivate the great and powerful, but it was his ability, leadership, and selfless industry that in the end led him to the summit of his profession, and not diplomacy towards his superiors.

No greater test of a young officer's abilities could have been devised than the Viceroy's triumphal march now surging ponderously towards its climax, for it boasted a variety of institutions among its tents that is today difficult to credit. Even safe deposit facilities were included, not to mention a post office, telegraphs, and a score of other items. The Viceroy's immediate entourage occupied 150 tents each night, and these were increased five-fold by the need to provide for troops, followers, stores, Commander-in-Chief and staff, together with a host of other requirements. Each day's camp had its exact duplicate in course of erection at the halt scheduled for the following evening, and all these duties fell within the administrative responsibility of Bobs, still a lieutenant of well under thirty years of age.

The most memorable as well as the most poignant of all the halts was Lucknow, for Havelock and Sir Henry Lawrence lay buried there, and the ensuing ceremony was one to which the landowners of Oudh could only be persuaded to come with difficulty, 'For, guiltily conscious of their own disloyalty during the rebellion, they did not feel at all sure that the rumours that it was intended to blow them all away from guns, or to otherwise summarily dispose of them, were not true.' Throughout that troubled year of '59 the wraith of Nikal Seyn rode the North, very erect and commanding, a retinue of phantom gunners behind him, the portfires smouldering in their hands.

The route must have seemed interminable as the entourage moved from station to station, and each with its quota of grand, outlandish names to be honoured. At Fategarh, the Nawab of Rampurh, a Muslim nobleman whose fidelity in the darkest days had meant so much. At Agra the Karaoli Raja, who had for escort 'four tigers, each chained on a separate car, and guarded by strange-looking men in brass helmets'. Then there was the 'Maharao Raja of Ulwar [. . .] seated on a superb elephant, eleven feet high, magnificently caparisoned with cloth-of-gold coverings, and chains and breastplates of gold.' Prince after prince came and went to the fanfare of trumpets, stately representatives of a now vanished age.

The tour was not without its domestic incidents, and Bobs was a keen observer, Chaucerian in his love of detail, though more discreet. Lord Canning, who looked well enough on his horse, was less imposing on foot, when 'his height, not being quite in proportion, rather detracted from the dignity of his presence'. Lady Canning, in contrast, emerged rather well, until the day when her stove caught fire and burnt down the tent. In due course Her Ladyship emerged, clad in the borrowed garments of a mere knight's wife, but Bobs kept a straight face. Only years later, when all concerned were dead, was it safe to confide to his memoirs that 'as Lady Canning was tall, and Lady Campbell was short, the effect was rather funny'.

Ceremonial parades followed one another profusely as the tour wound towards its close. Meerut was next on the itinerary, and then Delhi, where Bobs attracted the favourable attention of the Viceroy by acting as that great man's guide. With his own memories of the Mutiny still fresh and poignant, it was an easy enough task, though in the process Bobs learned more about the savage history of that ancient city—amongst the most bloodstained in the world. Less impressed by recent events were the inhabitants themselves, for though there was ruin everywhere, almost every wall being scarred by shot, the people 'seemed now to have forgotten all about it. The city was as densely populated as it had ever been: the Chandni Chauk was as gay as formerly with draperies of brightly-coloured stuffs: jewellers and shawl merchants carried on their trades as briskly as ever.' On all sides the Indians smiled, salaaming to the pale invaders whose kin, only two years before, they had as cheerfully butchered under cover of night.

Matters seemed for a time less satisfactory at Lahore. There, the elephants lined up in stately parade took fright at a shower of rockets and bolted incontinently, scattering their riders in the crowded streets and in the thickets outside. 'Howdahs were crushed, hats torn off', and even the Viceroy, though 'seated in a superb howdah', was shaken. Yet in the end, though eminent personages were tumbled in the mud and famous bones ached for days, only one rider was seriously injured. History does not record the comments of the British soldiers who watched the scene.

The Viceroy's tour was by now almost over, and Bobs was afire to serve in the China Expedition where Wolseley, deprived of the Quartermaster-Generalcy by the rigid operation of the seniority rule, still managed to lay the solid foundations of a brilliant career under the fatherly wing of Hope Grant. Bobs' ambitions, wholly creditable to him as a soldier, were perhaps less complimentary to him as a husband, for Nora, who till February had dutifully followed the camp, was now far advanced in pregnancy. One who did not fail to note the fact was Sir Colin Campbell, now Lord Clyde, and he flatly refused to send Bobs to China. When, however, he made the mistake of telling Nora the reason, he was roundly snubbed for his pains. It was hardly surprising that in reply he should have 'burst out in his not too refined way: "Well, I'll be hanged if I can understand you women." ' The truth was that, deeply as he loved his family, the army came first for Bobs, and maintained this place in his esteem for the rest of his life.

On 10 March, their daughter was born, and not long after, Bobs rode up to Simla beside the *jampan** in which his wife and child lay. Though the trip exhausted her (and it was an age when 'the vapours' were fashionable) Nora survived. The house that awaited them at the top—'Mount Pleasant'—was all that they could wish for, with its approach road winding sharply upwards 'through the rhododendron forest, along a path crimson with the fallen blossom'. But the sight at the summit was still more entrancing. 'The wooded hills of Jakho and Elysium in the foreground, Mahasu and the beautiful Shalli Peaks in the middle distance, and beyond, towering over all, the everlasting snows [. . .].' The contrast inside was delightful, for there 'bright fires were burning in the grates', and breakfast was ready on a white linen tablecloth. By such flashes is the work of a lifetime remembered, long after the hardships and tragedies have fallen back into the kindly twilight of the past.

It was an idyll all too brief, for Bobs had now to rejoin the tour for the last few weeks of the march. By May, however, it was over and he was able to rejoin Nora and return to normal

* Sedan chair.

duty. In some ways it was a disappointing experience, for after the excitement of the Mutiny and even of the viceregal march, the work of a peacetime staff officer tended to pall. Not only that, but 'life at Simla was somewhat monotonous' for a couple having little interest in the perpetual round of parties and social gaiety. Fortunately there were compensations, such as 'a trip into the interior of the hills, beyond Simla', for both loved nature and the lonely grandeur of high mountains. With the heat of the plains replaced by the bracing upland air, Nora could enjoy the scenery. Loveliness abounded in the forests too, for Bobs noted that 'the scarlet festoons of the Himalayan vine stood out in brilliant contrast to the dark green of the solemn deodar.'

*   *   *

1860 proved to be a year of destiny for Bobs since at the start of it, despite the promises given to him, he remained a subaltern. In October, however, his gallantry, attention to detail, and discipline at last bore fruit, for in that month he was promoted to captain and then, for services in the field, to brevet-major, as the old Commander-in-Chief had promised. Bobs was not alone in discovering that Lord Clyde, gruff though he was, remained a man of his word. From Bobs' point of view it was a most important step in an age and service when captains of fifty were still commonplace, for he had achieved field rank, albeit brevet, well before his thirtieth birthday. Now firmly on the staff ladder, with a VC to his name and an impeccable background for those who gave such matters weight, a career of infinite promise seemed to be open to him.

Against such a background the next few years were of considerable importance since, though outwardly uneventful, they gave him the opportunity without which no professional soldier can hope to rise high—the chance to prove that distinction earned in war is balanced by efficiency in peace. He quickly earned the regard of his superiors, who learned that they had in him a staff officer to whom they could safely delegate responsibility; but it did more, for in accustoming him to the detail of staff work, logistics, and training, these years enabled him to emerge as an expert in all aspects of army command when the time came. He had enjoyed the best of both worlds—the regimental and the staff levels—in war and in peace, and this was a distinction enjoyed by few commanders during the middle years of Victorian rule.

It was in such prosaic though valuable tenor that the Roberts' life was spent during the years that ended in the autumn of 1863. Commanders-in-Chief had in the meantime changed in 1860, with the retirement of Lord Clyde and his replacement by Sir Hugh Rose, another Queen's officer, but one who was himself a Mutiny veteran of distinction and who now came straight from command of the Bombay Army. It was a bitter pill to an Indian Service already well accustomed to bitter pills but which, since India had become an Imperial possession, had hoped for more consideration in the chain of command. Sir Hugh, however, 'fifty-nine years of age, tall, slight, with refined features, rather delicate-looking', was at least a man of considerable experience of Indian conditions, and Bobs lost no time in making his mark with the new chief. Much as Bobs had admired Clyde the fighting commander, his plebeian personality and unrefined ways had sometimes irked the Etonian. Besides, Lord Clyde had made no secret of his partiality for Highlanders in emphatic particular and the Queen's Service officers in general; they were hardly sentiments calculated to please an Anglo-Irishman commissioned into the Company's force.

In contrast, no plebeian origins attached to Sir Hugh Rose, a man 'possessing a distinctly distinguished appearance', whose military abilities and successes were only slightly less notable than those of Clyde. Questions of division between the officers drawn from John Company's old force and the British Service were also, in theory, laid for ever with the transfer of the Company's troops to royal command. That theory in this differed from practice, young subalterns of as late as John Masters' day were frequently to find.* Nonetheless, the hope remained. Moreover, Sir Hugh Rose liked Bobs, admired his gallantry, and recognized his brilliance; and the compliment was returned.

The autumn of 1860 was the occasion of yet another viceregal march, this time a rather tedious affair, shorn of much of the pageantry and purpose that had distinguished its predecessor.

* *Bugles and a Tiger*, pp. 23–24.

Bobs was again chosen to be the Quartermaster-General's officer in charge of the camp, but there were compensations such as a tiger shoot at the Begum of Bhopal's palace where, as Bobs modestly put it, 'I could not resist having a shot, and was fortunate enough to knock him over.' They also visited Jubbulpore and the 'famous marble rocks at Nerbudda' where the cliffs rose a hundred feet sheer into the air, pure white at the base and a delicate grey at the crest.

The march over, life continued at Simla in the fashion common to Anglo-India of the day, with ceremonial, tiger-shoots, and pig-sticking highlighted, but always attended by the shadow of peril and disease. Early in March, 1861, Bobs had a reminder of this when he returned to a Simla layered in deep snow. His wife and baby daughter were 'pictures of health; but a day or two after my arrival the little one was taken ill, and died within one week of her birthday'. It was the first of many bereavements he and Nora were to suffer down the years.

Offers of civilian employment continued to come his way, but Bobs refused them all. To do so was not easy, for pay and promotion were notoriously better in the civil services than in the Indian Army. As a dedicated soldier, however, Bobs rejected them all, for he still craved action, and where would he have found his Kandahar in the Secretariat?

By the end of November 1861 Bobs was away on yet another march. 'Showing the Colours' was a well known and approved Victorian pursuit, increasingly popular since that never-to-be-forgotten day in '57 when the bullets had come crackling, like a swarm of angry bees, to break the long slow shadows of the Meerut sunset. This time it was the Commander-in-Chief alone who rode and Bobs, his staff officer, rode with him. Sir Hugh was a keen equestrian and a great champion of Arab horses, and it is not surprising, when his eye lighted on Bobs and his nutmeg-grey, that, 'from that moment he never varied in the kindness and consideration with which he treated me, and I always fancied I owed his being well disposed towards me from the very first to the fact that I was riding my handsome little Arab [. . .].' Bobs was being over-modest, for few senior officers were long in doubt as to his calibre, but it is from such small beginnings that great things grow.

Meanwhile the months passed in a sequence of different places

—Amritsar, Mian Mir, and Sialkot—and at each there were different events to remember, whether pig-sticking, parades, or the swift flying visits to out-stations in which Sir Hugh enthused. At Jamu the Commander-in-Chief crashed to earth, felled with his horse by a charging boar. At Jhelum, Nora was taken gravely ill. And in between, the cavalcade rode through the green sward of the countryside, its ranks a bright dazzle of different coloured uniforms. With drums thudding and the whistle of the fifes preceding them, it was a splendid spectacle.

> Ho! get away you bullock-man, you've 'eard the bugle blowed,
> There's a regiment a-comin' down the Grand Trunk Road.[3]

Even the evenings on tour were dramatic with bivouac fires gleaming into the night, lean shadows of the pacing sentries, and the still groups of sleepers clustered round the blaze, often with their rifles chained to them for security.

> Oh, then it's open order, an' we lights our pipes an' sings,
> An' we talks about our rations an' a lot of other things.[4]

Despite the hardship these were glamorous times; evenings in an age when British Imperial prestige had achieved a zenith never previously reached in Asia. Yet for Bobs the essential was missing. After four years of office routine and peace-time ritual, he was yearning once more for the activity of campaign. He had already been on the Frontier once, though in the relatively safe district of Peshawar. Now, with his Chief, he was to penetrate further, to the very fringe of 'Tribal Territory', for Kohat was a true Frontier post. Wrote Bobs, 'It was my first experience of a part of India with which I had later much to do, and which always interested me greatly [. . .] It was a wild and lawless tract of country.' Being Bobs, the fact that 'as we left Kohat we met the bodies of four murdered men being carried in, but were told this was nothing unusual' served only to whet his appetite.

When his chance of action came again, it did so in unexpected fashion, even though there was no element of surprise about the campaign itself. For months now the Yusafzai Pathans of the

Peshawar district had been giving trouble, raiding, murdering, and holding to ransom in true North-West Frontier style, whilst the authorities had scrupulously looked the other way. In a sense the whole affair was a by-product of the Mutiny, for the men behind the outbreak were in the main those same Muslim fanatics who in 1857 had raised the standard of a short-lived holy war, coincident with the Mutiny. Equally, however, a *casus belli* was superfluous in terms of Frontier warfare, as the British had more than once found to their cost during the previous half-century. When Pathans were ready for battle, legalistic formulas (which in any event they despised) had little to do with the occasion, and there was every sign that the Yusafzai Bunerwals were now set on war. Led by their spiritual head, the picturesquely styled Akhund of Swat, they were by mid-October already massing in ominous and familiar fashion along the Chamla and Buner peaks.

What was later to be known as the Umbeyla Expedition now started off in fine style, with Probyn and his famous cavalry pushing up the Umbeyla Pass, but difficulties of terrain exceeded all forecasts, and the rate of march was hardly more than six miles per day. By 24 October, with glowering enemy concentrations opening fire from the spurs of the Guru Mountain, the British advance guard, as usual outnumbered, was in serious difficulties, and though in the end they succeeded in holding their ground, they felt little optimism. Their positions could be held but that was all. It was at this stage that the Government of the Punjab lost its head and, by-passing the Commander-in-Chief, sought to order up troops without even ascertaining his view.

Sir Hugh Rose was normally an equable man, but he was now thoroughly incensed. As a soldier he had no objection to an expedition, but it must be a properly planned and organized column and not the sort of *ad hoc* collection now being canvassed by the amateur strategists surrounding the Viceroy. To organize properly also implied the possession of 'exact information respecting our position at Umbeyla, the means of operating from it, the nature of the ground—in fact, all details which could only satisfactorily be obtained by sending someone to report on the situation [. . .]'. The remedy was obvious, and by 24 November Bobs and Colonel Adye were already approaching the pass.

Despite the romance which has for so long enshrouded the grey Frontier peaks and their unquenchable tribesmen, warfare there was savage and unyielding, for in the finer arts of inflicting pain there were few races capable of teaching the Pathan anything. Perverse alike in their loyalties and their treasons, the lean Semitic mountaineers defied logical assessment, for Quixotic fidelity, even to the death, was as much part of their national character as murder. The sight of young Pathan villagers, *chappli*-shod* and armed with *jezail*† and *tulwar*,‡ springing like antelopes from rock to rock, was a sight not easily forgotten. With their fine carriage, hawks' eyes, and natural athleticism they were memorable figures. They were also dandies, delighting in splendid turbans, embroidered waistcoats and, as often as not, a red flower twined in the folds of their long oiled hair. This was the land of the *Zachmi Idil*—the 'Wounded Heart'—ferociously homosexual and indelibly individualistic. Boys might wander hand in hand in the morning, but by evening they could be in ambush, keen-eyed marksmen, vigilant behind their grey rocks.

It was a dramatic landscape, for the scenery, the climate, and the foe were all of epic dimensions. The Victorian redcoat, with his earthy humour and his unyielding courage, was a worthy adversary for these bizarre mountaineers. Even the names served to heighten this epic quality, for the struggle was hard fought among such landmarks as 'The Eagle's Nest' and 'Crag Picquet', as Yusafzai swordsmen hurled themselves, regardless of loss, into the heart of the British positions. With Neville Chamberlain, the British commander, severely wounded, the whole force was in sore need, for it was heavily outnumbered.

On 25 November, 1863, when Bobs and Adye rode in, the British position was in theory perilous, yet they found everyone in high heart. Gurkhas, Sikhs, and Europeans alike were fighting hard, and not one sepoy, even of the Pathan contingent, had deserted. Gurkhas and Pathans in fact seemed to take a delight in stalking the enemy, and Bobs records how one Buner sepoy found his own father among the enemy dead after a Yusafzai attack had been repelled. It was a shining example of the truth

* Frontier sandals.
† Pathan musket.
‡ Muslim sword.

of the Napoleonic saying that there were no bad soldiers, only bad officers, for the Pathan soldiery at Umbeyla placed loyalty to their regimental officers above the tie of tribe and religion.

It did not take the Commander-in-Chief's emissaries long to reach their conclusions, for both Bobs and Adye were men imbued with the spirit of the offensive. They were also well aware of the psychological perils of delay when dealing with ebullient tribesmen. The Bunerwals had endured serious losses and were dismayed by the reverses they had suffered at the hands of the tiny expedition. The least British hesitation would have brought them on again, the black and green standards of revolt massing afresh among the peaks.

In such conditions the two staff officers urged an advance into the Chamla Valley, and the answer was not long in coming. Having selected his aides, Sir Hugh Rose, like most commanders of capacity, was prepared to stand by their advice and, almost by return, Bobs was ordered to reconnoitre a camp near Attock, where the reserves could concentrate. Hardly had he returned from this mission before the royal forces swung into the advance. An enemy now heartened by the slight British delay had determined to attack on the 16th, but General Garvock (in charge pending the arrival of Rose) decided to forestall them and, as dawn broke on the morning of 15 December, the assault troops fell in below 'Crag Picquet'.

In theory the enemy had the best of reasons to expect success, for the line of the British assault was painfully thin. As the redcoats moved forward through the chill morning air, they could see the 'Conical Hill' ahead of them 'crowded with Hindustani fanatics and their Pathan allies'. As always, enemy forces far outnumbered the British, and they moreover included a good number of trained soldiers—men who had deserted the Company's service during the Mutiny. Now, barricaded behind *sangars,** standing at bay in a country ideally suited to the defence, Buners and Indians alike had splendid opportunities to deal the British expedition a crushing blow. The prospect of attacking any of the enemy positions seemed bleak but, above all, it seemed folly to attack 'Conical Hill', the focal point of the defence. Yet, not to attack would have been worse; it was an unhappy dilemma for the British commander.

* Stone barricades.

It says much for Garvock that he never hesitated. By 0630 hours, the whole operation was well under way as, with the screw guns of the mountain batteries snapping angrily from either flank, regiments of legendary reputation moved in to the assault. Fusiliers, Gurkhas, Punjabi Mussulmans took part, and with them the Sikhs, their red *puggarees* providing a bright splash of colour in the dawn sun. Even the cavalry were to have their turn, for the Guides and Probyn's Horse stood waiting in the wings.

The first to move was Turner's column as, with bugles shrilling the advance, the skirmishers swept forward to drive in the enemy picquets ahead. But the real test came as they approached the 'Conical Hill', its every approach and feature lined with waiting enemy musketeers. As Bobs wrote, it 'was a most formidable position; the sides were precipitous, the summit was strengthened by *sangars*.' Yet the attacking force made short work of the assault as Fusiliers, Guides, Pioneers, and Gurkhas with their *kukris* in their teeth, stormed up the bare face 'amid a shower of bullets and huge stones', and carried it at the point of the bayonet.

All these successes had been on the right wing, but elsewhere the day had proved as uniformly triumphant, for when the Pathans, massing in Umbeyla itself, swept out to scoop round the British left, the Gurkhas and Sikhs charged into them with the bayonet, and the mountain gunners took what was left. Sullenly the Yusafzai front recoiled, at first slowly and then with increasing impetus, until by midday the last enemy concentrations had dispersed and the screw guns were sweeping the few remaining elements from the approaches to Umbeyla village. Tribal *élan*, so formidable in the attack, had proved no substitute for discipline under the strain of reverse, and by 1400 hours British and Indian troops, led by Brownlow's 20th Punjabis, were surging forward to mop up and bayonet such tribesmen as remained.

Considerable though the success had been, few experienced Frontier hands made the mistake of regarding the campaign as over, for Pathan powers of recovery were as legendary as their skill in disappearing and merging with the countryside. Next morning, as British troops stood to arms in the grey light of dawn, it was without surprise therefore that they were able to distinguish the enemy massing once more on the ridges that covered the approach to Umbeyla itself. A frontal assault would have been costly, so Garvock turned their flank, and fifteen minutes later a troop of Bengal Lancers galloped in to fire the village.

If the setting was dramatic, the action was no less so as the 32nd Pioneers now found. The pall of smoke from the burning Umbeyla was already drifting across their front when a band of Ghazis swept suddenly from low scrub, their *jezails* crashing, *tulwars* bared. In seconds, the British officers of the Pioneers had fallen. In seconds more the sepoy survivors, panicking, would have broken completely. It took cool courage for Bobs and another staff officer to ride in amongst the fugitives, rally them, and drive the enemy back. Frontier warfare had its grim side, far overshadowing traditional romance for those on the spot, and to the wounded there would have been a ghastly reality in Kipling's advice, written years later:

> When you're wounded and left on Afghanistan's plains,
> An' the women come out to cut up what remains,
> Jest roll to your rifle an' blow out your brains[5]

had the Ghazis succeeded in their aim.

By now there were real chances of a settlement as the defeated enemy reeled back. The Bunerwals in particular were anxious to be friendly, though fear of the other tribes held them back at first. British terms were harsh, and wisely so, involving as they did the destruction of Malka (the trouble-centre), the dispersal of tribal concentrations in the Buner Pass, and the expulsion of the Indian agitators who had caused the trouble. Supervising these terms nearly cost a few hundred British and Indian soldiers their lives. On 19 December, eleven British officers, four companies of Guide Infantry and twenty-five of cavalry marched out along the track that led to Malka; amongst them rode Bobs.

From the start the omens weighed heavily against their success, for in place of the 2,000-strong Bunerwal escort they had been promised, the two colonels (both called Taylor) and their subordinates found a mere fifty waiting, and the anxious expressions of even these boded ill for the expedition. To cap all, cold soaking rain fell continuously out of a grey sky. It was a dreary little column that splashed out along the muddy path from Umbeyla that afternoon. By nine o'clock next morning, conditions were still worse, with large groups of heavily armed Amazais* hanging on their flanks. Far above them brooded Malka, fitting lair for a pirate tribe, its stone battlements defiant above the spur on which it stood. Almost impregnable, its rear secured by the summit of the Mahabun Mountain, its garrison looked out into the blue haze of the Hindu Kush, peak after peak rising to north and west of them, shading away towards Afghanistan and Chitral.

Nonetheless, Col Taylor's column had been ordered to destroy Malka, and as the last of the sunset beamed over them, they reached their destination. For a time it looked as if they would never leave, since 'the Amazais did not attempt to disguise their disgust at our presence [. . .] and they gathered in knots, scowling and pointing at us, evidently discussing whether we should or should not be allowed to return.' That night the sentries paced restlessly, and there were few in the British column who slept well, for they could hear ominous sounds through the darkness—the clink of metal on stone, the mutter of sullen voices, the stir of heavy concentrations of men.

By next morning, matters rose swiftly to a climax as the British party, obedient to their orders, fired Malka, 'And the huge column of smoke which ascended from the burning village [. . .] did not,' wrote Bobs, 'tend to allay the ill-feeling so plainly displayed.' Even the VCOs† of the Guides Infantry, tough veterans of a hundred border skirmishes though they were, were plainly nervous since, Pathans themselves, they understood only too clearly the trend of the Pushtu conversation around them. Unflinchingly loyal, they were prepared to pay the forfeit of their lives, but without enthusiasm.

It was at this stage that the inherent strain of chivalry, which so often and inconsistently distinguishes the Pathan race, was to exhibit itself. Matters could hardly have been more menacing, for less than 500 British and Indian troops stood at bay, under the thick cloud of smoke that blanketed the neighbourhood,

---

* A tribe of Pathans.

† Viceroy's Commissioned Officers, a status peculiar to the old British Indian Army, open to Indians promoted from the ranks. VCOs held a position mid-way between a Commissioned and a Warrant Officer, and formed the backbone of the old Indian Army.

surrounded by up to 10,000 Amazais, and each of these was himself a warrior in his own right. Big men with hooked noses and baggy trousers, they gathered, awaiting a propitious moment to sweep in. Had they done so, not a single soldier could have survived, for the tribesmen were already at close quarters, and every Pathan traditionally carried a musket, knife, and crossed bandoliers of ammunition.

Fortunately, the officer in charge, Reynell Taylor, was equal to the occasion. Ignoring the muttered threats and menacing gestures, he marched straight into the crowd. Though courage was one of the very few traits the tribesmen admired, they were by now too angry to be impressed, talking 'in loud tones, and gesticulating in true Pathan fashion, thronging round Taylor'. The colonel, a tall, erect man, was by now isolated from his men, and although he appeared wholly unconcerned, it was quite obvious to all that they were on the verge of tragedy. That it never occurred was due in part to the restraint of the British present, in part to fear of the retribution that the British Army would exact, and above all to the sudden intervention of the Bunerwals. There were only sixty of these with the British party, but they belonged to a powerful tribe. To offend them would, as the Amazais well knew, have been to provoke a vendetta and Pathan blood-feuds were endless and catastrophic.

The head of the Bunerwal contingent now came forward, thrusting his way through the crowd to the colonel's side. Grey-bearded, lacking an arm and an eye, he was himself a fearless and imposing figure. Now, as he reached the colonel, he did not hesitate, and his strong voice rang out across the crowd. 'You can, of course, murder them and their escort, but if you do, you must kill us Bunerwals first, for we have sworn to protect them, and we will do so with our lives.' It was a strain of Quixotic gallantry that appealed to the Amazais, spoken in a language they understood, and, temporarily muted, they stood aside while the British marched away.

There were to be other tense moments before they finally reached base, as when a fanatical Amazai charged downhill on them, waving a standard, watched by a thousand of his brethren, but even here the wiser of his fellow tribesmen caught him in time. It was with profound relief, nonetheless, that Taylor's contingent reached the Umbeyla Pass and the rest of the expedition once again, on 23 December. The orders which had sent them out in such small numbers had been reckless, and few of those waiting at the pass had ever expected to see them again. Angriest of all was the Commander-in-Chief, Sir Hugh Rose, for news had filtered back to him at Mian Mir. Tough though these Victorian soldiers were, it had proved an assignment that not even the bravest could relish.

On his return to Peshawar, Bobs settled back into garrison life once more. Though he had every reason to expect some advantage for his part in the Umbeyla expedition, he was to find his comparative youth an insurmountable bar. Ability and courage were all very well, but a recommendation that he be given a brevet lieutenant-colonelcy, sent in by no less a person than Sir Hugh himself, was tersely refused on the grounds that, at thirty-two, Bobs was too young. Gruff old Sir John Lawrence, brother of the hero of Lucknow, was Viceroy now, and the day when he and Henry had been the young lions of the administration seemed a trifle faded. With the emergency over, the establishment at Simla was again in the ascendant. Youth was fine enough in battle, but the well-tried rut of service was a good deal more suited to the hierarchy of peace.

It was a sore blow to Bobs, whose ambitions had not lessened with the years, but there were compensations to be found in garrison life. Hunting with what later became the 'Peshawar Vale' remained his principal delight during the few more weeks they spent there. Then came a posting back to Simla, with what Bobs characterized as its 'slightly trying gaiety'. Neither he nor Nora were socially-minded though, typical Victorians as they were, they enjoyed charades in private and kept open house for a small circle of friends. Donald Stewart* and his wife were their special intimates, but as time went on and Bobs grew more senior, he and Nora made a point of cultivating the younger officers. Many a lonely youngster, fresh from home, was to find in the Roberts' household something of the atmosphere he had left behind with his parents in England. In a sub-continent where self-restraint was not always easy nor always the rule, Bobs and Nora set a standard of behaviour that few could surpass, and his magnetism was such that the younger men were usually happy to follow his example.

* Later Field-Marshal Sir Donald Stewart, Bart.

But now Bobs' health was once again breaking down. As he wrote, 'Throughout the whole of 1864, I was more or less ill', and though he ascribed it to the effects of office routine, the truth was that overwork, the rigours of active service, and the effect of the Indian climate on a naturally delicate constitution were having their result. Not unexpectedly, the medical men recommended leave, and in January 1865 Bobs and his wife sailed for England on the S.S. *Renown*. It was an important experience for Bobs since he was given command of a batch of 300 time-expired men. Indian Army officer though he was, he had always felt a deep affection for British troops, and close association with these old soldiers, many of them Crimean veterans, brought out his powers of leadership to the full.

There was good cause for his solicitude, for the lot of a Victorian private was no bed of roses, with its brutal discipline, high death-rate, and poor pay but many found a return to civilian life still worse. Liberty and *laissez-faire*, those proud landmarks of freedom extolled by the rulers of Britain, were splendid fare for the affluent, but for the poor it had its darker side in the crime, hunger, and unemployment that flourished amid the urban slums. It was small wonder that when the *Renown* landed at Portsmouth between flurries of snow, Bobs at the final parade noticed that, 'Some of the poor fellows were already beginning to be anxious over their future and to regret that their time with the colours was over.' Kipling's vision of the old soldier seeking re-enlistment in 'a tickey ulster an' a broken billycock 'at'[6] was no poet's fantasy but a tragic and disreputable fact.

Though far from being a social reformer, Bobs was a man of rich humanity and unswerving patriotism. As a professional soldier, moreover, he had seen the rare courage with which British troops fought, and he had often been sickened by the brutal conditions to which they were needlessly subjected in the name of discipline. Very early in his military career, he had been horrified by a flogging parade—'The only one, I am glad to say, I have ever had to attend.' Reflection on this 'barbarous and degrading custom', to which British but not native soldiers were subjected, had started a train of thought which, by 1890, was to make him the hero of all British troops. A high Tory, he also had the moral courage to distinguish between the good and the bad of past ages, and to come out strongly for what he believed to be right, even though in so doing he appeared at times almost radical to the military reactionaries of his day.

Now, on board the *Renown*, he had the chance as early as 1864 to demonstrate his views with a leniency practised in the teeth of the officers' opposition. Characteristically, he did not hide his motives. 'I told the men that we had now met for the first time and I was unwilling to commence our acquaintance by awarding punishments; we had to spend three or four months together, and I hoped they would show, by their good behaviour while under my command, that I had not made a mistake in condoning their transgressions.' Nowadays such an approach is trite, but in 1864, 'the officers seemed somewhat surprised at my action.' Nonetheless, the soldiers showed that he had been right, 'For they all behaved in quite an exemplary manner throughout the voyage.' In his disciplinary attitudes Bobs was far ahead of his time, for even in the British Service itself the officer corps regarded such ideas as radical. For a major of Indian Artillery to take an interest in the welfare of British troops was almost unheard of in an age when the rank and file were regarded as little better than criminals. The sentimentalists who harp upon the proclaimed sufferings of the natives under British rule are, historically, on dangerous ground for the truth is far otherwise. Despite sharp reprisals during the Mutiny and occasional excesses elsewhere, the British guardians treated their native charges more gently than the authorities at home treated Britons and better by far than the natives treated each other. The real sufferers were the British soldiers and their families, and it is upon their blood and sacrifice that the British Empire was built. Bishops and missionaries endlessly intoned the rights of African and Asiatic, but there were few men besides Bobs and Kipling to enter the lists on the side of the waifs of the Industrial Revolution who took the Queen's shilling.

The Roberts now spent a year in the United Kingdom, with Bobs slowly recovering his strength and enjoying his favourite sport with several packs. The old General, his father, was still hale, and the more affable for having been made a KCB. All in all, Bobs spent a happy leave and it was with something of an effort that he tore himself away in May 1866 to sail for India, leaving Nora to follow afterwards.

Allahabad was his station for the next year, and few places

could so well have illustrated the perils of life in India. Nora, when she arrived, chose to stay there with him, ignoring the usual hot-weather exodus of officers' families to the hills, and this in itself was an act of great courage in an horrific year during which cholera decimated the European population. In the end, conditions became so bad that the special camps in which the troops were kept, well away from the ordinary cantonments, degenerated into mere charnel houses. Men doubled up, screaming and blue in the face, died in hours, for there was no known cure—whilst those not yet afflicted drank hopelessly, awaiting their turn. It was part of Bobs' duty to visit these camps daily, and there was much to be done, not least the arrangement of recreation and entertainment, 'For if once soldiers begin to think of the terrors of cholera, they are seized with panic, and many get the disease from sheer fright.' Such was the prevailing medical ignorance that this belief was widely held and precautions accordingly varied from the primitive to the non-existent. Inevitably, these camps were hideous places, yet Nora, courageous as ever, chose to accompany Bobs on his rounds for there was work to be done for the living and letters to be written for the dead. It was an example of the Roberts' practical brand of Christianity, a brand more eloquent than any homily from the pulpit.

CHAPTER VIII

The Small Wars

ONE of the least known of all Britain's Imperial adventures, as well as one of the best organized, was the Abyssinian War of 1867. In its origins it was simplicity itself. Theodore, Emperor of Abyssinia, was three parts lunatic and wholly despot. A criminal, an interloper, a fanatical Christian and, for all his madness, a shrewd tactician, he had come to the throne in 1855 by the simple expedient of defeating and (usually) slaughtering other legitimate contenders. Like all such men when they first achieve power, he had sought to cast a veneer of legality, or at least of popular justification, over his usurpations. Behind the scenes, rivals were dismembered and the dangerous eliminated, but in public at least, all was carefully stage-managed in the initial years of his reign.

At first all seemed promising, for he had a wife who exercised some measure of control over him, and a British consul—Plowden—whose advice he followed. Reform was the word of the moment; slavery was to be abolished, and taxation drastically altered. By 1862, however, all this was past, for the wise wife, Tavavich, was dead, her twelve-year-old successor a mere cipher, and Plowden had been murdered by dissident tribesmen. With discipline relaxed, sexual promiscuity and alcohol began to occupy an increasing part of the Emperor's life and, under the strain of debauch, a mind never distinguished for balance began to break down.

All this was a familiar story, and one responsible for British intervention in places and decades as widely separated as the annexation of Oudh and the war against Lobengula, King of the Matabele. Plowden had been kindly, a father-figure to whom the half-crazed despot had looked for advice, but Capt Cameron, his successor, though also dutiful, proved less sympathetic to the Emperor's excesses. A terse military man, he gave respect where it was due but to the brooding Theodore, teetering on the brink of insanity, it seemed that Cameron's manners were perfunctory. Without further ado, in January 1864, Theodore cast him into prison, adding for good measure the inevitable crop of hapless missionaries.

The Victorian era is today popularly associated with what the politicians call 'Gunboat Diplomacy'. The slightest trouble and the navy sailed, sailors and marines disembarked, and the whole affair was swiftly and gruesomely settled amid a flurry of bayonet charges and brass bands. So at least the legend runs. Generalizations are, however, often painfully inaccurate, and the swiftness of retribution by 'Gunboat Diplomacy' is no exception to the rule. Cameron had been seized (and tortured) at the beginning of 1864. By July 1867, emissaries were still vainly negotiating for his release, with Theodore alternately threatening and abjectly supplicating their forgiveness. As Bobs wrote, quoting the British agent at Aden, the delay had been fatal, for in Abyssinia the belief had become general that 'England knew herself to be too weak to resent insult.'

The exact course of the incidents leading up to the expedition are of little moment here. Like all paranoiacs, Theodore could be as persuasive one moment as he could be atrocious the next, and the British Government was in consequence kept in alternate hope and frustration. By August 1867, however, the Cabinet had been forced to the point of decision and in that month an expedition was firmly agreed. An officer of the Bombay Army, Lt Prideaux, was already in Abyssinia, and the news spread quickly through Simla, as the ambitious and the daring raised their heads. Active service meant promotion, a campaign medal, and even the chance of a decoration—important considerations in a service where promotion was still slow and distinction hard to come by.

Among the first to react was Bobs, and in typical fashion. When the news came through he 'called upon the Commander-in-Chief and told him that, if my battery was sent on service, I wished to join it and was quite ready to resign my staff appointment.' Once again he was fortunate for though Rose had retired in the previous year, his successor was Sir William Mansfield, the Anglo-Irishman, Chief-of-Staff to Lord Clyde during the Mutiny, who had first sent Bobs off on a mission during the retirement from Lucknow, and then forgotten about it. This time Sir William proved neither forgetful nor disappointing but 'particularly kind in his reception of me'. Mansfield's failure to promise anything definite was irritating, but in the end everything turned out well, and Bobs' lifelong friend Donald Stewart was appointed to command the Bengal Brigade with Bobs as his AQMG.

By mid-August everything was in train for the landing, with none other than Bobs' old dragon of Mutiny days, General Napier, as expeditionary commander. But even this could not damp Bobs' ardour with a fight in prospect, and the preparations forged ahead with remarkable efficiency. The credit for this must undoubtedly go to Napier, an officer who combined knowledge and experience with an energetic and forceful nature. It could fairly be claimed that the Abyssinian Expedition was one of the best organized and equipped expeditions in the history of British arms. With ice-making machines, water condensers, a light railway, and large quantities of Maria Theresa dollars (but only Maria Theresa, since the Abyssinians admired the outline of her breasts) the campaign seemed fairly set for success. At least the Government at home was determined to avoid the commissariat and ordnance scandals that had followed the outbreak of the Crimean War. No other British Army of comparable size had ever sailed to action with the profusion of stores enjoyed by Sir Robert Napier's men.

All this augured well, and even the intelligence branch was of high calibre. Unfortunately for Bobs and his brigadier, neither was destined to experience the joys of such luxurious campaigning, for no sooner had they landed at Zula than their brigade was broken up, Stewart posted as station commander to Senafé, and Bobs ordered to remain at Zula itself as Senior Staff Officer. Wrote the frustrated warrior mournfully, 'The disappointment was great, but, being the last-comer, I had no unfairness to complain of.' Nonetheless it was a devastating prospect. To miss action was, in Bobs' eyes, bad enough, but the conditions of life and work at Zula must have seemed even worse. At a time when the rest of the expedition was marching inland, in fine weather and through gorgeous scenery, winning glory and renown, Bobs spent four months poring over returns and indents. Yet if 117 degrees in the shade was enough to damp the most exuberant professional zeal, even in Zula there were some compensations to be found. In Bobs' case they were all on the S.S. *Euphrates*, where George Tryon, another and hospitable Old Etonian, provided excellent dinners and even better baths.

By the beginning of July, when Sir Robert Napier returned to Zula, the whole campaign was long over. Theodore, abandoned by his army, had committed suicide, the missionaries and Cameron had been released, and the troops, in fine fettle after an easy victory, had re-embarked. Even from Bobs' own viewpoint all was not in vain, for with that uncanny flair he possessed for being in the right place at the right time, he had attracted the favourable attention of Napier. Whether the General had pangs of conscience over his earlier attitude at Lucknow is not clear, but at all events he now showed the utmost cordiality towards Bobs, insisting that he voyage with him as far as Suez and, most important of all, that he be the bearer of Napier's final despatches to London. The advantage of the latter may at first have seemed doubtful when, arriving at the 'town' door of the old, royal, and crusty Commander-in-Chief, the Duke of Cambridge, Bobs was sent about his business by the butler after handing in the despatches. Even that, however, turned to advantage, for the Duke, all contrition when he realized his servant's *gaffe*, at once sent for Bobs and introduced him to his guests, who included the Prince of Wales. Six weeks later Frederick Roberts was gazetted brevet lieutenant-colonel.

It was a promotion which could be regarded as a parting of the ways. Till now he had been a junior officer, albeit of field rank—promising, courageous and popular—but still junior. With years of staff work behind him, the threat of a return to regimental duty, with all that it would have meant in terms of retarded promotion, was tending to loom ever larger. Much as he enjoyed regimental work, with its closer association with the rank and file, it is questionable whether as just another gunner officer Bobs would ever have marched as commander first to Kandahar and years later to Pretoria. British history would have been the poorer and military tradition would have been robbed of one of its brightest personalities. As matters transpired, the promotion, though brevet, was decisive, for he was now offered

1 Brigadier-General John Nicholson. (*National Portrait Gallery*)

2 Major-General Sir Henry Havelock. (*National Portrait Gallery*)

3 General Sir Colin Campbell. (*National Portrait Gallery*)

4 Hindu Rao's House, Delhi

5 Officers of the 60th Rifles inside the Palace of Delhi, shortly after its capture

a new and senior staff post created in the QMG's Department, and acceptance proved decisive. Henceforth he was to be a staff man and thereafter a commander. The days of regimental soldiering were over.

By February 1869 Bobs and his wife were back in India, though at heavy cost, for on the way out their six-month-old daughter died. It was the second such tragedy they had suffered, but they were not alone in their bereavement. The garrison graveyards of India are filled with the small and pathetic tomb-stones of British children, and before the year was out the Roberts were to lose a third child, this time a baby boy, at Simla. Understandably, these were shattering blows to Nora, and Bobs, a kindly and devoted husband, was deeply upset. Both knew, as all who served in Imperial India inevitably knew, that this was the price exacted from those in the Queen's service in the tropics, and they paid the price without complaint.

Nonetheless, the canker had bitten deep. Both loved children passionately and longed for the family till now denied them, and the effect of their grief was to make them withdraw still further from the gay life of the hill station. Neither had ever taken to Simla 'society', and the Anglo-Indian social round held many elements alien to Bobs' nature and of which he disapproved. Honourable in everything else, the British in India were often strangely lax in matters of sex in an age when at home sexual restraint was ferociously enforced.

Both the climate and the shortage of European women had a great deal to do with this. In the older days, the problem of women had been solved simply and logically by the acquisition of native mistresses, but as the living standards of the British rulers soared, so did their dislike of miscegenation. In the old disreputable days, they had lived on close, almost intimate, terms with the ruled but now in the respectability of their closed cantonments, the pulsating, fertile, murderous life of the Indian cities passed them by. As Francis Yeats-Brown was to write of the period immediately before the First World War, 'Outside, people prayed and plotted and mated and died on a scale unimaginable and uncomfortable. We English were a caste [. . .] It was pleasant enough to be a Prince.'[7] Yet this isolation also had its disadvantages. The sternest critics of miscegenation were, understandably, the wives of Britons serving in India, yet few bachelors are designed for chastity. As the same author wrote, 'When one sense is thwarted, others are sometimes freed and quickened, although at what cost to the mind's rhythm I do not know. I do not know how far discipline of the sex life is a good thing. But I know that a normal sex life is more necessary in a hot than a cold country. The hysteria which seems to hang in the air of India is aggravated by severe continence of any kind.'[7]

Among the British in India, the result differed sharply between individuals, though the cause remained the same. Among wives, the sensuous took advantage of their husbands' absences in a fashion impossible in England, and of the rest, the weakest still went to the wall, overborne by the pressure of white men who outnumbered white women by ten to one. Not even the 'fishing fleet'* could alter these proportions to any appreciable degree. Sexual life among the cantonments remained, in consequence, illicit and intense, for the Mrs Hauksbees were numbered in their dozens and the Mrs Reivers† in their hundreds across the face of India. All this was inevitably at its most flamboyant in the hill stations to which the grass-widows escaped during the flaming heat of the Indian summer, while their husbands continued to toil in the plains. To bachelors, starved of a sexual outlet for months, sometimes years at a time, places such as Simla offered blissful opportunities. Though philanderers and wolves were probably as plentiful as in any society and age, it nevertheless remained true in essence that the British in India were a fine community, whose faults derived from their situation and the climate rather than from vice.

In judging the weaker among his fellows, Bobs was less intolerant and a great deal more just than the present age. Blessed by a happy marriage, he applied the rules a great deal more strictly to himself than to others. Those of whom he disapproved, he avoided, though when he reached high office he also took care not to promote them for in India a man's private life was never exclusively his own. Popular social events, holding as they did little interest for Nora or himself, were in the main avoided, and the circle of friends whose company they enjoyed were always people with similar standards to their own.

* The large number of single girls who came to India in search of a husband.
† *Plain Tales from the Hills*, Rudyard Kipling.

His great interests lay in his profession and in field sports; in both he excelled. Pegging across the dusty *maidan*, with lance awhirl, cantering at the head of a column of cavalrymen, hunting the wild boar with spear—these were the delight of Bobs and his circle. Yet, throughout all these years, Bobs was also steadily maturing in his profession, gaining that intuitive touch—*fingerspitzengefühl*, as the Germans call it—without which no commander can ever hope to achieve the zenith. He had never been a rigid, mechanical soldier, but a profound student of tactics and strategy. Now, with a thorough knowledge of staff work, he was invaluable to senior officers in peace and in war—for he was icy cold in action.

Some of this was the fruit of book-work, for as Wolseley remarked later, what was needed for the mental training of an officer was a limited amount of reading and a lot of thought. In Bobs' case, these requirements were fulfilled. His experience of war had been wide and varied, and he had had the chance to observe a number of generals at close quarters and to study their methods and dispositions in action. Now, when still comparatively young, he had risen high in the QMG's Department, and his star was still in the ascendant. Even his aversion to alcohol and his love of field sports were to help him further, for at an age and in a climate which sent men quickly to seed, he retained his fitness in body and brain. Hot weather, which made most Anglo-Indians drink deep, had no effect on Bobs, the blue ribbon man.

In 1870 the Indian Army officers won the first round in their long struggle for equality with the British Service, for in that year Lord Napier of Magdala, commander in the Abyssinian campaign, was appointed Commander-in-Chief, India—the first Indian Army man to hold the post since Clive. It was an appointment of immense significance, not merely to Indian Army officers but to British arms, for Lord Napier was a man who knew his job. He was also, in striking contrast to not a few British Service nominees, a soldier who knew India, her conditions and her troops, and the results were swiftly apparent. At a time when the British Army in England was still shackled to obsolete drill evolutions on the parade ground—'Barrack Square Ballets' in Wolseley's contemptuous phrase—the Indian Command under Napier's direction had brought in a system of realistic tactical training manœuvres. He was also meticulous in personal supervision. As Bobs wrote, 'No Commander-in-Chief ever carried out inspections with more thoroughness than did Lord Napier [. . .] he spared himself no trouble. On the hottest day he would toil through barrack after barrack to satisfy himself that the soldiers were properly cared for; Europeans and natives were equally attended to [. . .]'

With such a man at its head the Indian Army rose swiftly in efficiency and morale, and even the British regiments there, freed from the hand of the Duke of Cambridge, at last had the chance to better their fighting techniques. It was not the first time, nor yet the last, that the British officers of the despised 'Native Army' were to act as pathfinders for their more privileged compatriots of the British Service.

By now Bobs was a confirmed admirer of Lord Napier, for they had a common bond in their scientific outlook on the business of war, and (though Bobs was too discreet to reveal the fact in his memoirs) on the claims of the Indian Army to full recognition. When they had first met, Bobs 'used to think he was not very favourably disposed towards me', and with good reason, since Napier was that wounded colonel who, lying on a couch in the Lucknow Residency of Mutiny days, had 'wrathfully asked me whether I had measured the openings,* and on my saying I had not, he added: "You had better wait to give your opinion until you know what you are talking about," ' and much more in the same vein. The Abyssinian expedition, however, had changed all that, for Napier, a tough old veteran, all walrus moustaches and broad features, was a good judge of character, and it had not taken him long to assess Bobs as foremost among the junior leaders of the Army. His nomination of the young major to carry despatches to London was proof of that, for it had given Bobs the opportunity to make valuable contacts and to take some merited leave. Napier was shortly to give still more signal proofs of his favour.

Meanwhile the months passed at Simla, with hot summer and cold invigorating winter alternating—that wonderful winter of the northern hill stations when, towards evening, 'The snow takes the most gorgeous colouring from the descending rays of the brilliant Eastern sun [. . .] opal, pink, scarlet and crimson.'

* Made in the walls, for the purpose of letting guns and carts through.

He and Nora used to stand and watch it together until the sunset had died and 'the whole snowy range itself' turned 'cold and white and dead against a background of deepest sapphire blue'. Then it was time for them to retreat 'indoors, glad to be greeted by a blazing log fire and a warm cup of tea'. It was a quiet and idyllic existence which suited them both, with Bobs, anxious as ever to add to his military accomplishments, learning telegraphy and morse, whilst Nora, inevitably, became pregnant again; and 'in September a daughter was born'.

By next year, another minor expedition was in prospect, this time on the far side of India. There, well inland from Comilla and north-east of Chittagong, the southern tip of Assam points down in an accusing finger towards the Arakan across country that may conservatively be described as uninviting. The least inviting part of all was the high ground called the Lushai Hills, yet this was to be their goal, for the hills were the home of a tribe of brigands. For years they had proved a thorn in the flesh of the tea-planters, but in accordance with the British precept of too little and too late, measures to date had failed. Now, however, the Lushais had gone too far for they had kidnapped a little English girl, Mary Winchester, and even the Lieutenant-Governor of Bengal must needs bestir himself. Simla had been duly apprised, the wheels of routine had ground, the army had been advised, and in September 1871 Bobs found himself journeying towards Calcutta with his old friend Major-General Donald Stewart.

This time it was to be an expedition shorn of all the heraldic symbols; no lancers, their pennons fluttering, their lanceheads glinting in the sunlight; in fact no cavalry at all, for this was jungle country in which no horse could live. Only infantry could manœuvre here—infantry and the fierce little screw-guns of the mountain battery carried on mules. Six battalions, 200 armed police and one battery was the force available, the whole split into two columns. Each was led by a brigadier—Bourchier, based on Cachar, and from Chittagong that Brownlow whose leadership of his regiment as a major had already excited Bobs' admiration during the Umbeyla Campaign a few years before.

Few participants had any illusions of what awaited them, for there was little glory to be found in 'the vapour-bath-like atmosphere of the valleys [. . .] a succession of hill-ranges covered with jungle forests, made almost impenetrable from the huge creepers [. . .]' For Bobs himself, there was enormous preliminary work entailed, since, as senior staff officer to the force, supply was his responsibility. It was mid-November before he had organized everything sufficiently to leave Calcutta. By then, after gruelling exertion in a harsh climate, he was down to eight stone—'Rather too fine a condition' as he put it 'to enter on a campaign in a mountainous country, so thickly covered with jungle as to make riding out of the question'. Yet by early December, he was already deep in the jungle approaches to the Lushai Hills, as part of Brownlow's column. Even with the advanced medicine and comparative comforts of 1942–45, campaigning in Burma and Assam was cruel, but in 1871, with few drugs, no air transport, and a sketchy supply system based largely on elephants, it was a hazardous, often desperate undertaking. However, neither cholera nor the swirling fever mists of the low-lying valleys could halt them as, hacking their way through almost impenetrable jungle, the column reached the Tuibum River on 22 December, 1871. They had covered 104 miles in twenty-nine days in fearful conditions and, the next afternoon, forward troops went into action for the first time, a young policeman being killed at Bobs' side.

Even before this initial battle, climate, disease and terrain had taken a fearful toll, with the column already down to 250 fighting men. Despite their lack of numbers they went briskly into action and a few days after Christmas the offending chief, Lalbura, opened negotiations from his capital, Vonolel village.

There was, however, to be another round of fighting, this time decisive, in January 1872, when the mountain battery opened up with such devastating effect that Lushai resistance collapsed entirely. To students of modern warfare, it seems little more than a police action, but like so many of the small wars of the Empire, it is remarkable for the light it throws upon the hardihood and courage of British officers and men in face of appalling conditions. By 1 April, Roberts was back in Simla with only the memory of bamboo-bridged chasms, towering forests and unwavering valour to mark the end of yet another minor campaign. But it was an experience Roberts was never to forget and he called his famous Arab charger 'Vonolel' in tribute to the man whose son, Lalbura, the British expedition had defeated. He, himself, had come back with his reputation still further enhanced, and fortune had smiled on him in other ways, for on New Year's Day, while on campaign, he had received the news that Napier had personally appointed him DQMG.* A few days later had come the news that he was now father of a son.

Now, as he arrived back in Simla, he found a domestic crisis raging. Nora was suffering her usual ill health (though for one so delicate she contrived to live to a ripe old age). Far more serious was the attempt made by the *ayah* to murder Bobs' new son by pushing sharp pieces of cane down his throat. The baby had only been saved by the vigilance of his British nanny, and the cause of it all had been the *ayah*'s desire to change her job and her husband's reluctance to let her do so. Incredibly, the little boy survived, despite internal haemorrhage, and grew up to win the VC posthumously.

In his professional life, Bobs continued to move forward. At the age of forty, he was now a CB though, as he wrote bluntly in his memoirs, a brevet would have been more useful. He was also henceforth to act intermittently as Quartermaster-General. Only lack of rank prevented his being appointed to the substantive post when Lumsden vacated it early in 1873, for as a lieutenant-colonel Bobs was regarded as being too junior. Though he did not know it at the time, his lack of seniority was a deficiency Napier himself had determined to remedy, for the old field-marshal rarely stood on ceremony when the right man was to hand for a post. Though, for the time being, the Quartermaster-Generalship went to Edwin Johnson, Lord Napier ultimately had his way and Bobs succeeded to the post on an acting basis until January 1875, when he became a substantive colonel, and thus able to fill a major-general's vacancy.

Otherwise the next years passed pleasantly enough in routine work and in the field sports that were his delight. Now pig-sticking at Jamu as guest of the Maharajah of Kashmir—for Bobs revelled in one of the most dangerous sports in the world—now sight-seeing with his wife, he was an essentially happy man, at peace with himself. Nothing could have been more breath-taking than the mountain scenery near Simla and it was among these high peaks that Nora loved to wander with Bobs and their old friend, the artistic Col Baigrie. Only the death of

* Deputy Quartermaster-General.

his father, now almost ninety, cast a brief sadness over his life. Father and son had spent little time together, for Bobs' youth had been spent in England while the old man had served in India. Nonetheless, strong ties of affection bound them, for the Roberts were a united family.

In 1877, the proclamation of Queen Victoria as Empress of India provided a major opportunity for the type of lavish pageantry on which Anglo-Indians prided themselves and which all the world still secretly loves. There was something of a vanished feudal splendour in the ceremony and its surroundings, in the huge pavilions, bright banners, and caparisoned stately elephants. A woven palace, with a satin dome for canopy in the blue and white colours of the Star of India, brought a touch of romance to even the dullest viewer, though Roberts described 'The Throne Pavilion' a shade prosaically as 'a very graceful erection'.

It was an age of full-blooded, unequivocal imperialism, with the percussion of massed bands and the tramp of marching battalions to hypnotize its adherents, and no one who watched could fail to read the lesson of Imperial strength in the scarlet of the Line, the green of the Rifle battalions, and the bright shimmer of thousands of bayonet points. True, the elephants cast a temporary blight on proceedings when, alarmed by the massive artillery salute, they fled, trumpeting, in every direction. But all men love a pageant, and a few minutes saw the crowds reassembled once more, feasting their eyes on the princely and the great in this Victorian Field of the Cloth of Gold. There were material benefits too—honours, decorations, and more practical still, a general Indian Army pay increase—to mark the creation of a new Empire. Maharajahs swore fealty, and the assembly broke up in an atmosphere of pride and good will.

CHAPTER IX

Frontier General

Le Roi est mort. Vive le Roi! First the Viceroy, Lord Mayo, had died in the Andaman Islands, murdered by a convict, then old Lord Napier had retired as Commander-in-Chief, to be replaced by Sir Frederick Haines. It says much for Bobs' abilities that within weeks of their taking office, both Haines and the new Viceroy, Lord Lytton, should have had the fullest confidence in him. Doubtless he himself lost no opportunity in strengthening first impressions, but time and experience were to prove them right.

1872 was a year in which the need for good men in India was more than ever paramount, since trouble was once again building up far off to the north-west. For some time there had been peace with Afghanistan because Dost Mahomed, the Amir, had in his later years come to accept the worth of the British connection. With his death in 1863, however, turmoil had begun to brew, with Sher Ali, the unworthy son of an able father, covertly stirring the pot whenever occasion offered. Within a few years, he was himself in trouble, for he lacked any capacity to rule and the Afghans were never a people to overlook defects in deference to lineage. Revolt followed revolt as other members of the royal family sought to take advantage of his weakness, and by 1873 it was clear that not even the red-herring of anti-British senti-ment was likely to save Sher Ali's throne for long. This in itself was nothing new, for the whole history of Afghanistan is saturated in blood and treachery, and to have conceived an Amirate of Kabul and Kandahar free from intrigue would, in the nineteenth century, have been naive.

The real trouble lay with the Russians who, then as now, were unable to resist the temptation of fishing in troubled waters,

waters rendered ever more ominous by the inconsistent policies followed by successive Viceroys. In particular, the views of the one proconsul who might have been expected to cope with the Afghans had proved altogether the most disastrous. Sir John Lawrence had once been a good administrator, but time and responsibility had robbed him of his talent for dealing with the wild men of the north-west. Nothing could have been more disastrous to British prestige (and therefore to British interests) among men with the outlook of the Pathans and Afghans than what was sarcastically called his policy of 'Masterly Inactivity'. In the first place it repelled those who might otherwise have been friendly, for they knew that they would get no support. Secondly, it encouraged the Russians and thus confirmed certain of the Afghan nobility in their belief that Moscow was the centre to which they should look. In the third place, inaction was, in Afghan eyes, synonymous with fear, and they had not forgotten the dark days of 1841 when they had destroyed Elphinstone's army.*

It was therefore the deficiencies of British policy—its timid omissions rather than any positive action—which had brought danger flooding in from the north-west. Lawrence had made the mistake of appearing to recognize all three claimants to the throne (they were brothers) with the logical result that none of them trusted him.

Although by 1873 Lawrence had been four years retired, and Lord Lytton sat in his place, the disastrous results of Sir John's policy still lingered on. With the Shah of Persia intriguing in the west and Russia manœuvring on the Oxus, the stage seemed set for a full-scale crisis and Sher Ali, the reigning Amir, was just the man to set match to the train.

1876 saw a further heightening of tension, with the British Government, prodded at last into activity by Sir Bartle Frere, making definite overtures to Sher Ali. By this time, however, the boot was on the other foot with the Amir, who had been too often snubbed in the past, now firmly on his dignity and precise in his rejection of Simla's sudden courtship. As a foreseeable gloom descended on the Secretariat, another typical Victorian reaction was equally capable of being forecast; the time was not far distant when the columns might be expected to

* In the 1st Afghan War. Only one man had survived.

march again. During these preliminary negotiations, the Commander-in-Chief and Bobs had both been heavily engaged with the ceremonial which attended the creation of the Indian Empire, but as soon as they could decently disengage themselves they were away, visiting such strategic centres as Kohat, Bannu and Dera Ishmail Khan.

Sher Ali for his part had, by February 1877, worked himself into a frenzy and the butt of his fury was the British Government. A holy war would, he assured the world, be proclaimed without delay. Afghanistan would fight to the last man. He had 7,000,000 rupees, and each one should be hurled at English heads. The Treasury in London remained unimpressed.

In India the reaction was rather more practical, for the Viceroy also had to consider the 50,000,000 volatile Mussulmans in his domain, co-religionists of the Afghans. Memories of Frontier disasters were still recent, and as a first step towards permanent pacification it was proposed to bring all Indian Territory west of the Indus under a separate district, to be governed by a Chief Commissioner. With war more than a mere possibility, moreover, a competent fighting soldier was the obvious choice. It was a reversion to the Nicholson tradition, and who better to fulfil the role than the Indian Army's foremost young officer, a man who had also been one of Nicholson's closest friends? It was this post, Lord Lytton told Bobs, 'as much to my surprise as to my gratification, that he meant to offer to me, if his views were accepted by the Secretary of State.'

There was no mistaking Bobs' reactions for 'It was above all others the appointment I should have liked. I delighted in frontier life and frontier men, who, with all their faults, are men, and grand men too.' Even the fact that it meant departure from his beloved army seemed at the time to be a small price to pay, for the truth was that after years on the staff, duty at the higher reaches was beginning to pall, and he longed for a more active life.

One condition of the Commissionership which might have proved fatal in the case of another man was that he should first take over command of the Punjab Frontier Force [PFF]. Yet Bobs was acting as major-general, whilst command of the PFF gave only the rank of brigadier-general. It was a condition over which Bobs never demurred, and those of his friends who 'expressed surprise at my accepting the position of Brigadier-General, after having filled an appointment carrying with it the rank of Major-General' were very wide of the mark. As ambitious as the next man, Bobs was still in love with his profession rather than with its ranks, and above all, with the exhilaration that living dangerously can bring. He longed for a command—and Piffa* tradition held a unique place in Indian Army lore, for it was hallowed by association with John Nicholson, Neville Chamberlain, and a dozen other names almost as rich in legend and romance.

When the offer was made Bobs never hesitated for, as he wrote with prosaic euphemism, 'The Frontier Force offered opportunities for active service afforded by no other post.' The truth was that not merely the PFF but the Frontier itself had him in its grip. It was a disease common to the best Anglo-Indians, soldier and civilian alike, for there was a clarity in the fierce air of the hills that fined men down, a taste in the lonely perils of the Khyber and Kurram which, once acquired, set its devotees as a race apart. The Tochi Scouts, lean, hard Pathans themselves, knew it, and so did the sweating crews of the mountain batteries as they hauled their mule-teams towards the clouds. And Kipling had it all to a nicety—

> The Eagles is screamin' around us, the river's a-moanin'
>   below,
> We're clear o' the pine an' the oak-scrub, we're out on
>   the rocks an' the snow,
> An' the wind is as thin as a whip-lash that carries away
>   to the plains[8]

The PFF was, above all, a command quite liable to bring him face to face with the Russians, for by now they were perilously near to British-controlled borders. Even twenty years before, the danger had seemed remote so vast were the areas of Central Asia; by 1870, however, Tashkent, Yani-Kargan, and Bokhara were Romanov property, and with Russian agents fanning out through the passes of Central Asia to spread sedition and hatred along the borders of Imperial India, there were problems in plenty to keep the best brains in Simla at work. Clumsy diplomacy had intensified the problem, since it had placed many

* Anglo-Indian term for Punjab Frontier Force.

trumps in Russian hands. Friends of Britain were hard to find in the Afghanistan of the 1870s, and for this London and Delhi had to thank their own ham-handed behaviour. Bad as he was, Sher Ali could perhaps have been brought to follow his father's policy, however uncertainly, during the early days of his rule had not her ungracious attitude deprived Britain of the least expectation of his friendship. Most damaging of all was the lack of decision apparent in British policy, for it had deprived the Raj of the respect which most men, and especially the Afghans, accord to strength.

Still, for all her importance, Afghanistan was a mere pawn in a game whose contestants were Britain and Russia. Not infrequently it was a struggle carried out silently amid the gaunt hills by grave and nameless spies. To the casual reader, Kipling's *Kim*, with its tale of Tsarist machinations, must seem a good story and little more, but to the British of Imperial India, Russian border intrigue was an ever-present source of anxiety. Romanov methods differed little, at the perimeter, from those of their Soviet successors today and to parry their many designs, as also to counter the agents who infiltrated down through the Kilik and Baroghil passes in all manner of disguise, became a major task of the Survey of India. Hurree Chunder Mookerjee (though that was not his name) was as real in his day as the 'Great Game', whose devoted exponent he was.

There was, therefore, little surprise when it was learned, in June 1878, that General Stolietoff had descended on Afghanistan with a large Russian mission, but when the British, not to be outdone, sought to despatch their own diplomatic representatives, the way was provocatively barred by Afghan troops. To the Victorians, only one answer was possible, and Bobs was appointed commander of a hastily assembled Kurram Field Force. Characteristically, he plunged straight away into a fury of organization, counterbalancing his lack of tactical experience as a field commander with thorough administrative preparation. With 116 officers, 6,550 men, and eighteen guns, his was the smallest of the three columns and the quota was by no means generous even for the others. Donald Stewart, commanding the Kandahar Field Force, with 265 officers and 12,600 men, was only relatively better off though he had four times as many guns. Moreover, to bring the largest column of all up to the

AFGHANISTAN &
THE NORTH WEST FRONTIER
1870 — 1880

RUSSIA

RUSSIA

R. OXUS

Baroghil Pass

Kilik Pass

KASHMIR

N

HINDU KUSH Mtns

NORTH WEST FRONTIER

SWAT

Chitral
Malakand
Pass

Malakand

Takht-i-Shah

Sherpur

KABUL

Jellalabad

Khyber Pass

Nowshera

BLACK
Mtns

Gandamak

Alikhels

SAFED KOH

PESHAWAR

Shutargardan Pass

Peiwar Kotal

KURRAM VALLEY

KH

RAWAL PINDI

Matun Fort

Thal

Kohat

Bannu

Dera Ishmail Khan

LAHORE

Maiwand

Kelat-i-Ghilzai

Baba-Wali-Kotal

KANDAHAR

I

N

D

PUNJAB

BALUCHISTAN

R. TARNAK

R. INDUS

0   50   100   150

miles

Quetta

JW

strength thought necessary to guard the Khyber, the authorities had had to take men away from the other two columns. Even then the 'Peshawar Valley Field Force'—as it was called—totalled only 16,179 men of all ranks and forty-eight guns.

Nonetheless, troops and commanders awaited the order to march in high spirits. The three generals (Sam Browne was commanding the Peshawar Force) in particular were old friends whose shared memories stretched back to beyond Mutiny days. There were, too, old scores in plenty to settle with the Afghans; the greatest fear to which many of the military owned really was the possibility that one side or the other might climb down before a decision had been reached in the field.

By 19 October, 1878, such anxieties were, for practical purposes, killed by the arrival of the Amir's reply to the Government of India's letter sent in August, since its purport was plain. Sher Ali was, he said, 'astonished and dismayed by this letter, written threateningly to a well intentioned friend.' Particularly disgraceful was the fact that it had been written at a time when the Amir was 'assaulted by affliction and grief at the hand of fate', and he ended by placing the matter 'in the hands of God'. 'God,' invoked by a fanatical Muslim in such circumstances, had a familiar ring. The whole tenor of the Amir's communication was, in truth, to beg the issue, for he made no mention whatever of the fact that when Major Cavagnari (as forerunner of the British mission) had sought to traverse the Khyber Pass, he had been warned by the Afghan commander that the whole mission would be immediately attacked if it proceeded further. In the eyes of Simla, the affair allowed of only one interpretation, and the Government of India prepared for war. Though the Secretary of State in London continued to hold back at the eleventh hour, hopeful that even now the Amir might make amends, all caution had been thrown to the winds in Kabul and the chance was allowed to slip by. Even Westminster was at last convinced that there was no alternative to the use of arms and far off in the mountainous north-west of India, British and Indian troops prepared to march.

*　　*　　*

'It was a proud, albeit a most anxious, moment for me when I assumed command of the Kurram Field Force; though a local major-general, I was only a major in my regiment, and save for a short experience on one occasion in Lushai, I had never had an opportunity of commanding troops in the field.' In one short passage, Bobs had summed up the disabilities that have, throughout history, attached to the generals of a British Army always congenitally short of men. Bobs' position was far from happy in most other ways, for there were already strong reasons to suspect the loyalty of the Muslim sepoys, whilst his only British infantry regiment, the 8th Foot, was 'sickly to a degree [. . .] largely composed of quite young, unacclimatized soldiers'. When he rode out to inspect them, he was horrified by the vast tail of *doolies* and ambulance carts that followed them. Even transport was chaotic, for mules, bullocks, and camels had been purchased haphazardly by the commissariat and were now streaming into the concentration points in every stage of malnutrition and disease.

With every arm of his column deficient, Bobs was well aware of the dangers confronting him, and he wisely lost no time in advising headquarters of the fact. Though at first they regarded him as merely importunate, in the end he was to win a signal victory for, having grudgingly allowed him to retain a battalion of pioneers that had been earmarked for the Khyber Force, Simla retreated still further under the joint fire of the Viceroy and General Sir Neville Chamberlain, to the extent of allocating him half of the 72nd Highlanders and half a battery of the Field Artillery. Small enough numbers in terms of modern warfare, but they were troops of tried worth, and when the time came their presence sufficed to tip the scales. Without them, there is little doubt, that faced with the opposition he found at the Peiwar, Bobs could never have won.

The truth was that the headquarters staff had quite made up their minds from the comfort of Simla that the main issue would be fought out at the Khyber, and it was only the intervention of great men on Bobs' behalf that won the day. Even then the staff did not forgive, for disregarding the intelligence that Bobs, as the man on the spot, had sent them, they insisted that he leave half of the 5th Punjab Cavalry, the 2nd Mountain Battery and the 28th Punjab Infantry as a garrison at Thal. With Highlanders, Sikhs, and Gurkhas the only really reliable troops

6 The Secondra Bagh, Lucknow, after its final storming and capture.
(*Imperial War Museum*)

7 Wheeler's entrenchment, Cawnpore, on the day Havelock's column
arrived, 16 July, 1857. (*Imperial War Museum*)

8 General Sir Frederick Roberts and his staff in India, 1878

9 The Boers, after the defeat of their organized armies, turned to guerrilla fighting, successfully prolonging the war. The illustration shows three of their most resourceful and elusive commando generals, Christiaan De Wet, Louis Botha and de la Rey. (*National Army Museum*)

under his command, Bobs found most comfort in his staff, since they at least were all hand-picked men. Badcock, Collett, and Kennedy were his own nominees, the last two being members of the QMG's Department, whilst he was equally fortunate in his ADCs and Orderly Officers. He also had a large staff from the civil administration, headed by another Old Etonian, Col Waterfield.

In such circumstances, Bobs now prepared to march. With a grand total of 5,335 British and Indian troops under command, there was nothing to spare, and no unnecessary risks could be taken. British troops especially were in short supply, but—apart from the young soldiers of the 8th Foot—they were of fine quality, including as they did, horse gunners, field gunners, and hussars. There were also famous Indian regiments available, such as the 12th Bengal Cavalry under Hugh Gough, a battery of screw-guns, and the 5th Gurkhas. Above all, with the exception of some Mohammedan troops, the whole force was in the highest spirits and impatient to be off. Few had any doubts of the odds they would encounter, but fewer still doubted the outcome.

By midday on 20 November it was clear that the Afghans did not intend to answer the British ultimatum, and at 0300 hours on the 21st the spearhead crossed into Afghan territory. As the first rays of the sun lit down upon them, Bobs could see a magnificent panorama spread out ahead. On either side rose the mountains, high and profusely wooded, whilst ahead marched the infantry, their scouts, outflanking the column, astride the crests. And over all hung the skirl of the Highland pipes, seeming to linger in the thin air before it faded across the green-polled spurs. Pin points of flame whenever the sun shone, the bayonets of the advance party could be seen far ahead in a solid phalanx, their skirmishers thrown out to either side.

By noon next day the column was deep into the Kurram Valley with village headmen, anxious to please, laying out sumptuous meals for the General as he passed. Through such scenes had Iskander* marched two thousand years before. Though Bobs ate the chicken—he had a hearty appetite despite his lack of inches—he was in no way deceived. Reliable intelligence was proving a great deal harder to acquire than the pilau†

---

* Alexander the Great.

† A spiced chicken dish.

he relished, for the Afghans were hanging back. Not animosity but fear prompted them, fear that the British might pull out again, for they knew only too well the fate that awaited the friends of the English Queen once her armies had gone. Somewhere ahead, amid the grim mountain terrain the Amir's troops lay concentrated, and who could foretell the outcome?

The column reached Kurram on the 25th, and Bobs received striking confirmation of his belief that the main engagement was to be fought by his column as, reconnoitring to Habib Kila, he learned that an Afghan regular force of 18,000 men was moving with eleven guns into position on the Peiwar Kotal. Next day the column was hard at work forming a depot hospital, stores section, and garrison at Kurram. On the 28th they marched out under the pre-dawn starlight, 'chilled to the bone by a breeze blowing straight off the snows of the Sufad Koh.' By 1000 hours they were in a worse plight, oppressed by heat and clouds of dust, whilst the need to manhandle the guns over one *nullah* after another reduced the speed of the advance to a snail's pace.

Nonetheless, by afternoon they were approaching the site of what Bobs already knew would be the decisive battle. Rearing 2,000 feet above them into the blue sky, the Peiwar Kotal was an obstacle from which it would be almost impossible to dislodge well-trained and determined troops. On the face of it, Bobs and his column had no hope of success for the Afghans outnumbered them by three to one in men and by an almost similar measure in artillery. Even the single discernible path was virtually impassable, flanked as it was by glowering spurs from which riflemen could bring a decimating fire to bear on any advance. The enemy right flank was equally menacing, and he could see nothing of their left, for it was screened by a forest of deodars. Wrote Bobs, 'I confess to a feeling very nearly akin to despair when I gazed at the apparently impregnable position towering above us, occupied, as I could discern through my telescope, by crowds of soldiers and a large number of guns.' A further reconnaissance by his CRE* showed that the immediate route round the left flank was as hopeless as that on the right.

There were now two possible alternatives (apart from retreat); the task of finding another and wider flank approach or the more perilous choice of a frontal attack by night. It is

* Commander, Royal Engineers.

130

unlikely that even Wolseley, the victor of Tel-el-Kebir in years to come, would have opted for a night advance over such terrain, and there is nothing to suggest that Bobs ever considered it. Fortunately he was spared the need for, reconnoitring on the afternoon of the 29th, Major Collett discovered a wide flank approach round the enemy left, which involved storming another hill feature, the Spingawi Kotal, *en route*.

By the afternoon of the 30th all was ready. The townsmen of Kurram were by now openly mocking them, the women pulling back their veils in derision, the men ostentatiously spitting as they passed. Down in the bazaars, the talk was all of the coming infidel defeat, with the Gurkhas dismissed as mere beardless boys and the British column as a whole derided for its size. Though, as Bobs rather sententiously commented of the Gurkhas, 'They little suspected that the brave spirits which animated those small forms made them more than a match for the most stalwart Afghan.' The Kurram people had good reason for their doubts; 'There was no hiding from ourselves, however, that the force was terribly inadequate for the work to be done.'

Meanwhile the Afghans massed, boastfully confident of success, awaiting the frontal assault which they felt sure would come. Bobs himself was most careful to encourage them in this belief as, conquering his own inward panic, he arranged an ostentatious display of entrenching to their front and right. At the same time rumours as to the supposed direction of the assault were sedulously fostered among the Turi and Afghan camel-drivers, as well as among the Muslim sepoys whom Bobs suspected, with good reason, of disloyalty. Bengal Cavalry paraded endlessly, and gunners began digging battery positions in full view of an enemy who contemptuously awaited the British onslaught. As Bobs wrote, 'These attempts to mislead the enemy were entirely successful.' All the same, it was a perilous position in which the British forces found themselves for, unseen among the grey crags and timber-covered peaks, the tribes were massing around them and the slightest reverse would have brought them down for the kill. It would not have been the first British army to perish in the fierce Afghan hills.

'H' hour came on Sunday, 1 December. Troops fell in silently among the tents and not even the bivouac fires were dowsed, so anxious was Bobs to ensure deception. Then the long lines moved quietly out under the watery light of the moon. On either side of them rose the hills, gaunt and shadowy, and in front lay every conceivable obstacle as men fell over sharp boulders, crashed into holes and hidden *nullahs*, splashed waist-deep through ice-cold streams. There were worse hazards to come. Bobs had allowed adequate time for the march to bring them to the foot of their first objective well before dawn, and it was with consternation that he found the vanguard slipping well behind schedule. There seemed at first no reason for it but, on catching up with the 29th Punjabis, his 'suspicions were excited by the unnecessarily straggling manner in which the men were marching', and almost immediately afterwards, two shots rang out, one after the other, from a Pathan company.

It was a nerve-racking moment for the extended British line was at its most vulnerable. With his scanty force split into two groups, the main unit under Bobs himself and the minor column under Brigadier Cobbe, it was essential that the outflanking movement should be completed before dawn. For first light to have revealed them still on the march would have spelt almost certain defeat. Fortunately Bobs' nerve held, the Sikh companies of the 29th closed in, muttering grimly at this treachery, Gurkhas loosened *kukris* in their sheaths, and the men of the 72nd Highlanders moved quietly up to the Muslim troops, bayonets fixed and lowered.

By now night was almost at an end, and as Fitz-Hugh's Gurkhas marched in to the foot of the Spingawi Kotal, the first hint of day lit the horizon. At almost the same moment the enemy picquets on the Spingawi opened fire, and instantly all was noise and fury where before there had been furtive silence. With mountain guns already hurling shells at the crest, Gurkhas and the 72nd charged in to the skirl of pipes. First one trench was taken, as its defenders fell to the *kukris*, then the Highlanders were over the top, mixing with the little Mongol riflemen, carrying the second and the third line of positions at the point of the bayonet. The Afghan soldiers broke and fled, leaving even their sheepskin overcoats behind them in the panic of the moment. The British and Indian troops found almost impregnable positions deserted. Had even moderate enemy determination been shown, Bobs and his men would have been in the utmost peril. As it was, a night advance to this flank objective had won the decision. Night action was out of favour among the great armies of the European continent, but a British general had now shown that—not for the first or the last time—it was a tactic to which the professionals of the British and Indian line were well suited. It was a lesson which Wolseley was soon to emphasize at Tel-el-Kebir in an action no more notable, though a great deal more publicized.

The Spingawi won, the troops of the Kurram Field Force swept on to consolidate along the plain that lay beyond, but almost immediately Bobs thrust forward once more, remorseless in pursuit, determined to destroy the Afghan striking force completely before it had time to regroup. The scenery was magnificent, with its vast peaks, tumbling chasms, and rich green pine forests, but it was no country for the advance in an age when lack of wireless-telegraphy made contact between battle units tenuous even when conditions were ideal. In terrain such as this, even semaphore and heliograph were almost useless, and the units had to make their own way forward as best they could.

In such circumstances Bobs, up in front with the 29th Punjabis (who were still the leading regiment), found himself separated from Gurkhas, Highlanders, and mountain guns at the same time as he was heavily committed to action with the Afghan rearguard. With thick jungle all round, and enemy numbers even more preponderant than usual, there seemed every chance of disaster, for the Pathan element of the 29th, freed from the menace of Gurkhas and Highlanders, were now quite definite in their refusal to fight. Bobs was left to fight it out with a handful of British officers and a tiny party of loyal Sikhs. Fortunately, the enemy was slow to discover his advantage, and by the time that he had begun to exploit the British weakness Bobs' fighting padre, the Reverend Adams, had found the missing units and brought them on. It was symptomatic of Bobs' extraordinary good luck as a commander that the first of the lost units, the 23rd Pioneers, should have arrived at the very moment when the enemy, skirmishing up the rising ground towards the 29th, looked like securing a real advantage. Equally symptomatic of Bobs was the loyalty that he occasioned in his men; when under fire and struck by a spent bullet, he turned round to find one of his Sikh orderlies, a giant of a man, standing with his arms outstretched to shield his tiny general. Even the Pathan orderlies served him with devotion and courage during this campaign, for there were few soldiers of any race who did not love Bobs.

The stage was now set for an advance on the main Afghan positions high on the Peiwar Kotal, and Bobs' plan of attack bore the unmistakable hall-mark of almost all his operations involving as it did a flank movement and a resolute rejection of frontal assault. The very manœuvre which had almost cost him his life when the 29th Punjabis came under Afghan attack now emerged as the cause of ultimate victory. Reconnoitring for a way round the hill on which the enemy rear-guard stood, he discovered a route which did far more, since it took them behind the Peiwar Kotal itself. A penetrating eye for ground, a passionate regard for his soldiers' lives, and scrupulous preparation before action were all hall-marks of military capacity which, allied to a gift for instant decision, were destined to raise Bobs to the apex in years to come.

The second battle group under Brigadier Cobbe, meanwhile, was not faring well and casualties mounted under a curtain of Afghan fire that masked the direct approach. With Cobbe himself wounded, and the forward elements pinned down in front of the Peiwar Kotal, everything now hinged, as he had always known it would, on Bobs' flank attack from the Spingawi. It was a classic manœuvre of its kind. Time was now more than ever of the essence and, delegating his less reliable units for garrison duty on the Spingawi and elsewhere, Bobs pushed resolutely on towards the rear of the Peiwar whilst troops in front of the enemy position, headed by Hugh Gough and elements of his Bengal Cavalry, swept up the crest. At the same time a swarm of predatory Turi tribesmen, avid for loot, pushed still further to the enemy's right, under the command of Major Palmer.

Assailed from so many directions at once, Afghan troops first wilted, then broke entirely, and fled down the Alikhel road hunted by enthusiastic *sowars* of the 12th Bengal Cavalry. All units in the final assault had contributed magnificently to the final decision, not least the screw-guns of the mountain battery, but there was no doubt that the sight of Bobs' own group, edging its way to cut off their line of retreat, had finally unnerved an ill-trained and irresolute enemy. By nightfall the decision had been won and, after a night spent in the open in twenty degrees of frost, the regiments marched unopposed into the main enemy *sangars* next morning. Though the casualties had been light by modern standards, the odds had been heavy; even today the action stands as an epic of skill and courage fought out against the dramatic background of the towering hills.

A few days' pause was now inevitable, but Bobs drove the men of his command only a shade less than he drove himself in the advance, and by 6 December they were marching on to Alikhel. This time it was an advance with a difference, for the British regiments were no longer despised. Indeed, as Turis and Jajis swarmed in, anxious to offer their services, it was clear that, for the time being, in Herbert Edwardes' Mutiny phrase, 'Friends were as thick as summer flies.' Congratulatory messages were pouring in from India too; from England, the Queen expressed herself as proud and satisfied with 'the decisive victory of General Roberts, and the splendid behaviour of my brave soldiers'. Overnight Bobs, the unknown little Indian Army general, had caught the imagination of his countrymen.

Applause is heartening to any man, but there was little opportunity and, in Bobs' case, less inclination to bask in a limelight several thousand miles removed, for the dangers surrounding them were still pressing and formidable. Even the terrain, unrivalled in its beauty and breath-taking in its dramatic content, was a source of peril for cavalry and mountain gunners alike. At Sapari, descending the mountain meant a drop of 3,000 feet in two miles, down which the sweating troops often had to manhandle the pack animals.

> There's a wheel on the horns o' the mornin', an' a wheel
>   on the edge o' the pit,
> An' a drop into nothin' beneath you, as straight as a
>   beggar can spit:
> With the sweat runnin' out o' your shirt sleeves, an'
>   the sun off the snow in your face . . .[9]

Even the fighting was not over, for though the Afghan regular army had been decisively defeated, tribesmen still shadowed the column in time-honoured Afghan fashion, seeking plunder to seize and stragglers to geld. Bobs, exploring an alternative route back to Kurram via the Hariab river and Sapari, was for a time in danger of annihilation, as he and the elements of three regiments were caught in a narrow defile. They had already been long delayed by sheets of ice, considerately prepared for them by tribesmen at a point where the path was steepest but now, as they clambered down 'a way which can only be described as a ruined staircase', Bobs knew from the warnings of some friendly Maliks that the worst was still to come. Even he, however, was hardly prepared for what he now saw, for the only way open to them was a defile 'five miles long, and so narrow that the camels' loads struck against the rocks on either side'. Nor were precautions possible at the summit, since the cliffs above were too serrated with deep *nullahs* to make it possible for sentries to patrol them. Had the Afghans caught Bobs' men in such a death-trap, it is debatable whether even one would have escaped. Yet there was no way round.

Fortunately for the column, they gained the summit before the enemy, and as the 23rd Pioneers, whom Bobs had pushed ahead, debouched from the defile, they were met by hordes of Afghan warriors who, seeing their prey now already deployed, hastily sought to ingratiate themselves with the invaders. After the Peiwar Kotal, there were few tribesmen prepared to tangle with British or Gurkha troops, except with the most favourable odds.

Matters were less congenial at the rear of the column, as native transport drivers panicked and fled, leaving animals and stores to the mercy of sniping Afghans. But for the quality of his rear-guard, Bobs might have been in serious trouble. With Gurkhas and Highlanders to hold the rear, however, there was no immediate danger to the column as a whole. For the individual, matters were different since, as always in Frontier warfare, sniping was an incessant feature of the action. With the tribesmen continuing to mass, however, it was only the discipline and pugnacity of the rear-guard that averted a major attack. One gallant little incident, such as Newbolt would have loved, took place when Sgt Greer and four Highland privates rescued a wounded transport officer from certain torture and mutilation, defending him against hordes of tribesmen until rescue came. Though the officer later died of his wounds, it did nothing to detract from the heroism symptomatic of the whole force.

To win an engagement was one thing, but to wage a full

campaign on the limited resources allotted him was a very different matter, as Bobs was well aware. By Christmas, for all his skill, the force was in serious difficulty. With pack animals dying in their scores, equipment wearing out, and sick and wounded multiplying, the whole outlook was darkened still further by the ever-present concentration of tribesmen hovering on their flanks. Though in retrospect, the picture of Frontier warfare seems romantic enough, there was small comfort to be found there by the rank and file. A good deal of the savagery of those far-off Frontier struggles is recaptured in Kipling's sad little tale of the two drummer boys, Jakin and Lew, in *The Drums Of The Fore And Aft*. Certainly no experienced soldier was under any illusion about the fate of the unlucky. To straggle was to invite capture and that, for an NCO or private, meant a slow death of unmitigated torture. Officers were sometimes more fortunate, if the tribesmen judged them likely to produce a ransom, but this was far from being the rule. Even well into the twentieth century, after the First World War, when a British officer of Indian Infantry was captured by Pathans during a Frontier campaign he was castrated and flayed, his skin thereafter being pegged out for his regiment to see next morning.* In the nineteenth century, conditions were even worse, for it was an age when medical care was of a low standard, transport primitive, and the soldier a human pack-mule who had perforce to carry his every comfort upon his back.

Fortunately for Bobs, at this stage Sher Ali chose to flee from Kabul, after addressing a grandiloquent letter to the British Government in which he announced his intention of seeking the protection of the Tsar. The result was an immediate lessening of tension for the new ruler, Yakub Khan, was popularly supposed to be more amenable than his father, and the British looked forward to the dawn of a new relationship between the two countries. How optimistic an expectation this was, time alone would prove. Meanwhile, still pulsing with energy, Bobs rode out towards Khost at the head of a squadron of hussars, 200 Highlanders, two Indian battalions and two batteries of screw-guns. On paper it was a formidable force, but so wasted were the units by the campaign that their combined roll-call was little

* For an excellent account of Frontier Warfare during the 1930s, see *Bugles and a Tiger* by John Masters.

larger than that of two battalions at full strength. On the way they visited Matun fort, where a hospitably-minded Governor first invited Bobs to tea and then surrendered after suitable arrangements had been made for his welfare. He also warned Bobs that the Kurram Field Force was about to be attacked by a large number of tribesmen.

The warning was timely, and Bobs' subsequent comment that they were in 'for a scrimmage' was somewhat of an under-statement; for when dawn broke next day, the neighbouring hills were black with hostile tribesmen. Bobs had taken the precaution of putting the camp into a square with all-round defence, but despite this the situation at first seemed desperate, for the odds against them were enormous. Worst of all, a reconnaissance group sent out from the camp was in imminent danger of being cut off, and there seemed to be only one way of rescuing them. Never a man to leave his subordinates in the lurch, Bobs now rode to their rescue at the head of 225 British and Indian sabres, one mountain battery, and a few hundred infantrymen. In theory none should have returned, but in the event their casualties were light, due principally to the fact that the tribesmen, all fire and fury when they thought they had the upper hand, were rarely prepared to stand their ground against a determined foe. Others, more cunning, took advantage of Bobs' absence to attack the camp in a preponderance of numbers which would have horrified any other defenders. It was a situation, however, to which Victorian soldiers were well accustomed, and the Highland garrison remained unconcerned. Bobs, hastening back to the sound of the guns, with a bag of 100 prisoners and 500 cattle netted by a cavalry charge, found the situation in camp well under control.

A graver threat not to Bobs' life but to his career developed on the following night. It was a threat against which the valour of his troops was not proof. A group of Waziri prisoners, taken in the fighting, attempted to overpower the guard and escape. After repeated warnings had been ignored, the guard finally opened fire, and six of the prisoners were killed. The whole attempt had been carefully concerted with a plan, hatched by their kinsmen outside, to break in and rescue them. Amongst Waziris themselves, accustomed to generations of bloody ven-detta, the incident was hardly more than interesting, but to elements in the House of Commons, it offered a heaven-sent opportunity to defame the military. The allegations of Radical politicians against the guard commander (himself a Pathan) bore only the faintest resemblance to the facts. Bobs was now to experience for the first time what afterwards became a familiar occurrence—to find himself the principal target of the British left-wing politicians. On this occasion one MP went so far as to allege that the prisoners had been bound together as a preliminary to slaughter, and that thereafter 'the dead, the living, the dying, and the wounded were left tied together, and lying in one confused mass of bodies'.

Fortunately Bobs had strong nerves and was as morally as he was physically fearless, for he was already in expectation of criticism over his attitude towards the mutinous Pathan soldiery of the 29th Punjabis. These were the sepoys who had either deserted in the face of the enemy or had fired the shots during the night advance to the Spingawi Kotal. Tried by court martial, one had been condemned to death, and the remainder had received sentences of between one and ten years. Such punishments—and they were promptly and rightly confirmed by Bobs —were just the ammunition for Radicals anxious to prove the iniquity of imperialism, but strangely, they do not appear to have used it.

The public relations of the Kurram Field Force seem to have been dogged by misfortune, for Bobs also had to contend with the reporting of an over-sensational and wildly inaccurate press correspondent attached to the expedition. As incidents, they were part of the cross which a military commander habitually has to bear, and Bobs proved himself equal to the occasion. The reporter was sent smartly to the rear, a court of enquiry cleared the jemadar* whose guard had shot the escaping prisoners, and the little column marched triumphantly back to Kurram, disposing *en route* of 3,000 aggressive tribesmen with some smart cavalry work by Col Hugh Gough.

As Bobs rode back at the head of his force, he had every reason to be proud, for he had broken into an entirely new sphere. In the past he had proved himself a magnificent fighting soldier, as well as a staff officer in Berthier's tradition† of

* The lowest grade of Viceroy's Commissioned Officer.
† Napoleon's Chief of Staff.

excellence, but he had always been a subordinate. Now, however, he had proved himself as an independent commander in the most difficult circumstances, and the Queen's telegram of congratulation lying safely in his pocket proved that his action had been noted in high quarters. The Peiwar Kotal had opened new horizons to him and a knighthood, that almost mystic symbol of military success, lay only a few weeks off.

All this was splendid, and personally gratifying to the little general but, despite the success the column had achieved, no one who knew the Frontier—least of all Bobs—was deceived into believing the campaign conclusive. It was therefore unfortunate that the British Government, sweeping expert opinion aside, should have determined to conciliate under the stress of opposition tactics in Westminster. As usual in such conditions, it was the man on the spot who had to pay the price. In saying goodbye to Major Cavagnari and the mission which the Cabinet had ordained he should now take to Kabul, Bobs was far from unique in his forebodings of disaster.

Few men would have been more amused than Bobs to find himself described as fey, yet his own account of his final meeting with Cavagnari is interesting enough, for when he shook hands with that officer in July 1879 on the crest of the Shutargardan Pass, 'My heart sank as I wished Cavagnari goodbye. When we had proceeded a few yards in our different directions, we both turned round, retraced our steps, shook hands once more, and parted forever.' Nor was this all, for his presentiments had been so strong that when, the night before, he had been asked to propose Cavagnari's health in mess, he had been unable to speak. Cavagnari himself, though he affected nonchalance, must have had similar thoughts, for as they climbed the Shutargardan Pass, he had drawn Bobs' attention to that omen of disaster, a solitary magpie, and had begged him not to mention it to Cavagnari's wife.

The truth was that only a home government grossly ignorant or grossly callous of its servants' lives and safety could so far have swept aside expert advice as to send a mission at such a time to Kabul. Yakub Khan, the new Amir, might write flowery letters pleading that 'the friendship of this God-granted State with the illustrious British Government may remain constant and firm', but few men with any knowledge of the Afghan

140

character took such protestations seriously. The ink was, in fact, hardly dry upon the paper before a very different letter, also signed by the Amir, fell into British hands. In this he praised the Khagiani tribe for their rabidly anti-British attitudes, and quoted a verse which ended, 'Kill them to the extent of your ability'—an ordinance which nicely reflected the Khagiani's intentions.

To Bobs and many others, all this was proof of what they had already strongly represented—that the Afghans had not been sufficiently defeated and, indeed, still considered themselves more powerful than the British. Memories of the British reverse in 1841 were still fresh in Kabul, and amid the mud hovels of the capital, *Ghazis** came and went unceasingly, proclaiming God's preference for a *Jehad*.† Even the Pathan intermediary, Bukhtiar Khan, who acted for the British Government pending Cavagnari's arrival, placed it firmly on record with his superiors that it would be unsafe for the British mission to come to Kabul as things stood.

Unfortunately for Cavagnari and his men, the British Government was disinclined to take the obvious course. Pressure was put on the Viceroy, virtuous attitudes struck and, largely through the skill of the men destined to be Westminster's sacrifice on the altar of propitiation, the Treaty of Gandamak was signed in Sam Browne's camp. It was useless for Bobs and others like him to point out that Yakub Khan had no intention of keeping his word, for the stark fact was that the British Government did not care. The form and not the substance of an agreement was what Westminster sought, and if it sufficed to defeat the tactics of the parliamentary opposition at home, the Cabinet was prepared to stand out for no more. In such circumstances the realists' warnings went unheeded. Bobs' own argument can be seen, in retrospect, as irrefutable. 'Had we shown our strength by marching to Kabul in the first instance [. . .] and there dictated the terms of the treaty, there would have been some assurance for its being adhered to.' As it was, Bobs felt, 'The chances were against the Mission ever coming back.'

So Major (soon to be Sir Louis) Cavagnari marched,

* Champion warriors, slayers of infidels.
† Holy war.

outwardly cheerful, along the desolate roads that led to Kabul. A knight *sans peur et sans reproche*, he was an officer of the greatest ability, who knew the Pathan and the Afghan to perfection. There must have been few doubts in his mind as to what lay ahead when he parted company from Bobs on that July day so long ago. In riding to his fate, he was one of a long line of soldiers who have, through the years, been sacrificed to the wish of British politicians to achieve short-term political advantage.

Bobs had not long to wait for the fulfilment of his predictions. He had seen Cavagnari leave in mid-July, and by the morning of 4 September, the mission's bodies, vilely mutilated, were rotting in the Kabuli sun. With them, faithful to the end and having ignored all offers of surrender, lay the seventy-five Indian soldiers of the Guides Cavalry and Infantry who had marched as their escort. The exact degree of Yakub Khan's personal implication will never be known, but if he had no hand in the planning of the massacre, it is quite certain that the Amir had inflamed the passions of the Kabuli populace in general and of his soldiers (who did the deed) in particular, until this attack was the logical outcome. To Bobs, only recently created KCB, the news came as no surprise but Headquarters were, inevitably, caught unprepared. With Sam Browne's Khyber Force dispersed, and Donald Stewart's Kandahar Column greatly reduced, the Kurram Field Force was the only substantial striking group still in existence. The curtain was about to rise on the first stage of the most dramatic of all Bobs' campaigns.

*   *   *

One of Bobs' greatest accomplishments lay in the fact that he created a legend. Before him, the Frontier was an area of shadow known only to a few but, after the march from Kabul to Kandahar, it became a name redolent of Imperial glory and prowess. Bobs was, above all, human, and in capturing the imagination of his countrymen, he won their love as well. Perhaps more important still, he was dashing and courageous and invincibly patriotic, and to the Victorians he represented all that the best of them had been brought up to revere. There was romance in everything linked with his name, in the high peaks of the Hindu Kush, in the kilted Highlanders who charged under his command to the skirl of pipes, and in the dark bearded faces of the *sowars* who trotted behind him, their lance-heads gleaming under the Eastern sun.

It has sometimes been suggested that Bobs consciously publicized himself,* but no direct evidence has ever been brought to substantiate such an allegation, and to the end of his life he remained charming and natural to an extraordinary degree. He was fortunate to have reached the first pinnacle of his fame at a time when young Kipling was about to descend upon India. John Nicholson and Wolseley had no Kipling to write about them, and the poet disliked Kitchener intensely. But Father Bobs was every man's hero.

Whatever the reasons, however, the fact remains that before Bobs, 'The Frontier' was a term unknown to more than a small group of Anglo-Indians; by the time he died, it was a name on the lips of every schoolboy as a synonym of courage and romance. For all who loved bravery and hardihood and achievement for their own sakes, 'The Frontier' remained a symbol that was to have a powerful influence on the British pioneering spirit throughout the Empire.

* * *

For once the Viceroy's Council acted with speed and decision, ordering the formation of a full-scale expedition, to be called 'The Kabul Field Force', as the treachery surrounding the massacre became apparent. Bobs, as commander-elect, did not hesitate to press his position by demanding that specified officers, on whom he knew he could rely, be appointed to key positions. In some instances he succeeded. With Elphinstone's† melancholy shade forever at their shoulder, the powers in Simla were not disposed to be awkward. At the same time, there were other gods to be propitiated, and in Bobs' eyes some of the expedition's senior appointees left much to be desired.

For an Indian expedition, it was mounted with extraordinary speed. Bobs had first received news of the atrocity early in the morning of 5 September. By afternoon on the 6th, his major arrangements all completed, Bobs left Simla for Kurram, where

---

* See *Goodbye Dolly Gray*, Rayne Kruger.
† Commander in the First Afghan War.

his force was concentrating. With Yakub Khan maintaining the pretence that the whole affair was the work solely of mutineers over whom he had no control ('My true friendship and honesty of purpose will be proved as clear as daylight') an elaborate and convenient façade was continued, the Amir being informed that 'a strong British force under General Roberts will march speedily on Kabul to his relief'.

It was in such vein that the ritual continued, but it was already wearing rather thin, for reports were filtering through of emissaries sent out by the Amir to rouse the tribes. Bobs himself had no illusions about the Amir's innocence, for reliable information was becoming progressively more plentiful, and all pointed to Yakub Khan's duplicity. The proclamation that Bobs published on 16 September before leaving Alikhel was therefore correspondingly blunt, and could have left the Amir with few doubts about British intentions for, after reciting 'the lack of power of the Amir and the weakness of his authority in his capital', it stated specifically that 'the British troops are advancing for the purpose of taking a public vengeance on behalf of the deceased as well as of obtaining satisfaction of the terms entered into in the Treaty'. Requests by an evasive Yakub Khan that he be allowed to punish the murderers himself were firmly brushed aside, and on 27 September Bobs handed over the Kurram Command and rode out into Afghanistan as leader of the Field Force. The great adventure was now about to begin.

In the present century of mechanized warfare, it is hard to re-create in imagination the romantic vision of an army on the move in an era when the horse was still the principal means of movement. As he rode up the track that led to the Shutargardan Pass nearly a century ago, Bobs saw round him a wonderful scene. Ahead rode a squadron of the 9th Lancers—bronzed British regulars—and to his rear the 5th Punjab Cavalry, whilst on either side rose the fierce hills, silhouetted against a pitiless sky. The infantry marched in tight columns, the beat of their drums echoing from rocky spurs, whilst far off could be seen the tiny figures of the flank picquets, clambering along the skyline on the flanks from vantage to vantage.

Bobs was not himself with the vanguard, for that was already at Kushi under Brigadier-General Baker, one of his own nominees. Yet first blood was swiftly drawn, for hardly had the column entered the Shutargardan Pass before a party of 92nd Highlanders brought a note which warned that an attack was imminent. Within minutes they had reached 'the narrowest part of the defile' and there Bobs found a body of 2,000 Afghans drawn up. Almost immediately another party of Afghans, concealed in ambush behind rocks, opened fire, scything down the medical officer who rode at the general's side. Commented Bobs laconically, 'I was told afterwards that it was intended for me, but I remained unscathed.' What to some men might have been a conversation point for the rest of their lives remained merely an incident to him.

The tribesmen now swarmed to the attack, and a spirited engagement developed as the column wound its way through the forbidding pass. British and Indian troops alike fought hard, and two junior leaders who especially distinguished themselves were Colour-Sergeant Hector Macdonald of the 92nd Highlanders, later to command a Sudanese brigade at Omdurman, and Jemadar Sher Mahomed, himself an Afghan of Kabul. Nothing more clearly illustrates the extremes of Pathan character than Sher Mahomed, who won the Indian Order of Merit in action against his own kin, contrasted with others from the Imperial side of the border who had committed treachery and desertion some months earlier, during Bobs' advance to contact at the Spingawi Kotal. Yet the very sepoys who had deserted in the face of the enemy were themselves men who would have murdered their fellow tribesmen without a qualm in perpetuation of some impersonal blood feud generations old.

With small arms fire crashing from the walls of the pass, the crescendo of sound suggested an engagement far greater than the numbers indicated. The British forces available were considerably outnumbered but, deployed in skirmishing order, they pressed grimly on. It was no accident that tactical conceptions in India Command should have been decades ahead of those prescribed by its counterpart in London, for at a time when the emphasis at home was still on the parade ground, the square, and the old mass formations, keen-eyed Afridi marksmen had long since taught the troops on the Frontier that to bunch was to invite an early grave. Highlanders, with the tradition of centuries of conflict coursing through their veins, needed little encouragement or instruction to move in open order.

By next day the picture had changed anew, for the Amir alarmed at British military success, had hurried to Baker's camp at Kushi and was there waiting to ingratiate himself with the force commander. Yakub Khan was loud in his protestations of friendship, but Bobs was not deceived. 'An insignificant-looking man', he recorded bluntly, 'with a receding forehead, a conical shaped head, and no chin to speak of.' The Amir's conciliations were equally unpalatable, for they amounted to no more than the suggestion that British troops should delay 'that he might have time, he said, to restore order among his troops, and to punish those who had participated in the attack on the Embassy'. Bobs, whose own gaze was as straight as a lance, noted that His Highness 'was possessed, moreover, of a very shifty eye . . . [He] could not look one straight in the face . . . [and] his appearance tallied exactly with the double-dealing that had been imputed to him.' It was a matter of minutes to put the Amir firmly in his place, and thereafter to frighten him further with ominous hints that women and children would be better evacuated from Kabul in case it should prove necessary to attack it.

Though the Amir was unaware of the fact, nothing was more distasteful to Bobs than the prospect of fighting through the narrow lanes of Kabul, for he had lively memories of the storming of Delhi and of the losses it had entailed. Fortunately, the warning served. Yakub Khan was frightened and, attended by this fawning and perfidious Apollo, the Kabul Field Force advanced rapidly until 3 October, when they sighted the capital.

It was now necessary for Bobs to move with care and decision if the burgeoning fears of the populace were to be allayed. The objects of the invasion had to be made clear, potential allies courted, and causes of friction removed. With these aims in mind, he now issued a forthright proclamation to the people of Kabul. It was not, he stated, the practice of the British Government to 'make war on women and children', but those found in arms, in or about the city, would 'be treated as enemies'. To Afghans accustomed to the direct methods of their own régime, there was no mistaking that warning.

Bobs was also equally explicit to the British troops. The causes of the 1841 disaster had been diverse, but the immediate fuse that had ignited the explosion had undoubtedly been the sexual vigour of the British Tommy. Troops abroad rarely grow into plaster saints, and the Victorian redcoat (and not infrequently his officers) had proved no exception. To the oppressed Afghan women, treated more as brood mares than as human beings in a ferociously homosexual society dominated by men, these pale-skinned invaders had offered an irresistible appeal, and the capital had throbbed with unwonted heterosexual intrigue. It was not a situation which a race of the Afghans' stamp could be expected long to endure and the net result, as hatred built up on a national scale, had been disaster.

Bobs had already thought deeply about such matters, and his orders to the army were succinct. Troops were to behave themselves, to refrain from intrigues with women, and 'to cause the British name to be as highly respected in Afghanistan as it is throughout the civilized world'. It was a policy that paid early dividends for, impressed with the discipline of the force, local notables began to arrive with offers of help, some genuine, others as false as the Amir himself. The anti-Yakub faction was particularly anxious to ingratiate itself and it was something of a struggle not to accept their offers, for, as Bobs admitted, he was unable 'to feel quite at ease about the proceedings of my Royal guest'.

Indeed, matters were far from satisfactory, for if the force had secured an initial advantage by thrusting deep into enemy territory, there was every sign that Afghan resistance was stiffening. Behind them, the guardian of the Shutargardan Pass, Lt-Col Money, had already found it necessary to disperse one enemy attempt to occupy the commanding heights. Above all, the Amir, still an unwelcome guest in the British camp, was proving an expert angler in troubled waters, and his attitude, which vacillated between the arrogant and the servile, constituted a good barometer of Afghan intentions. The needle currently pointed to 'Stormy'.

By 5 October the trend was plain, and Bobs had clear intelligence pointing to an Afghan attack. (The Amir's manners were also noticeably worse.) Though the surroundings were idyllic— 'The pretty little village of Charasia, nestling in orchards and gardens, with a rugged range of hills towering above it about half a mile away'—the British troops knew that they were going to have to fight for their lives, and soon.

By the evening of the 5th it was already clear that the tribes were gathering and, next morning at first light, Bobs could see concentrations of regular Afghan troops taking up position. With only 4,000 British and Indian soldiers and eighteen guns to oppose the massed enemy, Bobs knew that his one hope lay in taking the initiative. It was a case of *periculum in mora*. 'The Afghans had to be dislodged from their strong positions at any cost, or we should have been surrounded by overwhelming numbers.' Still more dangerous was the fact that by having, perforce, to accept the Amir as a resident in the British camp, every military disposition made by the invaders was known to the enemy.

Today the column's vulnerability could easily be remedied by the simple expedient of an air strike followed by a parachute drop but in 1879, with neither aircraft nor radio to comfort them, the British troops were on their own. The gap between the Afghan army's equipment and that possessed by the British force was also of little consequence, not least because of the limits imposed upon the column's ability to transport heavy material. With peril and deficiency on every side, Bobs enjoyed only two material advantages over the enemy—his own genius, and the courage and discipline of the troops under him.

A less hopeful situation for a commander was difficult to imagine, yet the means Bobs used to defeat his enemy were classic in simplicity and devastating in effect. Never a believer in allowing his opponent the first blow, he now feinted to their left, giving them sufficient time to concentrate their forces at this point, then launched Brigadier Baker with Highlanders, Gurkhas, and Punjabis round their right flank. In doing so, he showed shrewd psychology as well as tactical command, for Afghan morale was always somewhat shaky. Experience had proved before, and was to prove again, that they could be formidable troops in the attack but defence was not their *métier*. They were especially sensitive to any movement which threatened to cut them off from their line of retreat, and the appearance of Baker's column from the woods in which it had concentrated, spread immediate alarm among the enemy ranks.

At this stage the Highlanders and Gurkhas came into their own. Hillmen all, they swept forward with bayonet and *kukri*, amid a landscape as dramatic as any artist could wish to paint.

It must have seemed at first that even the Afghan outposts were invulnerable, positioned as they were on almost inaccessible spurs, with unrivalled fields of fire. One by one, however, they fell, either to kilted Highlanders or to Gurkhas in rifle green, and as they did so the enemy echelons began to lose heart.

The truth was that though the main Afghan position on a crest of hills was of enormous strength, the quality of the enemy troops was far from matching this advantage. The British and Indian infantry carried everything before them, a fact that did not pass unnoticed by the hordes of tribesmen who crowded the nearby hills, waiting on events. As the enemy forces broke and fled, the civilian spectators began to shred away, all hope of loot gone, and by evening, with the Afghan Army everywhere in full retreat, the British troops could afford to relax. By dawn, their indefatigable commander had them once more on the move, his cavalry blocking the route which, accommodating Afghans assured him, the defeated enemy intended to take.

One interested spectator who did not have the opportunity to shred away was Yakub Khan himself. Wrote Bobs, 'Throughout the day my friend(!) the Amir, surrounded by his Sirdars, remained seated on a knoll in the centre of the camp watching the progress of the fight with intense eagerness, and questioning everyone who appeared [. . .]' Later, in impish vein, Bobs was to send an ADC 'to His Highness to convey the joyful intelligence of our success', but, to Bobs' disappointment, the Amir 'received the news with Asiatic calmness [. . .] merely requesting my Aide-de-Camp to assure me that, as my enemies were his enemies, he rejoiced at my victory'.

Bobs had laid his plans shrewdly, but not even British cavalry could compete with the speed of an Afghan retreat. The cavalry brigadier, Massy, seems moreover to have approximated to the popular caricature of a senior officer of the *Arme Blanche* for, as Bobs remarked succinctly, it had not 'struck him that the enemy might attempt to escape during the hours of darkness'. The result was that the steel jaws of the carefully laid British trap clamped on thin air, while in the hamlets of the Chardeh Valley and the slums of Kabul, Afghan soldiers shed their uniforms and melted into the background of civilian anonymity. Baker, the Brigadier commanding the 2nd Infantry Brigade, had done his best to intercept their retreat, but the Kabul River stood between him and the enemy, and it was no easy business to get even a fighting patrol over, though at about midnight he succeeded under the pale light of a new moon.

> There's the river up and brimmin', an' there's arf a
> squadron swimmin'
> 'Cross the ford o' Kabul river in the dark.[10]

With the Afghan Army disintegrated, there was nothing now to prevent Bobs from moving cautiously in towards the capital though he was disappointed by his failure to ensnare his enemy. Had his trap succeeded, his own casualties would almost certainly have been higher but, crushed between the upper and nether millstones of the British brigades, Afghan powers of resistance would have ceased to exist, a moral as well as a physical victory would have been won, and in all probability the Kandahar District would never have risen in revolt. As it was, the Afghan soldiers who had gone into hiding awaited only their opportunity to re-emerge, for they were experts at the art of living to fight another day. Ahead of the tiny British force, meanwhile, lay Kabul, 'the place I had heard so much of from my boyhood, and had so often wished to see.' Now as quiet as the grave, its sullen glowering bazaars, with their narrow lanes and 'extremely fanatical, treacherous and vindictive' people, could on the spin of a coin become a death trap for British soldiers.

There was little in the British programme designed to soothe the emotions of a volatile populace, for the serious business of retribution for Cavagnari's murder was now about to begin, and Bobs' instructions were plain. The punishment of individuals, intoned the Government of India sonorously, was to be 'swift, stern and impressive, without being indiscriminate or immoderate [. . .] You will deal summarily in the majority of cases with persons whose share in the murder of anyone belonging to the British Embassy shall have been proved by your investigations [. . .]' The 'execution of justice', concluded the despatch ominously, 'should be as public as possible, it should be completed with all possible expedition.'

Bobs set up the necessary courts without delay. Their procedure, as usual in military tribunals of that type, was swift and justice implacable. By strict juridical standards there seems at least to have been room for a plea as to jurisdiction, but the instructions of government were decisive, and no complications of international law seem to have clouded Bobs' straightforward, soldierly mind. There can be little doubt that, on the facts, natural justice for mass murder was performed.

Events now moved to a routine, as Bobs exacted first a general penalty from the Kabulis and then, through the agency of his court, from the individual offenders. A visit to the ill-fated British Residency, with its multiple scars, bloodstains, and piles of unburied bones did nothing to engender feelings of mercy in officers who had in many cases friends and acquaintances among the dead. A slow and steady round-up of those directly responsible for the outbreak, as well as of Yakub Khan's more malign advisers, was taking place and the Amir himself was subject to close, if covert, supervision.

By the third week in October, Bobs had every reason to feel satisfied for, though too old a hand for complacency, he had done well. With the praises of Monarch and Viceroy alike in his pocket, he had just learned of his promotion to the local rank of Lieutenant-General. With all the troops in Eastern Afghanistan now under his command (two divisions totalling 20,000 men with forty-six guns) he was not unreasonably delighted 'at this proof of the confidence reposed in me'. What, despite his vigilance, he could not have foreseen was that within weeks he and his men would once more be fighting for their lives with their backs to the wall.

CHAPTER X

Kabul to Kandahar

THE worst was still to come. Kabul had been placed under formal British supremacy, the Union Jack run up, the National Anthem played—all the outward and visible signs of military rule displayed—but under the surface, tension was building up as Afghan hatred of the infidel smouldered on. Far back along the lines of communication, the first snows of winter were already clothing the Shutargardan, and there Money was standing at bay with his handful of British and Indian troops, in face of an enormous force of tribesmen. Hugh Gough, the dashing cavalry brigadier, arrived to relieve him in the nick of time, but it was not before the tribal confederation had offered the indignant colonel terms for surrender. A few days later, the Bala Hissar, a huge building in Kabul used by the Afghan Government as a magazine, and seized by the British during their occupation, blew up. The cause of the explosion was never discovered. It may have been a chance ignition of the gunpowder stored there, but to the sharp eyes watching from the hills it remained a portent.

Meanwhile Yakub Khan was at his old business again. To Bobs' face he was the suppliant who 'would rather be a grass-cutter in the English camp than Ruler of Afghanistan', but behind the scenes it was a different matter as intelligence reports continuously reaching Bobs emphasized. A smile might be reserved for the General himself, but out of his sight it was a night of the long knives for those who, tired of princely extortion and official misrule, had sided with the British as the one hope of securing fair administration and justice in their country. In the end, the Amir was to choose abdication for he reasoned, with some accuracy, that the Government of India could be trusted.

Though his dislike of the British remained as lively as ever, he had few illusions about his own race, and in the end he abdicated, shifty and prevaricating to the last.

There was a certain tragedy about Yakub Khan, a man with none of the gifts of character needed to rule a race such as the Afghans, and even Bobs, despite all the trouble Yakub had caused, felt sorry for him at the end as the Amir, stripped of possessions and money, made his way south-east to India under strong escort. It was to make little difference to the general situation. The Afghans, lively and disputatious as a basket of weasels, were by no means dependent on their king when it came to disorder. Recognizing this, the Government of India had already despatched reinforcements through the Khyber, reinforcements destined to arrive only just in time. Other storm signals were not wanting throughout the area of British occupation or down the lines of communication (where cutting telegraph wires had achieved almost the status of a national pastime). At Maidan, dissident tribesmen attacked the cavalry and murdered the British agent, Sirdar Mahomed Khan, whilst throughout the length and breadth of the country the *Mullahs* were denouncing the British in virulent terms. By early December, it was clear that mischief was afoot and Bobs, who had already concentrated his garrison in Sherpur, began making his plans to deny the enemy Kabul. With the Mushk-i-Alam, doyen of all fanatics, rousing the population with a vocabulary that belied his name,* there was every need for precaution.

By 9 December, cavalry reconnaissance groups were in contact with heavy concentrations of tribesmen, all armed and all spoiling for a fight, and next day the infantry of Macpherson's 1st Infantry Brigade went into action, Gurkhas and Sikhs carrying all before them in a series of charges. As ever, the Afghan tribesmen, faced with determined troops under good commanders, had little stomach for a fight. Few men knew their job better than Herbert Macpherson, a tough VC winner, and that afternoon the Gurkhas and Sikhs marched proudly back with seven enemy standards picked up on the field.

Bobs was now in high hopes, and with good reason, for his troops had emerged victorious from every battle to date. That night he sent Macpherson 'orders to march very early the next

* In Pushtu it means 'Fragrance of the Universe'.

153

morning', informing him over-optimistically that 'Massy, whom I had placed in command of the troops at Aushar, would [. . .] leave that place at nine o'clock to co-operate with him'. Bobs had, in fact, always had his doubts about Massy. A brave soldier, he had by his courage earned the nickname of 'Redan Massy' during the Crimean War, but courage was not the only essential in a cavalry brigadier, as Bobs was not slow to infer. To a disposition unsuited to senior command was also added the disadvantage of inexperience in recent battles. Bobs wrote carefully of Massy's appointment to brigade command, 'I could not say whether he possessed the very exceptional qualities required in a Cavalry Commander.' It was a question now to be put to the test.

Few officers have luck eternally on their side, and Roberts had to date had more than his fair share. The balance was now to be remedied, for on 11 December, the scales tilted sharply when Massy allowed himself to be manœuvred into action with 300 cavalry and four guns against 10,000 Afghans. On the face of it, Massy's action seemed to his indignant general to be a clear disobedience of orders though he preferred to assume in his memoirs that, 'Massy could not have clearly understood the part he was meant to take.' It is certain, at least, that Roberts would never have intended the steps his subordinate undertook and, behind the guarded words, one hears an echo of Wellington's remark, made seventy years before that, 'There is nothing on earth so stupid as a gallant officer.'

A desperate situation confronted Massy's cavalry, for the bulk of the men who came on were no rabble but 'the greater part of Mahomed Jan's army'. Man for man no match for the British and Indians facing them, they were, at odds of thirty to one, quite prepared to tangle in hand-to-hand conflict. The four British guns were also ineptly handled by the commander, first through the range being too great and then through danger of capture, and were unable to play their full part. With nearby villagers joining in the battle against the hated invaders disaster seemed imminent. Bobs, galloping to the scene, found a thick mass of Afghans, two miles long, bearing down upon the tiny cluster of soldiers. Quick thinking saved the day as, sizing up the situation immediately, he sent General Hills galloping to order the Highlanders up. Desperate rear-guard actions meanwhile held back the enemy, though civilian intervention exposed troops to continual attack from rear as well as front.

It was an action that nearly cost Bobs his life when, as he modestly put it, 'I was helping some men out of the ditch' (under virtually point-blank fire) and 'the headman of the village rushed at me with his knife, seeing which a Mohamedan of the 1st Bengal Cavalry, who was following me on foot [. . .] sprang at my assailant and, seizing him round the waist, threw him to the bottom of the ditch, thereby saving my life.' The plucky soldier received a well-deserved Indian Order of Merit and, in due course, promotion. It was one more example of the loyalty which, increasingly as the years went by, transcended the frontiers of race in the old Army of Imperial India.

Elsewhere, Macpherson's 1st Infantry Brigade, which had set out under a pre-arranged plan, ended by marching to the sound of the guns. It was one o'clock before Macpherson could get into battle, but his intervention had a powerful effect as his infantry, angered by the sight of gelded and disembowelled British corpses, swept into the charge. By night, nonetheless, though the army had held its own against heavy odds at virtually every point, the Afghan population was inflamed with the elation of supposed victory. Peace, however precarious, had been maintained till now only by the aura of success crowning British efforts. The prospect of British defeat was now building Afghan hopes high and it required only the slightest British reverse to set the whole country ablaze with revolt.

There were stormy scenes that evening, for intelligence had been profoundly at fault, and the General left his shifty local Sirdars in no doubt as to where the blame lay. Though they prevaricated zealously Bobs was not deceived and later wrote bluntly, 'I was unwillingly forced to the conclusion that not a single Afghan could be trusted.' It was not an unreasonable conclusion, for the facts were plain enough. Fraudulent intelligence and an obtuse (or disobedient) brigadier had lost Bobs the chance of trumping the game with a single card. Yet, ironically, that wasted opportunity was ultimately to provide the *raison d'être* for the most dramatic of all his achievements—the epic march from Kabul to Kandahar.

Epics were, however, hard to come by in the next few days, though there was hard fighting enough. Bobs 'could not help feeling somewhat depressed at the turn things had taken', and well he might, for his own position was on the surface none too secure. He was already a target for Radical spleen in England and Wolseley, the military darling of the Liberals, was casting covetous eyes on the command in this frontier war. Though the reverse had been suffered through no fault of his own, Bobs was the man in command, and as British generals from Moore to Wavell have discovered, it is the man in charge who pays. Afghanistan, moreover, was about to become a major political issue, as the Grand Old Man of British Liberalism fixed his eye unswervingly on the main chance. Election time was near and the Frontier far, and Gladstone, embarking on the Midlothian campaign, was waxing lyrical. 'Remember that the sanctity of life in the hill villages of Afghanistan, among the winter snows, is as inviolable in the eye of Almighty God as can be your own', rather too charitable a portrait of one of the most bloodthirsty and vendetta-ridden nations in the world.

Fortunately help was at hand as, on 12 December, the Guides marched in—and the Guides, in Frontier tradition, were a name to conjure with. The same morning, however, a set-piece attack by 1st Infantry Brigade on the massive hill feature known as the Takht-i-Shah, failed in the face of determined resistance, and Bobs, never a man to hurl troops to ruin in pointless frontal attacks, called the operation off. 'I perceived,' he commented, 'that the enemy were being reinforced from their rear, and to ensure success without great loss, it would be necessary to attack them in rear as well as in the front.' Bobs' tactical conceptions were rarely to be faulted. Economy of life, with a flair for manœuvre, were the keynote of his success; it is interesting to speculate on how his handling of conditions in the First World War would have differed from that of generals whose memory is now under continual attack for their prodigal use of Britain's manhood.

Neither tactically nor in any other respect could Bobs' action in calling off the attack be criticized, yet the whole affair was unfortunate in the sense that any inference of failure was bound to have unfortunate effects on a nation as afflicted with delusions of grandeur as the Afghans. By 0800 hours on the 13th, these were already apparent, as Brigadier Baker, attempting to out-flank the Takht-i-Shah, discovered heavy concentrations of enemy moving up a commanding ridge. With British and Afghans stretching for the same objective, it became, as Bobs put it, a race between the 92nd Highlanders, supported by the Guides, on the one hand, and the 'Afghans as to who should gain the crest of the ridge first'.

In the end the British won, but there were tense moments beforehand when, after ferocious hand-to-hand fighting, even the Highlanders hesitated. *Tulwars* gleamed on the bare hillside and, hundreds of feet below, observers could see first the leading subaltern, Forbes, then senior NCOs fall as the 92nd stood at bay, a little patch of scarlet and tartan, lapped by a sea of white and blue ten times as numerous. Then the Highlanders rallied and 'with a wild shout [. . .] threw themselves on the Afghans [. . .] driving them down the further side of the ridge'. As Highlanders, Gurkhas, Guides, and Sikhs edged their way forward under screw-gun and field artillery support, bayoneting Afghan riflemen who, defiant to the last, stood at bay behind their crags, junior leaders might be pardoned for their belief that they had won a decisive engagement.

About a mile to their rear, Bobs was under no such illusions, for it was now painfully clear to him that he was facing no mere remnant of a defeated professional army, but a general rebellion in which tribesmen from the wild highlands and townsmen from Kabul itself were taking part. Even while he watched those two incomparable units the 72nd and 92nd Highlanders racing each other towards the crest of the Takht-i-Shah, huge crowds were concentrating on the outskirts of the city, every man armed with sword and *jezail*. Though each individual action had been won, casualties in Bobs' tiny force were inevitably mounting, and reinforcements were few, whilst the enemy's manpower was comparatively inexhaustible.

That afternoon the British were treated to a splendid sight, redolent of the ancient pageantry of war as, trumpets pealing the charge and pennons fluttering, the Guides Cavalry and the 9th Lancers smashed into a large enemy concentration, crumbling it into ruin. Yet, by the 14th, all was in the melting pot again since, far from being deterred, the enemy was pressing in for the kill in greater strength than ever, and few men had any illusions about what 'the kill' meant in Afghan parlance. Afghan tactics had also changed, for not merely were their numbers 'far greater than I had dreamt was possible', but, 'foiled in their attempt to close in upon us from the south and west, the tribesmen had concentrated to the north, and it was evident that they were preparing to deliver an attack in great strength from that quarter.'

By 0800 hours the crisis was upon them as Baker and his 2nd Infantry Brigade moved in to capture a commanding feature known as 'Conical Hill'. Though it fell, the sequel was not a happy one; after Baker had passed on, leaving a tiny garrison under Lt-Col Clarke to hold the peak, Bobs, watching through his telescope, was horrified to see an Afghan knife rising behind a rock close to Clarke's position. Nowadays a swift exchange on the radio would have warned the men but in 1879 Bobs, separated by numberless *nullahs* and chasms from his outposts, could do little but watch with a sinking heart. He had not long to wait; 'Next I heard the boom of guns and the rattle of musketry, and a minute or two later [. . .] I only too plainly saw our men retreating down the hill, closely followed by the enemy. The retirement was being conducted steadily and slowly, but from that moment I realized [. . .] that we were over-matched, and that we could not hold our ground.'

The fault lay in neither leadership nor troops but in numbers. In quality Bobs' force was supreme. Yet, as the crews of the screw-guns of Number 2 Mountain Battery stood at bay, defending their guns to the last, Bobs' doubts vanished. From all sides, messages were pouring in of the enormous concentrations of Afghan manpower poised for the offensive. Flashed one daring young officer on the heliograph to his commanding general, 'The crowds of Afghans in the Chardeh Valley remind me of Epsom on the Derby Day.' By 1300 hours there was only one course open and Roberts took it, withdrawing his outposts and bringing the outlying columns within a shortened and concentrated perimeter. Wise though it was, the move, nevertheless, also had its disadvantages for the effect was instantaneous. Victory seemed to the Afghans to be within their grasp and they advanced with every semblance of ferocity to the kill.

Nothing was better suited to Bobs' strategy than a massed Afghan attack at a time when his small and highly professional force was securely entrenched behind the massive walls of Sherpur, but the retreat to Sherpur was a different matter.

Nothing could have excelled the steadiness of the troops, British and Indian alike, yet it was a perilous situation as swarming tribesmen, mad with the promise of victory, hurled themselves time and again at the retreating regiments. Fortunately discipline held, the units turned bravely into the fury of hand-to-hand combat and by evening the whole force, complete with dead and wounded, was safe behind the walls of Sherpur.

Had the Afghans attacked immediately, the danger would have been considerable for even inside Sherpur there was a fair amount still to be done to put everything in a state of defence. As it was, the enemy contented themselves that night by occupying Kabul City and the Bala Hissar, whilst the British busily put the finishing touches to their plans. Everything had already been planned; a considerable amount of constructional work had been done and large quantities of material stockpiled, for not the least of Bobs' virtues was his foresight. He had long before formed a committee that had decided the measures necessary to put Sherpur into a state of defence, and the physical work had thereafter gone quietly ahead. Unafraid to take unpopular steps, such as a retreat into laager, Bobs also believed in preparing for all eventualities. Now, with four months' food supplies and a large quantity of animal fodder within the walls, the British forces could face the future with relative unconcern. Relief columns should have no difficulty, if the worst came to the worst, in getting through within that time, but such a need was in any event remote, for a race of such mercurial temperament as the Afghans was unlikely to settle down to a prolonged siege of attrition. Even in the sphere of purely military equipment, the British force was excellently placed, for such deficiencies as had been imposed on them by the wastage of war and transport difficulty had been made good from captured Afghan material. Now, with the enemy passively watching, the troops dug and built with the pertinacity of beavers and, as strong-points rose, Afghan chances sank swiftly. Brigands by temperament, the tribesmen found Kabuli loot irresistible and so, as they raped and pilfered among their fellow-countrymen, the magic moment passed.

Inside the laager, Bobs, who left nothing to chance, installed every defensive refinement available to him. Each sector was connected by field telephone, and visual signalling provided for 'intercom' in case of the wire being cut. The laager was divided into five sectors, each with a colonel or brigadier in command, whilst Massy, the *beau sabreur* whose disobedience was in part responsible for the present difficulty, was allocated 'the centre of the cantonment, where were collected the forage and the firewood'.

For the next week a lull prevailed, with minor skirmishing around the enemy forward posts whenever Afghan snipers there became troublesome. Inside the fortress itself, a game almost of cat-and-mouse ensued, as Bobs watched his Afghan Sirdars and they, losing confidence in the British ability to win, watched their chance to contact Mahomed Khan and his national army outside. A still deeper cause of anxiety lay in the loyalty of the Pathan soldiers serving in the Guides and the 5th Punjabis. To date their loyalty and courage had been beyond question, but Bobs had not forgotten the treacheries of their fellow-countrymen in the 29th Punjab Infantry during the advance to the Spingawi Kotal, and careful as ever, he now placed a couple of Highland companies behind them. Check, if he had his way, would be transformed into checkmate.

By the 21st, there were unmistakable signs that the Afghans would wait no longer. With British and Gurkha reinforcements thrusting their way forward under Brigadier Charles Gough via Gandamak, the enemy wished to strike before their arrival. Gough was also well informed of the overall British position throughout Afghanistan, for though messengers were moving out almost daily, the total disappearance of some and the agonized death masks of others told their own grim tale. Only heliograph could be relied on, and cloudy days meant that even this was out. By the 22nd the bazaars of Kabul were echoing to the construction of hundreds of scaling ladders. With *Moharram** almost ended, religious fervour was at its peak, a fact of which the *Mullahs* were not unaware. Led by that picturesquely-styled and recurrent ancient, the Mushk-i-Alam, they thundered daily from their minarets, proclaiming a crusade. The 'Fragrance of the Universe' would light with his own hand the beacon signal for the assault that should destroy the infidel invaders to a man. It required no great perspicacity therefore to discern the morning of the 23rd as the likely time for the assault,

* A Muslim festival.

since this was the last day of *Moharram*. Intelligence from the bazaars moreover—and there was plenty of it to be had for a price—exactly pinpointed the time as immediately before first light.

With such detail to hand, Bobs acted swiftly. The most doubtful of his Afghan collaborators—Daud Shah, the former Amir's commander-in-chief—was clapped under arrest, sector commanders were rehearsed and, long before first light, the troops were standing to behind their entrenchments in the freezing darkness of the Afghan night.

It was an exciting panorama and one certain to appeal to the Victorian imagination, for all the elements of drama were there —the outnumbered, beleaguered Imperial forces, the swarming tribesmen, the dark forbidding peaks of the Asmai mountains, with the flame of the assault signal spurting from the topmost crest. Above all there was the isolation, the broken lines of communication, the hundreds of miles that separated the soldiers from their base, and the certain choice between victory and death. With Afghans for enemy, no other alternative was discernible. In fact, though it was a dramatic canvas, there was never any great danger, for the Afghan dispositions were thoroughly amateur. Song and signal fire had already locked the door on any prospect of surprising an alert garrison and now, as the enemy swept forward in massed formation, charging wildly for the walls, the British star-shells burst in silver radiance over the whole scene.

The *Ghazis* came on gamely enough, their swords held high, the volleys of their covering musketry battering at the walls, but they had no chance as first Punjabis, then Guides and British infantry opened fire. Artillery was also hammering at them and by 1000 hours the Afghan dead were piled high at the fringe of the abattis, marking the utmost point of their encroachment. When, an hour later, the enemy swept in with one more attack, gallantly pressed, Bobs turned sharply to the counter-attack, taking them in the flank with field artillery fire and the small arms of the 5th Punjab Cavalry.

It was the last phase of the battle as, under such unexpected determination, Afghan valour swiftly ebbed, and by 1300 hours they were everywhere hurrying for the safety of the mountains, with Massy's eager cavalry snapping at their heels. The arrival of a fresh brigade from Gandamak under command of one of the ubiquitous Goughs ended any semblance of immediate danger to the force, and the staff were able to enjoy the spectacle of 100,000 would-be Afghan conquerors racing from the attentions of barely 7,000 Imperial troops. British casualties, at eighteen dead and sixty-eight wounded, also told their own story when compared with the enemy figure of 3,000. Throughout, the British and Indian troops had been heavily outnumbered, and though the tribal combination played a big part, regular Afghan troops always formed a high proportion of the forces opposing them. Even in purely material matters, the Afghans at the outset enjoyed a positive advantage, and if by the end Bobs was the better supplied, this was largely because he had been able to capture his enemy's arsenal. It would also be a mistake to regard the Afghans' fighting abilities as negligible for, as the disaster of the First Afghan War showed, they were treacherous and implacable foes. Maiwand was soon to reveal that, even when faced with British troops, time had not robbed them of their sting.

For the time being it seemed as if the battle at Kabul had sufficed. Bobs issued reassuring proclamations ('Come and make your submission without fear, of whatsoever tribe you may be'), hospital treatment (such as it was) was offered to large numbers of grateful Afghan patients, and the respects of prominent locals were accepted. By New Year's Day 1880, everything was apparently peaceful and the prospects of an early withdrawal appeared good. Only those with knowledge of Afghan ebullience—and Bobs was one—knew that in that remote land of peaks and heat and freezing cold, nothing was ever what it seemed.

The two main problems were, as Bobs wrote, 'What was to be done with Afghanistan now we had got it?' and, 'Who could be set up as Ruler' to replace the departed Yakub Khan? With regard to the first question, Bobs was probably correct in his assumption that a division of the territory into its several states offered the best hope. Afghans had from time immemorial been predators and the kingdom, beset by anarchy, had almost never functioned effectively as a single unit. Bad communications, rivalry, and the very nature of the people seemed to favour the emergence of small local states, each ruled by its tribal head. It was equally true, as Bobs noted, that even if the improbable happened and a strong and capable government gained effective control, 'There would always be the danger of a Ruler, made supreme by the aid of our money and our arms, turning against us from some supposed grievance, or at the instigation of a foreign Power [. . .]'

In 1880, this was just the stuff to appeal to a British ruling class still, despite its vacillations, essentially Imperial in outlook. With Disraeli at the helm, a Tory Government saw no reason to play down its Empire and, as a general election neared and Gladstone grew ever more virulent, a decision in Afghanistan became imperative. Like many politicians before and since, Disraeli was finding the small wars of Empire an electoral encumbrance. It was hardly surprising therefore that Bobs' thesis should have made a strong appeal, for it had the advantage of offering a definite policy. There was also a good candidate for the throne, if not of Afghanistan, at least of Kabul, in the person of Abdur Rahman, cousin of Yakub Khan and nephew of the previous Amir, Sher Ali. Abdur Rahman had his weaknesses, but he was clearly head and shoulders above all other contenders. Within days the wires were humming and by mid-April Bobs had been authorized to hold a durbar* with the Afghan nobility. Faced with the hustings, even a British Government could move.

Unfortunately, as Bobs had already shrewdly foreseen, there was a strong faction opposed to Abdur Rahman, for the Afghans had correctly gauged him to be a British nominee. Equally unsuited to their plans was the fact that he was a strong personality unlikely to tolerate the intrigue which was an inseparable feature of the Afghan political scene. Whilst British negotiations with Abdur Rahman continued in cautiously optimistic vein, Bobs' own efforts to win over the nobles failed, and though the durbar was held, his blunt statement that Yakub Khan could not be permitted to return caused great disappointment. At the same time, it had the advantage of letting the Afghans know exactly where they stood, and that meant a great deal. As Bobs put it, 'All present felt that they had received a definite reply.'

From now on, events moved rapidly, with the Afghan Army and a certain number of the tribesmen prepared to accept Abdur Rahman, whilst others, notably Wardakis and Logaris, prepared

* A court.

163

to resist him and to fight it out on behalf of Yakub Khan. The British seemed, at the time, in a far better position than before to win their way, for both Sir Donald Stewart at Kandahar and Bobs at Kabul were men who had the Afghans' respect and, with a firm record of success behind them, their troops were in high spirits. What Bobs had never forgotten, however, the Kandahar contingent were now painfully to rediscover; in war it is the unexpected that is often decisive.

The background of the new disturbance was simple enough to understand, and should have caused no surprise. As a man, Yakub Khan was of little consequence, a fact that Bobs had good cause to know, but in his position as deposed Amir he remained a rallying point for all Afghan nationalists, whilst Abdur Rahman suffered from the proportionate disadvantage of having ridden in, as it were, amongst the British baggage train. The man of the moment in fact was Yakub Khan's brother, Ayub, and if Yakub could not return, the nationalists were determined that Ayub Khan would. With Abdur Rahman indulging in intrigues of his own, the British position was not happy, and only an early retirement could lay the spectre of fresh hostilities.

The first firm indication of renewed war occurred at the end of April, when a British column under Col Jenkins was unsuccessfully ambushed at Charasia, but by early May it must have seemed to Bobs that it was no longer his problem, with the arrival of his old friend and senior, Donald Stewart, to assume command at Kabul. As Bobs recorded, 'It was not in human nature to feel absolute satisfaction in yielding up the supreme command.' Though there was probably no one to whom he would have handed over with better grace than to Donald Stewart, he had some reason to feel aggrieved, for he had borne the burden of the day at Kabul alone for months. Now, at the moment when the stage was set for an early retirement, it seemed as if the laurels were to be snatched from him.

By mid-July, withdrawal from Afghanistan seemed a foregone conclusion. Agreement of a sort had been reached with Abdur Rahman, another durbar had been held to explain the Government of India's stand, and firm orders had been issued to the army to prepare to retire to the Indian border. Bobs himself 'was to withdraw my column by the Kurram route'; and, being an inveterate tourist, he rode off early as he was 'anxious to see something of the Khyber line'. All seemed as quiescent as Afghanistan ever was, for the promise of withdrawal ought to have done much to pacify the tribes, and there was no reason to expect disaster, yet once again Bobs' extraordinary sensitivity to the future, as in Cavagnari's case, was to forewarn him in the face of general optimism. As he himself put it, 'My intention, when I left Kabul, was to ride as far as the Khyber Pass, but suddenly a presentiment, which I have never been able to explain to myself, made me retrace my steps and hurry back towards Kabul—a presentiment of coming trouble which I can only characterize as instinctive.'

He was not mistaken, for as he rode back, he met the force commander, Sir Donald Stewart, and his own chief of staff, Col Chapman, bearing news that indicated a total reversal of the situation. Gone was the promise of peace and early retirement, for the news had just filtered through of Brigadier Burrows' total defeat at Maiwand. Worse still, the main British forces at Kandahar, under General Primrose, were now under siege in the city itself. With elation spreading amongst the tribesmen, and concentrations massing in the hills, the military barometer was once again set to 'Stormy'. Indeed, there was every expectation that within the week the whole British force in Afghanistan would be fighting for its life.

There were certainly special causes for concern, since it swiftly became plain that this was not even an ordinary reverse. Though varied accounts continued to circulate about Maiwand, the bare fact was that it had been a rout. As early as May, Sher Ali, the Afghan Sirdar of Kandahar, had warned General Primrose that he could not answer for the loyalty of his own troops, and Primrose had asked the Government of India for reinforcements. Yet by late June, the reinforcements had not come, and the Sirdar's Afghans did exactly as he had predicted, deserting *en masse* to Ayub Khan as he advanced to attack and they to intercept him. The result was that Burrows, who had marched out with a brigade of British and Indian troops to support the Sirdar, found himself isolated and unassisted by reliable troops. With two alternatives before him, those of retreat or battle, he chose the latter for he reasoned, not inaccurately, that he might be able to deal with the tribesmen piecemeal before the regular Afghan troops came up.

What happened is a matter of record. Ayub Khan arrived at Maiwand first, and his junction with the tribes had been completed before Burrows' vanguard reached the scene. A wiser commander might, in the circumstances, have retreated, but Burrows, a brave man if no Wellington, decided to fight. With 2,500 unflanked British and indifferent Indian troops to face 25,000 Afghans, the result was inevitable. The 66th Foot (2nd Berkshires) fought and largely died with a gallantry reminiscent of the Imperial Guard's last stand at Waterloo but, with Afghan swordsmen lapping round their flanks, the sepoy regiments broke and fled. Enemy troops were closing in, the guns were silent for want of ammunition, and panic spread through the whole force. Years later Kipling was to write of it, after a conversation with one of the British survivors,

> We was 'idin' under bedsteads more than 'arf a march
> away:
> We was lyin' up like rabbits all about the country-
> side:
> An' the Major cursed 'is Maker 'cause 'e'd lived to see
> that day,
> An' the Colonel broke 'is sword acrost, an' cried.[11]

Though Kipling did not claim for 'That Day' the accuracy of history, it was unpleasantly near the truth.

Bobs was the first of the senior officers to react, and he did so with characteristic clarity. The Government of India was planning to send up troops from Baluchistan direct to Kandahar, but, reasoned Bobs, 'belonging to the Bombay Presidency, they could not be composed of the best fighting races, and I had a strong feeling that it would be extremely unwise to make use of any but the most proved Native soldiers against Ayub Khan's superior numbers, elated as his men must be with their victory at Maiwand.' Plainly now was the time for a courageous decision, and Bobs, always personally as well as militarily a skilled tactician, played his cards well. The Government of India's tendency to look 'to Quetta rather than Kabul as the place from which Kandahar could be most conveniently and rapidly succoured' was wrong in military principle. Besides, it meant that Bobs and his men would be left out of the fighting.

A dextrously worded telegram, sent with Stewart's consent, produced lightning reaction in a fearful Simla, for at last they had a man ready to take the decision and the responsibility too. There was certainly no mistaking the terminology of the wire. 'Personal and secret. I strongly recommend that a force be sent from this area to Kandahar [. . .] the movement of the remainder of the Kabul troops towards India should be simultaneous with the advance of my division towards Kandahar [. . .] You need have no fears about my division. It can take care of itself.' Ten thousand fighting men were to be launched, unsupported, upon a vast country and a great campaign, at the very time when all reserves were being withdrawn. The small war-horse was straining at the bit with a vengeance.

There was little time to lose, for nowhere does news spread faster than along the caravan trails of the north-west, and throughout the hill regions of that great area the tribes were stirring. In the bazaars of Peshawar even, the rumours ran, as agents, lean and shadowy, slipped through lanes so narrow that two men could hardly walk abreast. Was British invincibility a thing of the past? Tsarist agents, sedulous as ever, were active in propagating the myth of British ruin. Even as far south as the Central Provinces and dreamy Madras, the impact was considerable, 'enough to make those who remembered the days of the Mutiny anxious for better news from the North.' All this was known to Bobs, both officially and otherwise (for Mahbub Ali was no figment of Kipling's imagination*), and he wasted no time. Authority to march to Kandahar was in his hands by noon on 3 August, and by the 9th the newly constituted Kabul–Kandahar Field Force of 10,000 men was marching to the relief of Primrose under its diminutive but pugnacious commander, Sir Frederick Roberts, VC. Bobs had certainly pushed himself to the fore, thereby securing himself the command, a strategy that he was to repeat with equal success soon after the outbreak of the South African War in 1899. Yet it would be wrong to regard Roberts as a vulgar careerist for not merely was he a patriot of the highest motives but, undoubtedly before volunteering for any command, he was at pains to satisfy himself of his ability to perform it. Certainly by the standards of 1880, the campaign he was about to wage savoured of *blitzkrieg*. It was

* See *Kim*.

also a feat of extraordinary endurance by the marching troops. For the cavalry, with their manifold tasks, it was bad enough, but for infantry, marching through a midday temperature of 110 degrees and providing flanking parties along the crests, the strain was appalling. In contrast, the thermometer by night fell to freezing, and the harsh winds of the Hindu Khush struck men and animals alike with a cruel intensity. It says much for the leadership of Bobs, therefore, that the force should from start to finish have retained a morale and *esprit-de-corps* rarely equalled in such conditions. Baggage and ammunition, too, had to be carried by the troops themselves, to a degree incredible today, for pack animals were scarce; and to add to their discomfiture, unseen tribesmen lurked among the crags, swooping to mutilate any who fell into their power.

The equipment restrictions imposed on the troops are almost impossible to credit, for British soldiers were limited to thirty pounds, and sepoys to twenty pounds, per man for their kit. British officers were more generously treated, with a mule apiece, but even VCOs were held down to thirty pounds. Food too was in short supply, with the bread ration at only five days' level. Like Napoleon's armies in the Peninsula, there was no option: the Kabul–Kandahar Field Force would have to live off the land—or starve.

'Before daybreak on 11 August, as I was starting from camp, I received my last communication from the outside world.' Nothing more clearly illustrates the nature of his task than Bobs' own words. Bobs and his ten thousand were on their own. From now on, until they had accomplished the relief, a waiting world would have to depend upon rumour, usually unreliable and often deliberately misleading, for its news. Some couriers would make their way through, but more would end their lives shrieking uncontrollably under the slow torture of Afghan knives. The chances were that the fate of the Kabul–Kandahar Field Force would be unknown until the decisive engagement was long over.

The troops forged slowly ahead. After four days they had covered forty-six miles. Eight thousand non-combatants and 11,000 animals marched with the fighting troops and these too had to be catered for. The result was that 'Reveille' had to be sounded at 0245 hours, and by 0400 the long lines of men, carts, and animals had fallen in and were marching off through the starlit darkness and the cold mountain air. Yet it was 1800 or 1900 hours before the rear-guard marched in, tired, their tunics coated with dust, but in close formation, their bayonets glinting in the flame of the bivouac fires.

Not the least of Bobs' troubles lay in the camp followers. Obsessed with caste, the Indian Army relied to an extraordinary extent upon unattested non-combatants to perform the menial duties of the day. To a Rajput warrior, cook-house fatigues would have come as a mortal insult, whilst to ask a Brahmin to sweep his barrack room would have been tantamount to inviting insubordination. The result was that every expedition had, grouped round the hard core of its fighting men, a vast amorphous body of water-carriers, cooks, sweepers, and others, lacking in martial spirit, underpaid, underfed, and slow to operate. It was a problem that had taxed general after general, but with memories of the Mutiny still fresh, there were few commanders, however alive to the tactical problem thus posed, who were prepared to risk religious agitation by excluding followers and requiring regiments to do their own chores. The best, like inevitably, 'Our regimental bhisti, Gunga Din', were very good, but the general standard was poor.

It was now Bobs' responsibility to shepherd these wretches nightly into safe keeping. By custom and acceptance they were non-combatants, but no one had any illusions about the Afghans' regard for such niceties. As the pace quickened, moreover, the inferior diet and physique of the followers told, and they began to straggle. Virtually expendable, it is likely that few questions would have been asked had they been left to their fate, but this was not Bobs' way, and the rear-guard had the responsibility of rounding up and herding them to safety. With tribesmen forever on the look-out for the chance to loot and murder, as well as to ambush small parties of troops, rear-guard duty was one of the less pleasant tasks in the Force.

Whatever the views of the tribesmen, there was no sign of Afghan troops, for the enemy's army, aware from bitter experience of Bobs' reputation, were loath to close. On 12 August, three days after marching, they crested the Zamburak Kotal, over 8,000 feet high and, on the 15th, the Governor of Ghazni hastened out with the keys forestalling even a formal demand for surrender. There was an added poignancy in the place for Bobs for it was here, forty-one years before, that his father had won his CB.

From Ghazni they pressed on, the 9th Queen's Royal Lancers to the fore and the pipes of his old friends, the 72nd and 92nd Highlanders, skirling through the hills. Ahead, at Kandahar, a demoralized garrison was making feeble and unsuccessful attempts to break out, attempts disdainfully repelled by confident Afghan besieging units. But none attempted to interfere with Bobs, who could write on 23 August, 'We have met with no opposition during the march.'* On the same day they reached Kelat-i-Ghilzai, the first British garrison post they had encountered, and Bobs, never a man to leave small groups of troops in isolated places, added the 900-strong British and Indian contingent there to his Field Force.

For soldiers without mechanized transport, in a ferocious climate, the pace of advance was fantastic. Conditions along the road were also far from good, with the cavalry and the metal-rimmed cart wheels churning up the dust into white clinging clouds. The younger members of the force could surmount the conditions but Bobs, in his late forties, had been weakened by years of campaign and tropical rigours. Indomitable though he was, the pace told in the end, and on 27 August, the pugnacious little general, knocked out by fever, made his shamefaced appearance in a *doolie*. It was, he admitted, 'a most ignominious mode of conveyance for a general on service; but there was no help for it, for I could not sit a horse.'

Not the least of Bobs' virtues was his selflessness on campaign, and he had lived too long with ill-health to allow it to rule his plans. Fever despite, the march went on, and on the 30th they arrived at Momund where Bobs was, surprisingly, able to telegraph Simla. The contents of his communication are illuminating, for they reveal his clear and logical military thought. After detailing his initial dispositions he continued, 'Should I hear that Ayub contemplates flight, I shall attack without delay. If, on the contrary, he intends to resist, I shall take my own time.' He concluded with expression of a sentiment which was the mainspring of his military personality—concern for the welfare and safety of his troops. 'This country he is

---

* The first despatch from him to get through to India.

occupying is [. . .] extremely difficult and easily defensible, and each separate advance will require careful study and reconnaissance to prevent unnecessary loss of life.' Bold in decision and swift in action, Bobs was painstakingly cautious in his study of the minor details which so often make the difference between a cheaply won victory and a bloody reverse.

The great day dawned on 31 August, when Bobs, gritting his teeth, crawled from *doolie* to horseback for his ceremonial entry into Kandahar. Behind them lay 314 weary miles of appalling terrain covered in just three weeks and applause from the beleaguered garrison was loud enough to lay any issue between them and the rescuers to rest. Bobs, however, was not deceived, for comparison between the sterling *esprit de corps* of his own force and the shattered morale of Primrose's men made further comment superfluous. As he wrote, 'The general bearing of the troops reminded me of the people at Agra in 1857. They seemed to consider themselves hopelessly defeated, and were utterly despondent. They never even hoisted the Union Jack till the relieving force was close at hand.'

In all the circumstances, it was hardly surprising that Bobs should have placed scant faith in either Primrose or, with some notable exceptions, in the officers and men who had served under him. It was bad enough for civilians in Agra to have displayed such unmistakable symptoms of panic in 1857, but here in Kandahar he found a purely military garrison of 4,000 able-bodied troops, amply supplied with artillery and sappers, crouching behind city walls 'so high and thick as to render the city absolutely impregnable to any army not equipped with a regular siege-train'. Worse still, the possibility of the Afghans capturing the city by storm had been actively discussed. It showed, wrote a horrified Bobs, 'what a miserable state of depression and demoralization' the British were in.

Few men with any knowledge of Bobs' habits as a commander could have expected a prolonged delay in Kandahar, but his speed still sufficed to leave hardened soldiers gasping, for he had marched in at approximately 0700 hours and by 1000 hours the 1st and 3rd Infantry Brigades, after a quick breakfast under the southern wall, were leading out again to take up commanding positions near the city. As he knew only too well, the Afghans had been shaken by the speed of his epic advance and it was essential to hit them before they recovered their wind. By 1400 hours a reconnaissance group was in action at Murghan.

From now on, his tactical development was classic, with high ground seized, the enemy lured into premature disclosure of their positions by a show of strength, and British and Indian troops poised to deliver a knock-out blow on ground and in circumstances of their commander's choosing. As usual Bobs relied upon a feint and, as was their wont, the Afghans fell for it. Before dawn, all attacking units were standing to, and by 0600 hours Bobs was explaining his plan to Primrose and the brigadiers—the Victorian equivalent of an 'Orders Group'. There was scant pretence at diplomacy, for Primrose and his men were bluntly detailed off to carry out the diversionary movement, whilst Bobs' own triumphant columns were given the real business of the day. With the Kandahar troops bombarding the Baba Wali Kotal,* the Afghans, till now concentrated for attack, were drawn towards the feint. Meanwhile, the British assault formations moved carefully round to the rear of the Baba Wali Kotal. Under command of Major-General Ross, the 1st and 2nd Infantry Brigades were buoyed with success, their morale magnificent, their training and discipline superb. With the 60th Rifles, and the Sikhs and Gurkhas of the 3rd Infantry Brigade forming at once a reserve and a defence against counter-attack from the Baba Wali Kotal, the attacking formations could also move in with little concern for their rear.

The sun was rising high over the hills as the attacking regiments moved forward. Ahead of them on the *kotal* they could see the white and blue shading of the massed tribesmen, and behind, the screw-gun batteries snapped waspishly. As Macpherson's 1st Infantry Brigade advanced towards their objective, the village of Gundi Mulla Sahibdad, the shells were bursting over it like dirty puffs of cotton-wool, grey against the blue of the sky. It was a hard-fought action, with Afghan *Ghazis* turning at bay and exacting heavy toll from the charging Highlanders, but the main body of the enemy seemed to have lost all stomach for the fight, for as British, Gurkhas, and Sikhs swept in, they sullenly retreated. Here and there, as behind the Baba Wali Kotal, Afghan swordsmen and musketeers stood to the end in fortified entrenchments, but the dash and *élan* of the

---

* A high pass on which the Afghans were entrenched.

172

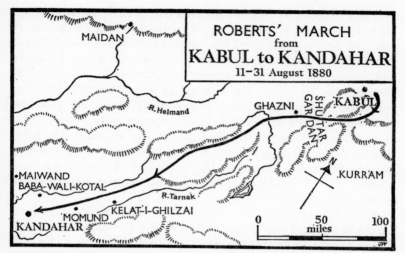

British attack was everywhere invincible, and by late afternoon
Anglo-Indian bayonets were sparkling on every vantage point.

The results were spectacular. For the loss of 40 dead and
210 wounded, the three infantry and one cavalry brigades of the
Kabul–Kandahar Field Force had captured Ayub Khan's entire
artillery, killing not far short of 1,200 Afghans and smashing
the enemy army beyond hope of repair. Blazing courage had
been commonplace, with Highlanders and Gurkhas on more
than one occasion storming enemy positions under point-blank
fire, yet the generalship had been of such a high order that such
incidents were the exception rather than the rule. As Bobs rarely
failed to stress, the duty of a commander was to win victory at a
minimum cost. To the true officer the lives of his men are sacred.

As the cavalry ranged far in pursuit, Bobs rode into the
abandoned enemy camp. Few victories could have been more
satisfying, but for the little general it had been success won at a
high price. For weeks his health had been failing, and will power
alone had enabled him to carry on. Now, as he rode into the
camp, the gutted corpse of a British officer captured by the
Afghans lying a few yards off, he was virtually in a state of
collapse. Weeks of stress, combined with the emotional climax
of victory, had proved too much and as his troops cheered him
to the echo, Bobs broke down. It was all he could do to make his
way back to his quarters in Kandahar.

173

Later that day he staggered to his feet to compose a telegram to headquarters. Typically modest, it was devoted to praise of 'the splendid infantry' and to details of the casualties suffered. Nothing was said of Bobs' own part, and the word 'I' occurs only twice in the entire message. After an achievement as dramatic as any since the Charge of the Light Brigade, the victorious General might have been forgiven had he dwelt on his own role, but that was not Bobs' fashion and, with as little display as possible, he made his way quietly back to India. There was also another duty to be performed, for he had promised his men that once they had won the campaign they could return from Afghanistan, and now he was scrupulous to redeem his word.

From Kandahar, the road lay south to Quetta, but even here he could not rest, for 'I found that, owing to indifferent health, I was unable to carry on my duty with satisfaction to myself' and 'applied to be relieved'. It was in such circumstances that in mid-October 1880, wrestling with a shattered constitution, he overtook regiment after regiment of the Kabul-Kandahar Field Force as he rode through the Bolan Pass.

It is difficult to bring back to life the strength and confidence of British Imperial might at its zenith, or the loyalty that inspired all ranks, British and Indian alike. For Roberts, however, it presented a dramatic spectacle as he overtook them, unit by unit, marching through the great hills, in their kilted or *puggareed* ranks, with their fiercely tanned and bearded faces. For the men too it was a moment of pathos and, as the little soldier who had won their loyalty overtook them, each regimental band broke into the lingering notes of *Auld Lang Syne*. Roberts was deeply touched for, if he had been brilliant, they had been brave, and in words memorable not least for their modesty he was years later to write, 'I have never since heard that memory-stirring air without its bringing before my mind's eye the last view I had of the Kabul-Kandahar Field Force. I fancy myself crossing and re-crossing the river which winds through the pass; I hear the martial beat of drums and the plaintive music of the pipes; and I see Riflemen and Gurkhas, Highlanders and Sikhs, guns and horses, camels and mules, with the endless following of an Indian army, winding through the narrow gorges'.

Pride was there and sorrow too for 'I shall never forget the feeling of sadness with which I said good-bye to the men who had done so much for me'. Few commanders have had the power to inspire devotion in the same degree as Bobs, but fewer still have so deserved it, for he was as thrifty of his men's lives as a miser of his gold, whilst they for their part were prepared to risk their all for him. And now it was over, and all that remained was the remembrance of the great hills and the narrow gorges, the regiments who had fought so bravely and won so much; above all, the remembrance of their valediction—the echo of the drums and pipes. There are worse memories for a man to carry with him to the grave.

CHAPTER XI

Top Brass

It was as hero of the hour that, not long afterwards, Bobs landed in England. Though Kipling had not yet lit the torch of Imperialism's last and most romantic era, the Victorians yielded to none in their love of country. Under the camouflage of watch chain and whiskers, moreover, they were possessed of a lively imagination. First Rorke's Drift* and then the pageant of the Frontier had touched the common man, with their echo of heroic encounters and historic ambuscades, and now Britain was determined to honour General Roberts, the man who had led the Tommies with such *élan* from Kabul to Kandahar. Bobs on his part, though he found the experience exhilarating, remained unaffected by the cheering crowds for no man could have been freer of vanity. There was also the old internal demon to remind him that all men are mortal, for his ulcer was giving trouble and, as he remarked, 'I was feted and feasted to almost an alarming extent, considering that for nearly two years I had been restricted to campaigning diet.'

As Bobs was quick to note, the British people had technically seized upon the wrong campaign to honour, for the initial advance on Kabul in the previous year had been much the more difficult operation. It was a point professional soldiers were quick to appreciate, though to the man in the street, innocent of strategic knowledge or logistic reflection, there was an essential drama in the daring swoop on Kandahar, a picture that touched the imagination, in the rescue of his beleaguered fellow soldiers. To the general public, moreover, the advance to Kabul was old hat, whilst Kandahar was the epic of the moment. Bobs, indeed, put his own finger on the point when he wrote that the reason

* 22–23 January, 1879, during the Zulu War.

was 'the glamour of romance thrown around an army of 10,000 men lost to view, as it were, for nearly a month'.

Lionized by the crowds, he found a significant silence at Horse Guards. It was an age in which the old aristocratic elements of the army, led by the Duke of Cambridge, still struggled for supremacy against the *avant-garde* of professionals led, in London, by Wolseley. To those who belonged to the court circle and who displayed distinction, Cambridge was quick to extend advantage but (as Wolseley had long since found) officers of less distinctive social position could win laurel after laurel without hope of promotion beyond a prescribed limit. In Bobs' case there were additional factors destined to hold him back for years. He had, for one thing, spent years on the staff—the fighting staff, it is true, but still the staff—and the Royal Duke had been heard to remark ominously that he knew 'these staff officers. They are very ugly officers and very dirty officers'. Although an Old Etonian and aristocratic in outlook, Bobs suffered the additional drawback of his Indian Army origin, a fact calculated in guards and cavalry circles to mark him as an 'uglier' and 'dirtier' officer even than if he had belonged to the infantry of the line.

Many of these were disadvantages from which his fellow Anglo-Irishman, Wolseley, had also suffered but Wolseley, though an impoverished career officer, was himself of the British Service. Despising the Indian Army, he was also personally jealous of Bobs, and perhaps with good reason for, if Wolseley was the profounder theoretician, Bobs was undoubtedly the better field commander. The rival 'Roberts' and 'Wolseley' schools of military thought and practice, which were such a feature in later years, had not yet sprung into prominence, but the seeds were already sown. Agreeing in little else, Cambridge and Wolseley found themselves for once united in their opposition to Bobs' advancement. If the GCB was the least they were able to give him, it was also the most they were prepared to confer, and behind them the titled ranks of London military society nodded in solemn assent.

The whole period of his leave proved, hardly surprisingly, an exhausting affair, though from time to time he was able to relax in the country with Nora and the children. Twelve years had passed since his last leave home, and 'two vacant places in my family circle—those of my father and my sister—cast a deep shadow on what would otherwise have been a most joyous return.' There was, however, little time for regret, for he had landed in England in November 1880, and by November 1881 he was back in India once more, having in the interim attended manœuvres in Hanover and Schleswig-Holstein as the guest of the Kaiser. More significant, since it set a seal upon his image as one of the foremost British commanders of the time, was his journey to the Cape (also during his leave) at the instance of Gladstone, then belatedly seeking a general to pull his Imperial irons out of the fire after the unexpected disasters of the First Boer War. Far more irritating to Bobs even than this waste of his leave was the fact that peace with South Africa had been made during his voyage out—'A peace, alas! "without honour" ' —and he found the Government at the Cape almost indecently anxious to rid themselves of him from the moment he arrived. Triumph in South Africa, for him as well as for Britain, still lay almost twenty years off; with Gladstone in power 'Humble Pie' was the prescribed national diet.

Bobs had been strongly tipped in certain quarters to replace Wolseley as Quartermaster-General on the latter's promotion to Adjutant-General, and for a time it seemed as though Bobs' Indian days were over. After thirty years of tropical heat, it was a tempting prospect, most of all for Nora, but in the end Bobs sailed for Madras and the London appointment went to another British Service officer. It is, nonetheless, interesting to speculate on how Wolseley and Bobs would have worked together had the latter stayed in England. Both Anglo-Irish, both modernist and wholly professional in their outlook, they had little temperamentally in common and there was already a strong undercurrent of rivalry between them. This was especially marked of recent months as, since Kandahar, Bobs was being spoken of as the only British general to rival Sir Garnet. In the circumstances, it seems unlikely that they would for long have worked in harmony. Had Bobs become QMG, the shock to Cambridge would also have been severe, for Bobs, a vigorous and far-sighted soldier, could have been expected to be as unsympathetic as Wolseley to the Duke's Peninsular reflexes.

In the end, the matter was not put to the test, and on 27 November, 1881, he landed in Madras. A presidency that had once been great, it now yielded pride of place to Bengal and the great areas of the north. To Bobs, fresh from almost legendary prowess on the Frontier, the Madras Army seemed a special disappointment, for though Clive had won his victories with the dark sepoys of the south, it took Bobs no time to discover how unfavourably Tamils, Telegus and Malayalams compared as soldiers with the tough yeomen of the Punjab and the Frontier. Though never a man to spurn promotion, in his heart Bobs regretted the move, for this was promotion to a backwater. The Madras armies were retained more in deference to tradition than for any practical military value. Only the Moplahs, of all the Madrassi peoples, showed the characteristics necessary for first-class soldiers, and they were not recruited.

The most satisfactory aspect of his whole command seemed the site of the headquarters, for the Commander-in-Chief traditionally lived at Ootacamund, and who in their right senses could complain of Ooty? Set amid the Nilgiri Hills, its climate was as good as any to be found in India and, for Nora at least, after the long years of illness, the green lawns and winding lanes of Ootacamund, Wellington, and Conoor must have savoured of paradise.

Madras was a command of which Commanders-in-Chief could make as much or little as they wished according to their temperament, for it was many years since urgent problems had ruffled the surface of the languid south. Bobs, however, with an outburst of his old energy lost little time in visiting the furthest limits of his command. Burma especially held for him, as it held for so many Englishmen of his era, a strange and almost mystic fascination. With its wild perilous beauty, green jungles, and inaccessible hills Burma enjoyed the attraction of the unknown, an attraction enhanced by the symmetry of its architecture and the supple charm of its slant-eyed women. For the despised British soldier, especially after the monotony of India, the Burmese towns provided a welcome relief. The jungles harboured malignant fevers, but life almost anywhere east of Suez tended to be short for a private of the line and Burma had many compensations. After the dustbowl of the Indian midlands it seemed, by comparison, a land of romance. Amenable women, ready liquor, and the piquant loveliness of golden pagodas—all these had a powerful influence and Kipling, with his genius for

mood and colour, etched the Tommy's reaction faithfully in a
score of memorable lines.

> For the wind is in the palm-trees, and the temple bells
>   they say:
> Come you back, you British soldier, come you back to
>   Mandalay![12]

There were also cogent Imperial reasons for watching Burma
with special care, for matters had a habit of boiling over on the
eastern as well as the north-western extremities of the Indian
sub-continent. In particular, Mandalay, where the mad Alompra
dynasty ruled, was a source of anxiety to successive British
Viceroys. The reigning sovereign just now was Thibaw, a youth
capable of most excesses in his own right but who, under the
tutelage of his Queen Supayalat, proceeded to extremes that sent
a thrill of horror through even the philosophical Chinese. British
troops were currently in occupation of Pegu, Rangoon, and
Bassein but it required no prophet to foresee that in the near
future they would be marching further north. Not imperialism
but common humanity and a duty to British subjects in Burma
rendered such a step inescapable. Bobs, busily inspecting
frontier posts at Thayetmyo and Toungoo, was well aware of
the fact.

Back in India again, he busied himself in laying the foundations of a reputation as a peace-time commander which was to
prove only less enduring than his exploits in action. Rifle-
shooting was the first point on which he laid emphasis.
Nowadays, small arms training is a subject so basic to infantry
as hardly to merit discussion, but in the British as in the Madras
armies of the 1880s, military thought still placed reliance on the
massed volleys, delivered shoulder-to-shoulder, that had won at
Waterloo. Intrepid realists were quick to point out that times
had changed, and even Cambridge in a candid moment admitted
that the British in the First Boer War had been defeated by an
'army of deerstalkers', but the old ways continued in England,
with emphasis as ever on the drill-sergeant and the barrack
square. The reformed school of thought, under Wolseley, did its
best but the opposition remained intense and the British Army
in consequence became increasingly anachronistic in the age of
Krupp and Nordenfeldt.

In contrast, Bobs, buried in Madras, was remarkably free of restraint. No gilded guardees rode down from the War Office to supervise him and the ocean put an effective damper even on the power of Cambridge to stifle military progress in India. The results were excessively good, for Bobs took full advantage of the situation and 'encouraged rifle meetings'. He did a good deal more, for personal example is infectious, and he 'endeavoured to get General Officers to take an interest in musketry inspections [. . .] I took to rifle-shooting myself, as did the officers on my personal staff [. . .]'. It was revolutionary enough, in an age which had forgotten the timeless lessons taught by Sir John Moore, for a Commander-in-Chief to try and make musketry inspections 'instructive and entertaining to the men', but for him actually to take part in small arms matches as member of a team that 'held its own in many exciting competitions' was unheard of in the 1880s.

His attitude towards field training was equally radical, though here he was following a precedent introduced by Lord Napier during his term as Commander-in-Chief. The Indian Army prided itself on a sense of realism, and there were always small wars to administer a salutary lesson when it forgot. In fact the Madras Command had been largely passed by, and the annual 'Camps of Exercise' which Bobs introduced were well overdue. Once again, the contrast between India and the mother country was marked, for Bobs and his colleagues strove continually for realism in field training at a time when manœuvres in England consisted of a few stylized 'Field Days' at which (as Wolseley wrathfully remarked), 'Ladies of all shapes and sizes' were wont to appear as spectators on horseback.

Above all, as Commander-in-Chief of Madras, Bobs had for the first time the opportunity to help his own countrymen in the ranks. In an age which prided itself on its patriotism, nothing was more scandalous than the Victorians' neglect and ill-treatment of the soldiers on whose loyalty the fate of the Empire rested. Nothing, moreover, was more outrageously shocking in Bobs' eyes for, Indian Army though he was, no man loved the British soldier more. He was especially scandalized by the appalling conditions in which British soldiers and their families were required to serve 'out East'. For the private of the line was an outcast in the social life of India, condemned, if a bachelor, to the cheap beer houses and brothels of the native quarters for the solace of his off-duty hours. If married, his fate was hardly better, for the death-rate amongst his children was appalling. Even in Britain itself, the soldier, on whose courage the country depended, was an outcast.

To Bobs' kindly and patriotic soul such conditions were indefensible, more especially since he knew the peerless loyalty and courage of the British ranks under fire. Kipling's 'Danny Deever' was a living—and dying—reality in the British Raj of 1882, and the little Indian Army general did not hesitate to reform the system. A relaxation of cruel punishments, the creation of a nursing service, and the maintenance of comfortable clubs and institutes were just a few of the humane reforms which Bobs and his wife pushed through during the years of his supremacy in Madras and, later, in India.

Kipling's claim, on behalf of Tommy Atkins, that Roberts was

> the man that done us well,
> An' we'll follow 'im to 'ell—[13]

was not as fanciful as it sounds. Many years after Bobs' death, Sir Bernard Fergusson was to describe Wavell as being, 'As much the soldiers' hero as Roberts half a century before.'[14] There could be no higher praise for either man.

Meanwhile the Imperial noontide was wearing on, though Bobs was not to survive to its evening. Russia was at her usual business on the northern frontiers, for Tsarist essays in the 'Great Game' were no less enthusiastic, if slightly less professional, than those of their Soviet heirs. In such a context the Romanov *Drang nach Osten* reached a sudden climax in 1885 with Skobeloff's victories in Turkestan, a shock for British sang-froid which was followed swiftly and unpleasantly by the Russian occupation of Afghan Panjdeh. All this seemed to Bobs to be a realization of his worst fears, fears moreover which had caused him and others like him to be characterized by a witty politician as suffering from 'Mervousness'.* For years the Tsar's envoys had been ceaselessly playing the Great Game among the distant passes of Gilgit, Chitral, and Hunza with the full support of their Government, whilst the British and Indian agents who had so faithfully combated them, could do so only

* A place called Merv was an initial Russian objective.

with the indirect and hesitant support of the Government of India. Now the pigeons looked like coming home to roost.

What British politicians, replete with knowledge of lands they had never visited, so often overlooked was that it was not merely a case of the Tsars coveting land east of the Oxus. This they did, but their statesmen also saw that creating discontent in India was a convenient way of applying pressure on London. As Skobeloff remarked, 'The greater the Russian strength in Central Asia, the more vulnerable is Britain in India and the more conciliatory will she be in Europe.' All this made nonsense of the Westminster view that discounted the need to safeguard Afghanistan from Russian influence, and it strongly supported Bobs and his school who favoured securing the Frontier passes against any possible invasion.

Normally Gladstone, pacifist by inclination and a 'Little Englander' in outlook, might have been expected to support the less belligerent line, more especially since it was also espoused by Sir Garnet Wolseley (who had never been to the Frontier). In point of fact, however, trouble in Afghanistan came as a heaven-sent distraction from Gladstone's troubles in the Sudan, and he lost no time in exploiting it to the full. With Britain's bewhiskered Prime Minister conducting, for his own ends, a passionate flirtation with the 'Fiend of Jingoism', war seemed inevitable and Bobs, to his unconcealed delight, learned that he was to have command of one of the two army corps scheduled for mobilization. Fortunately for all concerned a Tory Government, equally unequivocal and a great deal more resolute, now came to power. It was a time for tough dealing and strong nerves, and the Russians recoiled in alarm at Salisbury's bluntly worded opinions. It was not the last service to be rendered by the House of Cecil to their unappreciative country.

*   *   *

By July 1885, Bobs had reached the parting of the ways. He had proved himself a gallant soldier, an expert staff officer, and a fine leader of men. His Frontier and Afghan campaigns had also revealed him to be a highly competent expeditionary commander —at divisional strength. All this was known, but apart from the Kandahar Campaign, it was praise equally applicable to a dozen other brave and conscientious senior officers. Even his period as Commander-in-Chief of the Madras Army was no firm pointer to what lay beyond, for the Madras Command was by no means the brightest jewel in the Crown of India. The question was now whether he would join a thousand other Anglo-Indian officers 'on the shelf', or whether he would enter that select band of military peers who had won distinction in a score of battlefields over the last quarter of a century.

So far as Bobs was concerned, the omens in 1885 were not altogether favourable. On the whole, the Tory politicians liked him, but he had more than once been the target of Radical Members of Parliament. Above all, he was Indian Army, and this meant much in an age in which the court still exercised power and influence behind the scenes. Even Wolseley, detested by the court circle, had been loaded with decorations and promotion for his leadership in the Ashanti Campaign, and Parliament had voted him £25,000. Bobs, an Indian Army man, had in contrast received only a GCB for the much more difficult campaign which had culminated in the march to Kandahar.

Though there was no doubt of the Indian Army view in the matter—and it was an opinion held by not a few British Service officers—there would have been few prudent men ready to lay a bet on Bobs following his old friend Donald Stewart as Commander-in-Chief, India. Wolseley, freshly returned from his unsuccessful dash to Khartoum, had also laid claim to the India Command, and despite his unpopularity in some circles he had vociferous backers. It was, therefore, a very real tribute to Bobs' ability and status that he should have been appointed Commander-in-Chief in July 1885, and in India itself there were few dissenting voices from the officer corps of either British or Indian Services. Amongst the troops there was even less doubt, for the other ranks of both races loved him, and it was only among the London military hierarchy that a disapproving murmur arose. Bobs sailed for England and leave in August 1885, confirmed as Commander-in-Chief, India.

In Burma, meanwhile, matters had moved swiftly to a climax, as Thibaw, Lord of The Celestial White Elephant, Monarch of Ava, and Titular King of Burma, threw down his gage to the British. The Viceroy of India had been peculiarly patient in recent years, averting his eyes from massacres, disregarding the grossest scandals, placating where others would have gone to war. Recently, however, such benevolence had undergone a sudden change for France was fishing in troubled waters at Mandalay. For the next few months the French Consul, M. Haas, was to slide through the pages of Burmese history with the guile of a serpent, plotting, conniving, riveting together the ramshackle conspiracy which was to challenge the British Empire.

In himself, M. Haas was of little account. Diplomats have intrigued before, and will doubtless do so again. It is what they are sometimes paid to do. Few, however, have had to deal with monarchs of quite the style of Thibaw. Driven by his Queen Supayalat and encouraged by the illusion of French aid, the young King moved from one excess to another, until in the end the British were forced to take action. It had been possible to overlook red velvet sacks filled with the mutilated bodies of Thibaw's own countrymen, but now the great Bombay Burma Company was itself assailed, and the 'Bombay Burma' was British. Notes proved unavailing; ultimatums were disregarded. To Victorian statecraft only one answer seemed possible. General Prendergast, like Bobs a veteran of the Mutiny, marched north.

The campaign was short and decisive, as Burmese military power crumpled. The invincible Rat and Dragon regiments were soon no more, having emulated the former rather than the latter beast. Within two weeks of the start of hostilities, the Lion Throne was vacant and British Tommies were offering 'Soup Plate'* a light for her cheroot in Mandalay. Bobs could claim no credit for the tactical control of the advance for that belonged to Prendergast alone, but it was Bobs who had put Burma military establishments in a state of readiness. Above all, it meant that his tour of office had begun in a comfortable aura of success. No one could deny his shining qualities as a commander but he was also, as Curzon would have put it, 'emphatically Felix'.† At all events, by February 1886 Bobs was attending the Viceroy's formal annexation of Upper Burma. With lively memories of the monstrous despotism from which they

---

* The soldiers' nickname for Supayalat.
† A remark he made after inspecting the field of Wolseley's victory at Tel-el-Kebir.

had been delivered, the Burmese themselves were in no mood to protest. As Bobs ingenuously recorded, 'The People generally tried in every possible way to show their gratitude to the Viceroy [. . .]'. Anything was better than more red velvet sacks.

After hardly a pause, the Commander-in-Chief was off to the Frontier again to plan against that persistent and well-founded Victorian obsession, the Russian menace. One suspects too that the gaunt peaks which held his fame exercised no small fascination over him. Certainly his views on the defence of India, like his memoirs, reveal time and again his belief in the enduring nature of Britain's imperial destiny. Like most Indian Army officers with any experience of the Frontier, he had no doubt of Russian ambitions there, but unlike most he placed little faith in fixed fortifications. A belief in mobility is often the mark of the first-rate commander, and Bobs put his finger unerringly on the core when he emphasized the need for efficient lines of communication. Fortresses could be outflanked and surrounded, as other generals before him and since have found. The surest defence was a mobile force, well trained and efficiently led and equipped, with adequate supply lines. It is often the mark of timid and therefore second-rate military minds to take refuge behind fixed emplacements and Bobs, not surprisingly, found himself in a minority when insisting upon the importance of mobility. Nevertheless, as Commander-in-Chief, Bobs' opinions carried considerable weight, and though he did not get all he wanted, in the end his views largely prevailed.

Bobs' views were simply expressed in his own book,* when he wrote that lines of communication were 'of infinitely greater importance, as affording the means of bringing all the strategical points on the Frontier into direct communication with the railway system of India, and enabling us to mass our troops rapidly, should we be called upon to aid Afghanistan.' Other advantages, not exclusively military, flowed from this policy, for 'there are no better civilizers than roads and railways'. Emplacements had their part in the scheme, but less as the sort of line that bore Maginot's name than 'for the protection of such depots and storehouses as would have to be constructed, and as a support to the army in the field'. The fortress mentality was wholly alien to Bobs' temperament.

* *Forty-one Years in India.*

By mid-1886, more trouble had blown up in Upper Burma. With the death there of his old friend and comrade of Frontier days, General Macpherson, Bobs, in the midst of yet another seemingly interminable inspection, was instructed by the Viceroy, now Lord Dufferin, 'to transfer my Headquarters to Burma, and arrange to remain there until "the back of the business was broken".' Fresh from a pleasant journey with his wife through the Jalaurie Pass and 'the beautiful Kulu valley', the prospect of campaigning once more in fever-haunted terrain was not entrancing, yet Bobs went to work with a will. It did not take him long to draft explicit instruction 'for the guidance of General and other officers commanding columns in Burma' and these, issued in Mandalay in November, are eloquent of his gift for combining the gentler forms of pacification with an infinitely sterner approach to those who proved intransigent. 'Chief men of Districts' were to be treated with 'consideration and distinction' in common with informers and guides, who were to be well paid. Friendly villagers too were to be cultivated, but on those who took up arms 'against British Rule', the 'heaviest possible loss' was to be inflicted in any military action.

Officers commanding columns also had magisterial powers, where no civil officer was present, to imprison for up to two years or, still more salutary, to inflict up to thirty lashes. The orders had a stout Roman ring about them and were swiftly comprehended by the perceptive Burmese to such an extent that within three months the country was almost pacified. What must have been still more disappointing to his critics were the close personal friendships that he formed with a number of Buddhist priests, some of them indeed corresponding with him until quite shortly before his death. Bobs never found any difficulty about forming and maintaining friendships with Asiatics, though he also never fell into the error of false sentimentality and did not hesitate to strike hard when necessary. In this, though foremost, he was far from being alone in his age, for the Victorian Imperialists were on the whole of rigid integrity. They were also blunt, straight-spoken men and were undoubtedly admired by as well as devoted to the races whom they ruled and served.

During all this time, his preoccupation with the welfare of the British troops serving under him never waned, and in his efforts to improve their lot he had a constant supporter in Nora. She, indeed, launched out on her own account in 1886, when she drafted and achieved a scheme for the nursing of British troops in India. Nowadays, it is hard to credit that successive attempts to introduce trained nurses to the military establishment in India had been turned down by the government for no other reason than expense. In the end Nora, who had a knack of getting what she wanted, captured the Viceroy's ear and in due course even the Secretary of State in London capitulated. The scheme was modest enough in its inception, but the principle had been accepted, and by the end of the century proper medical facilities were an accepted feature of army life. As the packed military cemeteries of India proved, it was not before time. A year later, Bobs' own private campaign for improvement of conditions came to an end with Government agreement to 'my strong recommendation for the establishment of a Club or Institute in every British regiment and battery in India'. Fulminated the little General angrily, 'The British Army in India could have no better or more generally beneficial memorial of the Queen's Jubilee than the abolition of that relic of barbarism, the canteen, and its supersession by an Institute, in which the soldier would have under the same roof a reading-room, recreation room, and a decently-managed refreshment room.' Generations of long-suffering 'Presidents', wrestling with the accounts of the 'Regimental Institute' may not always have had cause to bless Bobs' name, but there were few doubts among the troops themselves.

> 'E's a little down on drink,
> Chaplain Bobs;
> But it keeps us outer Clink—
> Don't it, Bobs?
> So we will not complain
> That 'e's water on the brain,
> If 'e leads us straight again—
> Blue-Light Bobs.[15]

The spectacle of the Commander-in-Chief leading in person a crusade by a body whose forbidding title was 'The Army Temperance Association', was novel enough, yet so great was Bobs' magnetism and popularity with the British rank and file that by the time he left India, 'Nearly one-third of the 70,000

British soldiers in that country were members or honorary members of the Army Temperance Association.'

1887 opened proudly with Queen Victoria's Golden Jubilee, an excuse for renewed ceremonial and pageantry. In all this Bobs, as Commander-in-Chief, played an important part. No great lovers of the social whirl on their own account, he and Nora were, as they grew older, at some pains to entertain the young bachelor officers who thronged India and whose loneliness they understood so well. It was probably for such reasons rather than from personal inclination that they added a ballroom to their house, 'Snowdon', and on 21 June christened it with a fancy dress ball in honour of the Queen.

The Jubilee was sweetened for Bobs by a GCIE, but still no peerage, though men before and since have been ennobled for a tithe of his accomplishments. Meanwhile, there was plenty of work to be done, for all was not as secure as it seemed in the late Victorian age. As John Sealey, a Cambridge professor, had pointed out in 1883 (in published lectures that provoked a storm), the sands were running out for Britain, while new challengers arose. Security for Britain lay in the strength of her child-nations maturing overseas. Australia, New Zealand, South Africa, and Canada were the future sources of British strength— if Britain would allow it. Froude wrote much the same in 1886. 'The workshop of the world' seemed a proud title to the undiscerning, but Froude saw only too well that factory life was sapping the vitality of the British people. Already the yeoman had passed, and the troglodyte of the 'Black Country' was a poor substitute in the national hierarchy for tough peasant farmers.

These were views close to Bobs' heart, for though he was a Tory of the vintage years, his was a patriotism that transcended all other divisions. Like all Victorians he was a Briton proud in his national identity with the merest private of the line. Love of country was a vital inspiration for him to the end of his life. Such considerations, and not personal ambition, drove him ever onward, touring, planning, vanquishing his own fragility in the never-ceasing quest to secure the Empire he loved. By December 1888 he was on the Frontier once again, riding with an impressed Viceroy through the Khyber Pass and winning the Viceroy's consent for the digging of a strategic tunnel at

Kohjak. The tour ended at Rawal Pindi where, typically, he treated Lord Dufferin to a fine test of courage, with nine regiments of cavalry charging across the parade ground to within eight yards of him. The Viceroy (and his horse) came through with flying colours for though 'it certainly did seem rather close quarters', His Lordship remained 'perfectly calm and still on his horse in the face of such an onslaught'.

A great deal of hard office work now followed, as Bobs, in his capacity as chairman of the Defence and Mobilization Committees, planned the fortification of the major ports, the defence of the Frontier, and the construction of an efficient transport department, without which the mobilization of a single corps would be almost impossible. At a time when detailed staff work was still the exception rather than the rule, his careful planning of troop movements by rail was hardly surpassed and proved a model of its kind. Integration of 'State Force' units in the overall defence plan was also proceeding apace, and the loyalty of these units was of an extraordinarily high order. They also had a strong sentimental value, for though the age of splendid uniforms and bright trappings was fast passing away in face of increasingly scientific weapons, the Indian Princes' squadrons retained something of the old medieval heraldry, and if their efficiency rarely measured up to that of the central armies, they still provided a useful and enthusiastic reserve on which to draw in an emergency.

Bobs' last years in India therefore ebbed in an atmosphere of vigorous reform, as the old army achieved its sometimes painful metamorphosis into a modern fighting force under his control. The change was less radical for the Indian Service than for a British Army long and artificially retarded by Cambridge and his circle, for fieldcraft had always been a speciality of sepoy regiments, and the Hindu Kush was cold comfort for those imbued with the mentality of the Square. There had, indeed, been room for great improvements in uniform, musketry, weapons, and equipment, and within his limited financial scope Bobs made considerable progress during the final years. Above all, his emphasis on field manœuvres and realistic battle training raised tactical standards sharply. By the end of his service in India he could truthfully have claimed the major credit for raising the Indian Army from the level of a picturesque anachronism to the standard of a formidable modern fighting machine.

Though Britain had thrilled with delight at his prowess on the March to Kandahar, Bobs was still even at this juncture little known to the public at home, one of a score of Anglo-Indian soldiers whose names intermittently appeared in the popular press, in connection with distant exploits. By 1890, however, the picture was fast changing and through no action on the part of Bobs. For in that year, as Dr Bryant has written, there 'came the biggest literary sensation since the appearance of *Pickwick*. A young man of genius born in Bombay "between the palms and the sea" and bred half in India, half in England, painted the life of the Anglo-Indian community for his countrymen: the colour, scent and sound of the East, the crowded bazaar opening for the Sahib's horse'.[16] Rudyard Kipling was a great writer and, in his own fashion, a great man, and his gleaming stanzas were an immediate success. 'Since the day when Lord Craven drew his interminable cocoa trees for Harriet Wilson, the English had been bored by stories of their own Empire.' But Kipling changed all that. He also brought Bobs to the forefront of fame, with his vital word pictures of the oft-wounded little general, heroic in moral stature, and invincibly courageous. Within months 'Father Bobs' became a national figure.

When the two finally met there was a certain amount of hero worship on the one side and of paternal kindliness on the other. Kipling has described the proudest moment of his life as riding up the Simla Mall on his grey pony beside the Commander-in-Chief mounted on an enormous chestnut, and there were other social contacts between general and poet in such typically Victorian entertainments as amateur theatricals at 'Snowdon', the Roberts' home. Admittedly, relations between them were not always as smooth for Kipling in his own way was as blunt as Roberts, and sterling though his efforts in military administration were, there is no doubt that the General was happier in the field. In particular, he was inclined to appoint to important posts those on whom he knew from personal experience that he could rely. That in itself was commendable, but not all capable officers had had the good fortune to march with Bobs, and there were sometimes reproachful mutterings in the mess. Almost certainly Bobs, the soul of honour, had never intended the slightest injustice—had he not, when aged thirty-four, confided to his diary an ambition to be 'gentle with women, loving with children, considerate to [his] inferiors, kindly with servants, tender-hearted with all'? But Kipling was after all a journalist, and some stanzas in the *Pioneer* were undeniably sharp.

The truth was that Kipling never worshipped any god blindly, and he was quick to discern the weaknesses as well as the virtues of all his heroes. It was as much to the credit of the old soldier as to the credit of the young writer therefore that, despite differences of opinion, the foundations of their friendship never weakened. Each was big enough to accept the other's differences, whilst continuing to view major national problems from the same basic viewpoint, though Roberts might have been nettled had he known of Kipling's private opinion of *Forty-one Years in India*—'Remarkable for what it left out.'

Paradoxically, though Bobs was for the first time in decades beyond the serious possibility of personal action, the years of his command were far from quiet. It was a time of multitudinous small expeditions, to wild and lawless tribal areas such as Zhob, Miranzai, and the Black Mountain, and each was itself a minor epic such as Bobs would have loved to lead. The Russians were also at their old business of raising trouble on the Frontier, and Francis Younghusband, arriving late at the Commander-in-Chief's for dinner one night, was taken aside by the fire-eating little man and told that the Quetta Division had been mobilized 'just in case [. . .]'. For Roberts was no military gambler, ready to stake the national interest in a reckless throw, and he had gauged the Tsar's strength and weakness to a nicety. There were, he knew, as many dangers in timidity as in rashness and, giving the young officer's arm a confidential squeeze, he remarked, 'Now's the time to go for the Russians. We are ready and they are not.' In the event, conflict was avoided on a major scale by the success of British arms in the brilliant little Hunza Naga expedition against the Tsar's protégé, and the Russian bluff was called once more. It was all an excellent argument for the 'Forward Policy' which Bobs espoused and Wolseley deplored.

By 1890, Bob's Indian service was coming to an end, and he could look back on four decades of steady progress in every branch of the service, both British and Indian. At first it seemed as though he would not even see the year out in India for on New Year's Day 1890 he was offered the Adjutant-Generalcy in succession to Wolseley. After the long years of exile, it seemed almost too good to be true, and thus it proved, for though Bobs lost no time in accepting, the appointment was set aside by the powers that be on the pretext that a successor for India could not be found. It was a bitter reflection that though Wolseley had been a peer since 1882 Bobs, who had been preferred to him for the India Command, was not to be permitted to follow him in the post he had vacated. Even the way in which the affair had been conducted was singularly unfortunate for, after being told early in April that his London appointment had been agreed by the Cabinet and that he would be required in England that autumn, Bobs received another wire three weeks later, reversing the whole arrangement.

This whole incident was a bitter blow, for both Bobs and Nora were already feeling the effects of their long tropical service. It was also against his personal interests, since he fully realized that in doing so he was forfeiting his chance of employment in England. Unfortunately the Cabinet, in asking him to retain the India Command for two further years, had coupled the Queen's name with theirs. Faced with his sovereign's command, Bobs felt unable to resist, though 'I did not attempt to conceal from Mr Stanhope* that I was disappointed'. It is hardly necessary to comment that the Duke of Cambridge was, throughout the negotiations, hovering in the background. He had not rid himself of Wolseley in order to accept a 'Sepoy General' in exchange!

Meanwhile, old friends were fast slipping away. Most of those who had served with him in the Mutiny were gone now, dead or languishing in retirement at 'home'. The latest to leave, in April 1891, was George Chesney, whom Bobs had known for most of his service and who had been his colleague on the Viceroy's Council for five years. Worse still, Chesney was replaced by one of Wolseley's nominees, Lieutenant-General Brackenbury, that 'very dangerous man'† who had earned Cambridge's dislike. Brackenbury turned out to be a great deal better than Bobs had anticipated but the fact remained that the

---

* Secretary of State at the India Office.

† Dangerous, in Cambridge's view, because of his association with Wolseley.

old order was changing. Bobs yielded to no one in his zeal for modernization, but the call of 'home' was stronger than ever, and when on 1 January, 1892 the Secretary of State offered him yet another renewal of his term as Commander-in-Chief, Bobs' refusal was unequivocal. He had been without leave for a long time, he was exhausted, and though the pill was sweetened by the bestowal on him of a long-deferred peerage, the fact remained that the question of employment in England had been carefully allowed by the British Government to drop into the background. Bobs had no illusions about the poor prospects of an appointment at home.

A great deal remained to be done in order to bring the Indian Army finally into the ranks of the world's top fighting forces. It was already by far the best Asiatic army, but this was insufficient. There was dead wood to be cut away; certain units, retained through undue deference to tradition, had to be discarded and replaced by better material. Bobs recognized this, just as he saw the need to increase the establishment of British officers per battalion if the best results were to be obtained, for an Indian unit relied, to an extent undreamed of in a British regiment of the line, upon its British officers for tactical control and morale. As Bobs wrote, 'Nine to a Cavalry and eight to an Infantry corps may be sufficient in time of peace, but that number is quite too small to stand the strain of war.' Officer casualty incidence alone made it an unrealistic number, as Indian formations were to find in two world wars.

These and many other tasks, Bobs was to leave to his successors, and the man destined to complete the process was not even an Indian Army officer at all, though he had spent most of his career with eastern troops. Herbert Kitchener has often been hailed as the architect of the Indian Army as it existed until 1939, but in fact he was only one of a large and devoted if unsung band. He and Bobs were the greatest but there were others, stretching away into the dawn of John Company's supremacy, who had wrought and died with only cursory recognition.

The remainder of Bobs' time in India was relatively uneventful, and consisted of official visits to the many areas with which he had special ties. Khatmandu, capital of Nepal and home of the Gurkhas who had helped to win so many of his campaigns, was a special source of delight to him, and he and Nora were lavishly entertained by a ruling caste firm in its loyalty to the British tie. There were many other routine farewells also to be made; on the Frontier, in Burma, and the Punjab, for all India, white and brown alike, was united in its wish to honour the little man whose name had become synonymous with courage and chivalry. Some occasions, such as his last visit to the Peshawar manœuvres, were strictly professional but others, to old friends whom he might never see again, held that undertone of tragedy which is part of life; other visits, complimentary as they were, must have been frankly boring to a couple who set little store by formal dinners, though neither Bobs nor Nora would ever have given a hint of such feelings.

Forty-one years in India now closed with an incident typical of the man, which proved his courage unabated and his luck undimmed when, out for a last bout of pig-sticking he was able to save his host, Sir Pertab Singh, Maharajah of Kashmir, from certain death. Minor though the incident seems in retrospect, it was no mean feat for a small elderly man, dismounted, to tackle and kill an infuriated boar with a spear after it had already gored and was still tangling with his host.

By the spring of 1893, India lay behind the Field-Marshal and his wife, for at Bombay the ship was waiting to take them north to the islands which they called home but where for almost half a century Bobs, at least, had never really lived. It must have seemed to the Roberts, as they watched the receding shore, that his active military career was closed for ever and that soon he would be just another sepoy general on the shelf. At first he hankered after the Viceroyalty as did Kitchener in later years, and, unlike Kitchener, his would have been a welcome appointment by almost all shades of opinion in India, including the Princes. In the end, though at first he was optimistic and the press complimentary, his hopes were doomed to founder on a rock not fundamentally dissimilar to Kitchener's. Though there was no Morley to contend with yet, the Cabinet were unwilling to appoint a former Commander-in-Chief to the zenith of power in the sub-continent. Professional politicians are, as a breed, jealous of their perquisites. Lord Roberts, men said, had left the public scene. A day out with the hounds was the greatest excitement he could reasonably expect. Yet only six and a half years were to pass before his name would once more be on every lip, his genius reaching up to new and higher pinnacles of achievement. All this was unforeseen and in consequence unplanned. As he himself might have echoed, *L'homme propose, Dieu dispose.*

CHAPTER XII

The Queen's Commander

IN almost every country, the spectacle of an old soldier in retirement presents similarities. There is the same divorcement from civilian life, the same wistful nostalgia for past glories, the same instinctive conservatism and love of country. Bobs was in some ways more fortunate than most, for modest as it was, the half-pay of a Field-Marshal compared favourably with the pittance on which other less fortunate officers were retired. The truth was that the British Army had historically been designed to cater for the officer with substantial private means and, despite improvements over the previous half-century, it continued to be based on the same fundamental conception. The harsh laws of economics and the decline of the squirearchy had deprived the concept of its justification, but it remained convenient to a Treasury traditionally reluctant to support the armed forces to ignore this.

The result was that many officers faced poverty when they retired, and as the proportion of 'Professionals' increased and the pure 'Gentlemen' decreased among the commissioned ranks, more and more had to rely on their pay as a means of livelihood. Such a man was Wolseley, and amongst the Indian Army the proportion was even greater. Kipling's Troop-Sergeant-Major differed only in degree from those of his superiors who lacked a private income.

> But I'm old and I'm nervis,
> I'm cast from the Service,
> And all I deserve is a shillin' a day.[17]

Bobs' own financial situation was aggravated rather than alleviated by his peerage, for it was an age in which the stock of the aristocracy stood high, and the ways in which they could improve their finances were correspondingly limited. Various appointments were suggested, but none appealed, and he could never bring himself to canvass for personal advantage with Kitchener's rather graceless intensity. Time did not hang heavily on his hands for he was never a man to be bored, and in those halcyon days of Victorian prosperity, there were always hounds to follow. A flood of invitations also poured in for the public had taken him to their heart. Though traditionally hostile to the military, the British people could on occasion astonish even ebullient Continentals with the warmth of their feelings and, alone of Victorian soldiers, Bobs and Kitchener were both national heroes during their life-time.

In August 1895 Bobs replaced Wolseley in the Irish Command upon the latter's promotion to Commander-in-Chief and his period of unemployment came to an end. There was a remarkable similarity between the careers of these two great Victorian soldiers, so different in character, yet both so ardent in the service of their country. Bobs was immeasurably the greater man, and also the greater field commander, though this was not as obvious before the South African War as it later became. Their names were often linked by the press in a rivalry which, though unsought by either commander, was frequently coloured and emphasized by the attitudes of their staffs. It was said that a Roberts man could expect no promotion in a Wolseley sphere of influence, and that the reverse was also true. There is no doubt that Wolseley disliked Bobs and feared his distinction as a threat to himself. Even in politics their ways diverged, for Wolseley, though individually 'Jingoist' in viewpoint, was the military darling of the Liberal Party, whilst Bobs, who admitted no political affiliations during his service, could hardly have been other than the Tory favourite. His every word and action, no less than his patriotism, proclaimed him a Conservative of the old and upright school.

There was also an essential difference in the characters of the two men that goes far to explain how Bobs, the Frontier General from far-off, shadowy India, became a national hero, whilst Wolseley, the Gilbertian 'Model of a Modern Major-General', remained for all his victories a singularly unloved professional. Both were great soldiers in their own right at a time when the

British Army was only large enough for one genius, but whereas Bobs was transparently generous and of magnetic attraction, Wolseley's personality seems to have repelled more than it captivated. He could be mean and unforgiving on occasion, whilst the whole Army with few exceptions rightly adored Bobs. Wolseley loved his country, but Bobs worshipped it. Wolseley served the nation well, but in Bobs the ideal of service reigned supreme and dominated his life, to the subordination of ambition. It is upon such differences that the two men must be compared.

The months of enforced idleness had one happy result, at least for posterity, since they enabled Bobs to complete his memoirs. Autobiography, in which generations of generals have shown themselves ferociously enthusiastic, is also an art in which objectivity proves rare. Yet *Forty-One Years In India* is refreshing from almost every point of view, and not least for the light it throws on Bobs himself. Rarely can an author so unconsciously have revealed so much of his own character as he did. One has only to open the book to find on almost every page some proof of his courage, intelligence, and modesty, whilst here and there, hardly expected amongst the mass of terse, detailed prose, one discovers descriptive passages of rare beauty. There is no boasting—only a simple recitation of the facts, yet few readers can fail to be struck, even after three-quarters of a century, by the writer's character.

Press comment—apart from Kipling's caustic comment—was almost entirely favourable, and Henley the poet described it as the best book written by a soldier since Caesar's *Commentaries*. There were very few to contradict him, and Mr James' verdict* that the author's main fault lies in his 'extraordinary generosity' cannot be faulted. It was symbolic of Bobs that he should have let not merely his own colleagues, but outsiders, down very lightly. They were often persons who had small reason to expect his gratitude.

When finally the summons came to the Curragh, Bobs viewed it with unalloyed delight. He was also very fortunate to have been appointed since though he himself was unaware of the fact, the Duke of Cambridge had been zealously campaigning against him, pouring unfounded invective 'about Roberts, not in honeyed terms' into Wolseley's gleeful ear. By all the

* *Lord Roberts*, p. 25.

precedents, this should have been his last post, the type of job normally reserved for distinguished soldiers deemed worthy of an unexacting command as the finale to their careers. As Commander-in-Chief, Ireland, he was unlikely to be faced with any campaign (by all the laws of the Medes and Persians, Kabul-to-Kandahar should have been the climax of a talented life), but there would still be troops to train and, perhaps, though this was no pleasing prospect, a terrorist campaign to put down. For years Ireland had been the Achilles heel of the United Kingdom, with its Fenians and its guerrilla warfare and its black republican oaths, and now, with Gladstone determined on Home Rule, it looked as if the Green Isle was coming to the tragic end of an unhappy road.

To Bobs such problems would have come as nothing new, for though there were overtones of nationalism in Ireland not yet present in India, he had spent much of his life in contact with situations of basic similarity. There was much that was kindly and humorous about relationships between the Catholic Irish of the south and the landlords, who were mainly Protestant. As those crusaders who landed in Ireland, afire with zeal for the underdog, found, Major Yeates did not exist solely in the imagination of an Edith Somerville* and there was loyalty and good fellowship in plenty between the peoples there. At the same time, the Irish Command held its political risks in times of trouble, for the days of Lake's Dragoons† were long past. Soldiers had come a cropper there in the past and, as the Curragh incident was to prove during Bobs' lifetime, it could happen again.

In the event, Bobs' own time in Ireland proved quiet and unusually free of perils. For this the general political situation and, above all, the Parnell-O'Shea scandal were largely responsible. In a land traditionally inclined to condone murder more readily than adultery, the revelation of Charles Stewart Parnell's affair with Kitty O'Shea had split the Nationalist Party from top to bottom. In November 1890 Parnell, despite the mutterings of his henchmen, still led the Irish Nationalists, but by 6 December, ruined and disgraced, he was driven into the wilderness. All this had happened during Wolseley's tenure, but Bobs (as

* *The Irish R.M. Complete*, Somerville and Ross.
† Troops used by General Lake to put down an Irish rebellion in 1797.

well as his predecessor) was destined to reap the harvest—tranquillity. The British electorate had also rejected Home Rule for Ireland, and with it Gladstone. 'For five years,' the old Prime Minister complained, 'I have rolled this stone patiently uphill, and it is now rolled to the bottom again.'

With political unrest in abeyance, therefore, Bobs' years at the Curragh passed, agreeably free of hurdles if a trifle prosaically for one accustomed to the spur of great decisions. The hunting was excellent and Bobs, still a skilful and intrepid horseman, was an outstanding example of Kitchener's recommendation, made years later, that the encouragement of hunting and polo among army officers in time of peace was the best means of keeping them fit in nerve and sinew for the field. When Bobs told the Cabinet, on the eve of his departure for South Africa, that, despite his years, he had kept himself in condition for the task ahead, he spoke the literal truth, and horse and hound were not the least of his allies in that struggle. If, as Kipling remarked, he was 'a little down on drink', it undoubtedly made the conflict with a naturally delicate constitution all the easier for 'Blue-light Bobs'.

One highlight was the colourful ceremony in 1897 when Bobs rode at the head of the colonial contingent in the Queen's Diamond Jubilee procession, mounted on his old and spirited Arab charger, the stallion Vonolel. As the old horse, come home from India with his master, and a legend in his own right, pranced down the crowded streets, the pair were cheered to the echo by a people still proud of their Empire and responsive to its military pageantry. It was not the least attractive side of the old soldier's character that he should have refused to abandon the charger that had carried him so well, when the time had come for him to quit India for ever.

Meanwhile, in far-away South Africa, a problem that had been smouldering for years was soon to break into open flame. It was a land with which Bobs had already some familiarity, gained in part during his abortive expedition to the Cape at Gladstone's behest during the First Boer War. Only Colley's decisive defeat at Majuba had saved Bobs from the unenviable position of being forced to take over a demoralized and untrained force to fight a hopeless campaign. During a much more recent visit, foreseeing the likelihood of another war, he had studied the terrain and formed definite opinions on what should be the correct strategic approach. They were ideas that, though rejected by Wolseley and the reigning War Office clique, were to prove as correct as the official conception was faulty.

The causes of the South African War were many and complex, some reaching far back into the historic past but most centred upon the endemic rivalry between the two main European races —the British and the Dutch. To represent the trouble, as it is today fashionable to do, as merely a struggle between a humanitarian Britain, solicitous of native welfare, and a set of cruel and primitive farmers is quite inaccurate. The truth was that the Kaffirs,* as the black inhabitants of South Africa were commonly called, had proved infinitely more predatory towards one another and towards all white men than had the Boers towards the blacks. Equally true was the fact that the black tribes had no greater title to South Africa than the European, for the true indigenous peoples were the yellow Bushmen and Hottentots, now dying out through contact with civilization. The black Bantu peoples had entered the Northern Transvaal almost at the same time as Jan van Riebeeck's landing at the Cape, and it was only after the passage of decades that the first white-black collision occurred.

This was, unfortunately, never the picture which was presented to the British people, and only rarely to their government, during the sixty-eight years that intervened between the Great Trek and the final trial of strength, for there were expert propagandists at work. British missionaries were not above fishing in troubled waters, and they often had the ears of ignorant and prejudiced politicians at home. Glenelg was only the most famous of the latter and, as British settlers were not slow to discover, Briton as well as Boer became the target for evangelical spleen. The difference between them was that though the Englishman cursed, he stayed, whilst the Dutchman packed his bags and trekked. By 1870 two infant Boer republics were moving uncertainly forward, and by 1882 the whole Dutch cause in Southern Africa had been suddenly and dramatically advanced by the commandos' victory at Majuba.

It was during this period that a new and largely unexpected influence made itself felt. Whilst the Boer republics remained poor pastoral entities, British Imperial intervention was at best

* An Arabic term meaning 'unbeliever'.

half-hearted, for few party leaders felt inclined to explain away a rise in the income-tax upon the basis of moral duty. The converse remained equally true, for there were few people in Europe itself, including the Dutch, anxious to espouse the cause of a tiny group of backward and unimportant farmers across the Vaal and Orange Rivers. When, as happened in 1880, real trouble arose it was against the wishes of a British Government that regarded South Africa as the source of a great deal more anxiety than, fundamentally, she was worth.

All this, however, changed with the discovery of gold, for the trouble at once ceased to be parochial. As immigrants, avid for wealth, poured in, great combines were formed and great plans laid. It was all very well for the Afrikaner farmers to watch, horror-struck, as the pulsing centres of industry rose, but this was *Progress*, and a hastening century could not be expected to heed a few biblical farmers. Harlots, confidence men, and thieves hurried northward in a swelling tide to join the great rush and to batten on the miners of the Reef. The fact that many of these immigrants were a seedy lot seemed to 'Oom' Paul Kruger, President of the Transvaal, an excellent reason for denying all the vote. To Britain, in contrast, it seemed no reason at all. Commercial interests in London had at once become greedy, and behind both them and the Boers hovered the shadowy figures of international finance. Though, when the day of failure dawned, both Rhodes and his lieutenant, Jameson, were to find themselves abandoned, there is no doubt that before the disaster of the 'Raid', they had enjoyed powerful support, however covert it had been.

Greed there may have been, but there was no denying that Britain had her rights. Genuine British commercial interests undoubtedly required protection, and Hohenzollern and Hollander influences were only two of those that cast sinister and malign shadows across the scene. Imperial strategic and trading interests were unmistakably in danger, and the intrigues of Dr Leyds and other Boer extremist elements radically worsened an already explosive situation. There were abundant faults on both sides and in the end it was the fighting men, Briton and Burgher alike, who had to pay the price.

In all this, 1895 takes its place as the year of destiny, the year in which great decisions were made and great chances lost. It had opened with no expectation of the spectacular; it ended in the certain knowledge that war lay over the horizon. 22 June saw the formation in London of a new Administration under Salisbury, and if the Liberals under Gladstone had proved a disaster, there could be no mistaking the slant likely to be followed by a Tory Government with Joe Chamberlain in its midst. Both in Parliament and among the nation as a whole there was little disposition to bow before any country except their own.

Bobs had no part in such developments for though in private a confirmed Tory he was still a professional soldier, standing aloof from political movements. The mainspring of the crisis was, at the heart of the Empire, Joe Chamberlain, and at the perimeter, Cecil Rhodes. Rhodes, son of a clergyman, was an adventuring financier, Oxford student and hard-headed magnate, a creature of contrasts, almost incapable of analysis. 'What's your dream?' was a favourite question reserved for those he met for the first time. An Imperialist, he feared domination by an ignorant and misguided Westminster; a man who sought to destroy the power of the independent Boer Republics by fair means or foul, he boasted many Afrikaner supporters almost until the last, and he never veered from his view that the Dutch* were a vigorous and rising people in Southern Africa. Some men were to claim that he was a physical coward, yet he was not afraid to ride into hostile Matabele country without escort. An intellectual and moral giant, he could be as magnanimous at one moment as he could be petty the next, according to the mood that gripped him. Yet through it all, for all the minor flexions that circumstance imposed upon his plans, his main purpose remained unaltered, his will dominant and pervasive.

To assist him, Rhodes had many lieutenants, both industrial and political, but the most famous of them all was undoubtedly 'Dr Jim'. Leander Starr Jameson, a Scotsman, was clever and personable and figures large in the Rhodesian gallery of heroes, but he was also reckless and headstrong to a degree which belied his ancestry. His most notorious action was the ill-fated 'Jameson Raid', and few could have been more unfortunate. Don John of Austria riding to the war was a vision that certain British newspapers contrived to project at the time, but in truth Don Quixote would have been a more apt analogy. Without hope of

* i.e. South Africans of Dutch descent.

reinforcement, surrounded by a cloud of Boer sharpshooters, cut off from friendly territory, the outlook for the raiders was bleak. On New Year's Day 1896, Dr Jim set frontiers and the world at nought by riding across the Transvaal border in an attempt to force the issue. Two days later, everything was over, and Dr Jim in prison.

Bleak as the military outlook had been for the raid, the political results were bleaker still, for they meant that though war might be delayed, it could not now be avoided. From the day that Dr Jim marched over the border in his wild escapade, the second and incomparably the greater South African War became inevitable. None of these factors escaped Bobs, who took time off from his Irish command to do some hard thinking. There was much in the Boer character that struck an answering chord in Bobs as he was later to discover, but such considerations were far from his mind as, amid the golden fields of the Curragh, he plotted out the stages of his master plan for South Africa. All that mattered to him was that his country should once more be faced with the prospect of war there. She had already experienced one humiliating defeat at Majuba and Bobs, prescient as ever in military matters, could sense the likelihood of further disasters.

Meanwhile the clouds continued to gather, as relations degenerated on the Reef between Uitlanders and Boer Republicans. As Bobs knew only too well, there was no comfort to be derived from the state of the British Army at home. The years of Cambridge's rule from Horse Guards were still having their effect. Technique was backward and establishments antediluvian, whilst the 'Army of Deerstalkers' that had defeated Colley was able to take the field in incomparably greater strength than nineteen years before.

All this was known to Wolseley and the few scientific officers he had been able to gather around him, but he was able to obtain little assistance from the despised politicians. As early as 1895 he had demanded increases in both infantry and gunner establishments, and in July 1896 he had detailed to Lansdowne (then Secretary of State) the precise reinforcements he considered would be necessary in the event of war. All this, however, went unregarded and by August 1899 Wolseley was writing bitterly that, 'We are not locally prepared for war in

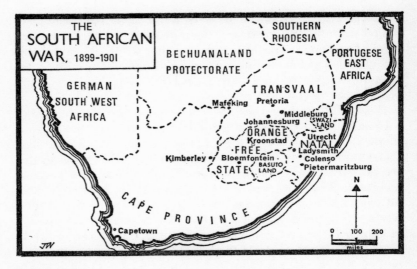

THE
SOUTH AFRICAN
WAR, 1899-1901

GERMAN
SOUTH WEST
AFRICA

BECHUANALAND
PROTECTORATE

SOUTHERN
RHODESIA

PORTUGESE
EAST
AFRICA

TRANSVAAL
Mafeking   Pretoria
                •Middleburg
Johannesburg SWAZI
ÓRANGE   LAND
Kroonstad   •Utrecht
•FREE   NATAL
Kimberley •/ •Ladysmith
Bloemfontein . •Colenso
\STATE/ BASUTO •Pietermaritzburg
         LAND

C A P E   P R O V I N C E

•Capetown

N

0 . 100   200
          miles

South Africa, so that if it comes upon us under present circumstances, we shall surrender the initiative to Kruger.' Neither in strength nor equipment was the British Army 'All Sir Garnet' in 1899.

Strategically, the position was even worse, for the War Office had deliberately averted its eyes from Bobs' careful plans. There were many reasons for this, but the principal was undoubtedly the jealous rivalry of Wolseley and his group. Wolseley had had little cause in recent years to love Buller, for the latter, though an old protégé, had in 1895 been detected in a shameless intrigue to secure for himself the position of Commander-in-Chief instead of Wolseley. Though the plan had not succeeded, it had been dangerous enough to give Wolseley a few anxious weeks. 'It is a horrible finish to my career,' Wolseley complained, 'to be superseded by one of my own lieutenants.'

Now, however, the appointment in prospect was that of Commander-in-Chief of the Expeditionary Force in South Africa, and there was little doubt that Wolseley's choice would be his old comrade of Red River days,* Redvers Buller, long one of the Wolseley School. He was also a popular figure in society circles, and the Cabinet was known to favour him. A man of gigantic physical strength and imposing appearance, Buller

---

* A Canadian expedition, led by Wolseley.

looked a typical Victorian military hero. In reality, a worse choice was hard to conceive, for though physically fearless Buller lacked both resolution and decision. He was also wholly unimaginative and distinctly indolent. Though long content to pose as a military progressive, he had no spark of Wolseley's genius and was quite unsuited for independent command against an aggressive and competent foe. It would, all the same, be wrong to stigmatize Buller as wholly without merit. A very brave man, he had been an excellent regimental officer and adequate in the lower reaches of field command. He was also a *bon viveur* of humane and kindly disposition and, like Bobs, imbued with an intense loyalty to the British soldier. Unfortunately, in Buller's case this led him to put his troops' comfort before operational necessities, and the results were distinctly unfortunate. His shortcomings were known to a small and select circle in the Army, and there were a few long faces at the news of his nomination. For neither the first nor the last time, British officers and men were to embark on a war in which at the outset every local balance except courage was weighted against them.

The outcome had been foreseen with remarkable accuracy by Bobs and it was in this knowledge that, in the period before the outbreak of war, he invited Kitchener to stay with him. Herbert Horatio Kitchener, just now Governor-General of the Sudan, till recently Sirdar of the Egyptian Army and victor of Omdurman, was already a soldier of international repute. It was a momentous meeting, for the two had never previously had the opportunity to exchange views. In character and appearance there can have rarely been two commanders so dissimilar, but it was these men who were now to form a partnership almost as famous as that of Hindenburg and Ludendorff. Enormous where Bobs was tiny, Kitchener was closest to the little Anglo-Irishman in the devotion to Britain and her army that was the guiding passion of both their lives. Bobs was by now a soldier on the very threshold of retirement, whilst Kitchener was regarded as the rising star in the military firmament. This meeting between the two great British soldiers at the Curragh in 1899 was to lay the foundation of victory in South Africa.

More surprising than their success, despite their contrasting characters, was their immediate mutual attraction, for Kitchener in spite of his inordinate ambition at once succumbed to the magic of Bobs' personality. It was a measure of their mettle that each, so exacting in his own standards, should so readily have accepted the other's worth. The value to Britain in the months to come was to prove incalculable. Without this partnership, whose foundations were thus laid in peace and tested in war, it is doubtful whether Britain could have staved off defeat, so low had military efficiency sunk under the twin disabilities of political hostility and court intrigue.

Throughout the Kingdom, a population at once ardent and vigorous awoke from the long sleep into which the last forty-five years had lulled them. Wars, which had come to mean the small wars of Empire, had traditionally been the business of a tiny force of underpaid professionals and here, quite suddenly, was a conflict which promised to absorb the patriotic energies of all that was bravest and best in the British spirit. In an age of pipe-clay, there was nothing muted in the appeal of military tradition, and the columns that swung through the country lanes to regimental march and ballad were still brave in their scarlet under the autumn sun. There was a new song, too, to add to the lilt of *The Girl I Left Behind Me*, *The Duchess of Gloucester* and a hundred others. The Boers had their *Saree Marais*, and here were the London crowds pouring down to the recruiting offices, cheering, waving, and singing a new tune destined to go down in history as one of the great war songs:

> . . . I can no longer stay—
> Hark! I hear the bugle calling,
> Goodbye Dolly Gray.[18]

By mid-December the bugle sounded a trifle tinny as the British Army reeled under a series of shattering defeats. Yet 'Black Week' occasioned no profound surprise to military experts. The weaknesses of British military organization were already apparent long before disaster brought them under the public eye, though vested interests had resolutely refused to admit their existence. When commanders such as Brigadier-General Arthur Hart led their regiments into the attack, massed as though on parade, despising deployment as unworthy, affecting to believe that assault in depth and lineal concentration was invincible, it is small wonder that casualties were high. The infantry, so loud in their denunciation of the 'brainless' cavalry, were now finding their own brand of mystique as deficient as that of the *Arme Blanche.*

To add to the difficulties, it was essentially a fraternal war; there were ties of kinship to link Afrikaners and British. In retrospect, it is also clear that both sides fatally underestimated their opponents. To the British, flushed with Imperial success, the Boer military organization seemed laughable, whilst to the Afrikaners the *Rooinekke* represented a stubborn but hopelessly inept foe, lost on the veld and more dangerous politically and economically than ever they were likely to prove in the field. Drafted to South Africa, the army in India would have taken to veld warfare rapidly. Unfortunately for the early success of Imperial arms, there were few British units from India available, and sepoy regiments were not permitted there.

The results were swiftly apparent. The overall standard of the expedition in such fundamentals as tactics, marksmanship, and logistics was low; indeed almost everything that made an army, except courage, was deficient and to most troops the terrain was wholly unfamiliar. The Boer commandos had a habit of going off to look after their crops (to the fury of their leaders) but when they were present they shot straight and kept their heads low, and the consequence for the British was disaster; in a minor key it is true, but still, unmistakably disaster. Regimental officers and men fought and died with valour, but they did so too often in vain. The essentials of tactical generalship were lacking and the position was not assisted by the total failure of the government at home to give the expedition any direction as to the limits and nature of the campaign they were required to wage.

In contrast, though strategically unsound, the Boer forces in the beginning were everywhere tactically successful. As brave and resolute as their enemies, they were even tougher, and unlike the British completely at home in the veld. They were also expert individual marksmen (the British troops still relied on mechanical volleys) and though their older and senior commanders lacked initiative, the junior Boer field officers such as Christiaan de Wet and de la Rey were magnificent leaders by any standard.

The result was that the British people had to watch with bewilderment as an outnumbered enemy shattered their brave and vaunted military *élite*. In professional circles the shock was almost as devastating, though from the outset a very few quiet voices had questioned Buller's leadership, and Wolseley had long been racked with anxiety. Now, as the measure of the government's and the field commander's failure became daily more apparent, these critics became increasingly more vocal and the problem of finding a successor more acute. It was a problem to which Bobs applied himself with zeal. To suggest that the fire of personal ambition still burned brightly in him would almost certainly be unjust, for he was well beyond the age at which he might have expected to go soldiering again, and his health was indifferent. But like many men of transcendent ability in any walk of life, he knew with an unshakable conviction that he was the best man for the job. In this he is to be distinguished from Wolseley, for though there had been little to choose between them in ability a decade before, Bobs' vital powers of intellect and vigour remained unimpaired by age, whilst Wolseley's were fading rapidly.

When, therefore, Bobs wrote from Headquarters, Irish Command, it was an offer of service almost sacrificial for, already sixty-seven, he was a man who by modern standards had never been physically suited to the army at all. Not only had he been delicate as a child, and tiny throughout his life, but his eyesight was defective and, as an intelligent man, he was fully aware of the chance that he would succumb to the South African climate and unsatisfactory medical services of the campaign. He knew, too, that his motives were almost certain to be misconstrued by jealous fellow soldiers. Yet he never hesitated, for he had foreseen the war years before, and had exhaustively surveyed its probable strategies. Having decided that he could fulfil the role, nothing else mattered.

His letter criticizing Buller's conduct of the campaign and offering to take over command himself did not, at first, commend itself to the Prime Minister (Salisbury) for though Bobs' ability was unquestioned, his age and stamina raised grave and immediate doubts. However, as day succeeded day, and 'Black Week' began (and never seemed to end) the Cabinet's doubts waned. Almost any of the available senior commanders must by now have seemed preferable to Buller, and Bobs was outstandingly the foremost general of his day. The public outcry was already gathering momentum and *periculum in mora*. With Kitchener as his Chief of Staff, Salisbury shrewdly conjectured, Bobs could yet pluck the Government's chestnuts out of the fire.

Events now moved rapidly, for there was no doubt what Kitchener's reply would be, and on the following Sunday morning Bobs personally accepted the command at 10 Downing Street. That afternoon, Lord Lansdowne brought him news of his only son's death in action at Colenso. It was a shattering blow both to Bobs and to Nora for theirs was a family of close and intimate ties; it was only a limited relief to know that the young officer's death, like his life, had been everything that his parents might have wished it to be. There was a magic, it must have seemed, in the Roberts spirit, for the boy—with a small group of others—had ridden out under scything Boer fire to rescue British guns whose crews had been killed. The fact that the episode, as indeed the battle itself, was symptomatic of faulty tactics in the higher command did nothing to lessen the bravery of young Roberts and his comrades, and never were VCs more richly deserved. By his posthumous decoration, Freddie, the gallant son of a famous father, had brought his family into the forefront of distinction, for only two other father-and-son combinations had won a VC apiece, and one of those (the Goughs) belonged to another famous Anglo-Irish military family. The tactical blunders which had brought young Roberts' sacrifice about were a less glorious story. Years later Bobs, visiting the scene, was to apostrophize the engagement as 'sheer murder'.

Young Freddie was dead, but his father lived on and there was work to do. It was a blow which would have broken many men, but Bobs, true to a soldier's sense of duty, held his job. Only when he took leave of the ancient and indomitable Queen did he break down a little as she commiserated with him. 'I cannot speak of that,' he muttered, 'I can of anything else.' The fact was that in his courage as in his determination to see the war through, he personified national character, for Britain was now thoroughly aroused in her amateur but immensely spirited way. Fears that the Empire might be faced with a Continental combination if peace was not made swiftly were scornfully brushed aside and volunteers for the army poured in. In many ways it was a period reminiscent of the Napoleonic Wars, with their haphazard volunteer organizations born of the French invasion threat. Though commissions could no longer be bought and sold, something of the old tradition still lingered on and units of every sort were formed piecemeal, some on private and highly individualistic lines.

It was with a spice of the spirit that was to prevail amongst their grandchildren after Dunkirk that a huge crowd gathered to cheer Bobs, as looking fully his age and dressed in the heavy black of mourning, he climbed into the train that was to take him from Waterloo to the coast. Still later, another crowd watched the *Dunottar Castle* cast off at Southampton, taking Frederick Sleigh Roberts, Baron and victor of Kandahar, to the last and greatest of all his campaigns. It was not the first and it was far from being the final occasion on which the Anglo-Irish were to provide from the crucible of their patriotism a great soldier to serve the British hour. So he sailed, with the wraith of another great Anglo-Irishman, victor of Talavera and Waterloo, nodding approvingly over his shoulder, and the grief of his own immeasurable loss to keep him company. Like Roberts, Wellington had once been a sepoy general. Like him, he had known the vagaries of fortune. The Duke had died in the very year that Roberts first sailed as a young officer for India, and Bobs was himself to die within the adult memory of millions still living today. It was a long and honourable tradition, and the pages of its roll of honour are yet far from closed.

Bobs disembarked at Cape Town on 10 January, 1900 to find all in confusion, for the glamour of their early success was still bemusing the Boers and a stalemate afflicted both sides. Time was on Britain's side if only Bobs could grasp his opportunity, and a jealous Europe neglect hers. There was certainly much to be done for Buller had proved a disastrous commander and British garrisons were besieged in places as widely separated as Mafeking and Ladysmith. There was no doubt either that the Imperial forces had been severely shaken, and not the least of Bobs' accomplishments lay in his ability during the evening of his life to restore the soldiers' confidence in themselves and to organize victory. In this as in much else, he was splendidly served by the ruthless determination and unparalleled drive of Kitchener of Khartoum.

Neither man had any illusions about the magnitude of the

problem facing them. Wrote Kitchener, 'My God! I can scarcely credit their taking the fearful responsibility of sending us into the field practically unarmed with artillery.' But the material deficit was in some ways the easiest to remedy; far more dangerous was the appalling deficiency in fighting skill amongst the commissioned ranks, for at the outset the spirit was incurably amateur. Wrote Major-General Fuller, himself a critic of high professional expertise, 'We then knew next to nothing of the art of war.'[19] As amateurs in spirit, their sense of honour and nicety was correspondingly as sensitive as has been true of other great amateur forces in British history, from Rupert's horsemen to the youngest ensign to flaunt his newly purchased commission in French faces at Barrosa. The same authority also wrote that officers and men 'knew how to die for the other', adding that, 'As wars go, the War in South Africa was probably the most humane ever fought.' But honour, humanity, and courage were not enough. More was needed if the serious business of battle was to be won.

Far worse, if certain talented observers were to be believed, was the state of leadership at the top. As Allenby, a future field-marshal and victor in Palestine, was to write, 'The more I see of our great generals, the more they sicken me. Every man for himself. I am beginning to think I am one of the few commanders out here that do not play to the gallery and tell lies to push themselves.' As one of the very few great captains produced by the British Army between 1901 and 1939, Allenby's opinion is entitled to respect.* There was little assistance to be had, moreover, from the military chiefs in England if Kitchener is to be believed—'We will do our best to pull through but evidently without help from the War Office. Utter disorganization [. . .] Lord Roberts is splendid.'

The truth was that Wolseley, back in London, was finished. For years he had sought army reform with all the fire and pertinacity in his nature, but when he succeeded to the Com-mandership-in-Chief, it was to a rump post with all the main powers withdrawn. By 1895 he was also ageing rapidly, the bright flame of his former genius burning low. 1899, which saw an extension of the process, found also a Cabinet rooted in opposition to even the flimsiest preparations for war, and when

* *Allenby*, Brian Gardner, p. 50.

battle was joined they impeded military expansion until at length Wolseley sent in his papers in disgust. 'As the Cabinet refuses to adopt the measures by which alone, I believe, you could raise the troops I conceive to be essential for national safety, I feel compelled to resign [. . .].' Added to the frigid relationship already known to exist between Bobs and Wolseley, it was not a glowing picture, whilst Kitchener had in his younger days fallen foul of Wolseley more than once.

The first need was to try and restrain Buller, and in this Bobs was undeniably unsuccessful. A gentleman in every sense of the word, the little commander sought to avoid imposing his will other than by way of advice upon the man whom he had, whatever the official explanation, unquestionably superseded. Advice, however, was just what Buller was not prepared to accept and, far from appreciating his senior's forbearance, he now resolved on yet another attempt to relieve Ladysmith. A commander by turns bull-headed and lacking in initiative, Sir Redvers' attack on 5 February was typically mismanaged and unsuccessful. Bobs had counselled against the assault from the beginning, but now with battle joined he saw nothing for it but to continue. In contrast, Buller, who had determined on the operation, suddenly and unaccountably withdrew his troops.

It was an unfortunate beginning, and Bobs was too old a hand to overestimate its gravity, yet he was, with Kitchener, already deep in the task of forging the weapon which should secure victory. It was a partnership of two opposites in character who yet had remarkable points of similarity. Bobs, the Anglo-Irishman, was old in an experience of war stretching back to the Mutiny and bore a name already revered by Victorians since his famous march to Kandahar. Kitchener, an Englishman, had spent much of his early youth in Ireland and was Britain's youngest, most vigorous, and certainly most dramatic general, something of an *enfant terrible* among 'Brass hats'. A giant, of romantic appearance and with hawk's eyes, he had leapt into fame only in the last few years, after active service almost exclusively Egyptian and Sudanese. Neither man had previously seen commissioned service against a European enemy, and both were dedicated Imperialists.

Their contrasts and similarities went still deeper, for Bobs, though determined, was invariably courteous, transparently humane, and a model of domestic felicity; Kitchener, who liked to appear tough and ruthless, was a sometimes indecisive celibate who liked his alcohol in moderation and did not shrink from brutality when he considered it to be in the national interest. It would be possible to enlarge endlessly upon the contrasts between them, and it was perhaps from this very conflict of character that they formed so fine a partnership. Certainly they were united in most of those public virtues that made the Victorians great.

Neither was long deceived as to the flaw in previous tactical concepts. As the Americans were to find half a century later in Korea, an undue reliance on fixed lines of manœuvre, dictated by emphasis on mechanical transport and a reluctance to live rough, is bound to be disastrous, for once the enemy spot your weakness they can invariably forecast your moves, which are thus correspondingly limited. If the obsession of the Americans in 1950 was with passable roads, that of the British in early 1900 lay in hugging the line of rail. Bobs—who had not campaigned in the far frontiers for nothing—determined to revert to free movement. With these aims, he now struck across the veld towards Bloemfontein, and the results were speedily and pleasantly apparent. Granted that the force lacked cavalry and trained staff officers, and that the infantry tactics were clumsy and quite unsuited to fighting the Boers; but these were not shortcomings for which Bobs personally could be blamed since he and Kitchener, called in only after catastrophe, had to improvise with what they found.

Certain it was that by now reverting to the true and timeless elements of war, he had profoundly misled the Boers, and the first fruit of his enterprise was no less than old General Piet Cronje. A great deal has been written of the battle of Paardeburg, where Cronje turned at bay, but there can be no doubt that in cornering him Bobs had scored a notable victory. More debatable was his decision to call off Kitchener's assault on the laager for, strategically, time was vital. If Kitchener's tactical deployment in the assault was clumsy, Roberts' decision to reduce the laager by siege—out of motives of humanity—did much to prolong the war. The surrender, when it did come on the tenth day, was a startling drama of contrasts as Bobs, immaculate in khaki drill and with his jewelled Kandahar sword at his belt, stepped forward to shake hands with the old, burly, slouch-hatted Cronje. Coming from some other officers, the victor's opening gambit, 'I am glad to see you. You have made a gallant defence, Sir,' might have seemed histrionic, but chivalry was as much a part of Bobs' nature as patriotism, and those present must have known that he would say no less.

Bobs' very courtesy was in fact one of his strongest weapons. Kitchener, sweeping men and material into his great mould, aroused respect but also fear and not infrequently hatred. Men likened him to a steam-roller, moving relentlessly forward, an organizer of victory who cared little for personalities. In contrast, Bobs was loved, for in place of Kitchener's bludgeon, he chose the rapier. Where Kitchener of Khartoum crushed, Lord Roberts charmed. Even their tactics exemplified their characters, for Kitchener's rather ponderous frontal assault at Paardeburg was transformed, in the hands of the master in all other operations, into the flank attack, the lightning manœuvre, the lineal dash rather than the sweep. Bobs had also a flair for the dramatic, an unconscious gift for public relations which is given to few soldiers, and which combined with his personality to make him the perfect leader. Men would fight for Kitchener, but they would die for Bobs.

From Paardeburg the march now continued unabated and, as Bloemfontein fell, Britain knew that her fortunes had been restored. Though there were to be minor reverses in plenty, the issue was never again seriously in doubt. Bobs himself would make mistakes, for all humanity is fallible, but they were not irrevocable and the national debt to him remained immense. From Bloemfontein the route lay north, with the khaki legions now avid for victory and 'Marching on Pretoria', in the words of the song. There were 38,000 men, with a hundred guns, in three columns under Bobs himself, with French and Kitchener in support. They must have seemed an invincible army to the 10,000 gallant, ragged Boers who had mustered vainly in defence.

Elsewhere the horizon was also lightening, for as Roberts rode into Kroonstad, Mafeking was on the point of relief hundreds of miles to the north, and only the persistent disruption of lines of communication by dogged guerrillas could now delay the onward-sweeping tide. Indeed, on 22 May, columns of dust showed Boer observation posts in the surrounding hills that Roberts was marching again. By the 31st they had reached Johannesburg, and a silken Union Jack, handworked by Lady Roberts for her husband, was being run up on the Court House. Few who knew either Bobs or Nora would have seen anything unusual in the act, at once symbolic of their patriotism and of their attachment to one another. Even in the Golden City itself there was little delay, and by 5 June they were in Pretoria. One phase of the war was now over, though there was still hard fighting to be done. By any standards it had been a fine achievement, and for a commander of Roberts' age it was outstanding. As Rayne Kruger writes, 'His march from Bloemfontein to Pretoria has a high place among history's great marches.'[20]

These were months of exhilaration for the British, as victory piled on victory. At Ladysmith, in February, Hubert Gough, as dashing a *sabreur* as ever, cantered forward in the teeth of his cautious superiors' orders to be the first to relieve the town. In Glasgow, Tory students chased Lloyd George and thrashed Keir Hardie when they held pacifist meetings. *Punch*, a little down-hearted during December, was now full-blooded in its pictorial denunciation of the Continental powers who had sought to intervene. Above all, on the main and decisive front, Bobs kept the enemy persistently on the move, sparing neither himself, his men nor his animals in the effort. The long lines of khaki-clad soldiers were parade-ground automatons no more. Dust powdered their sprouting beards; mud caked puttees, leggings, and boots; eyes were hollow with fatigue, bright with fever. But there was the scent of victory in the air, and they plunged ever onward, their marching songs ringing away across the veld to a dispirited and outnumbered enemy.

So they had marched into the capital, the pale clouds of dust rising from a myriad of iron-rimmed wheels, but it was not to stay. Christiaan de Wet was too active for comfortable celebrations, and Bobs would not wait. By the 11th he was marching again, his columns down now to only 14,000 travel-stained men, but enough he calculated to do the job. Ahead stood Botha with 6,000 indomitables, the hard core of resistance, led by junior leaders of the calibre of de la Rey.

It was a situation of enormous opportunity. The Boer force lay upon an extended line of hills masking the railway that led to Delagoa Bay, whilst behind the British gaped a long stretch of virtually uncontrolled terrain as far as Bloemfontein. Yet though his line of communication was tenuous, Bobs spotted the prize immediately. His interest did not lie in the acquisition of more ground, but in the destruction of his adversary. For it was the last Boer army that he was facing. If he could destroy it, victory was his, but if they escaped, Botha's men would carry the seeds of a renewed conflagration to the far corners of the Transvaal and Free State—and far more formidable than Botha in a guerrilla role were his two lieutenants, de Wet and de la Rey.

To achieve his object, Bobs resorted to what, with minor variations, had been a recipe for success throughout his career. Hamilton was to attack on the right flank, and French on the left, whilst Pole-Carew would deliver the final and knock-out blow in the centre. It was a skilful plan, carefully drawn, but as Bobs was now to discover the Boer command was infinitely adaptable. Unlike the Afghans who had fallen again and again for the same stratagem, the Boers had not suffered a series of stunning defeats at the master's hands without discovering the basis of his tactical conception, and Botha had this time guessed Bobs' intentions to a nicety.

The result was that as each wing of the British assault swept forward, they were met with a furious resistance from Boer positions sited to protect the very flanks on whose envelopment the British had relied. There was no disaster, no reversion to the bad days of 'Black Week', for once infantry had been brought up, field gunners and line regiments quickly hustled the enemy away. Nevertheless, results fell far short of the complete victory for which Bobs had hoped. Though for two days the hills sparkled with fire, British losses were only 200, due to improved tactics and the skilful control exercised by their commander. Their satisfaction at dislodging Botha's men was, however, tempered by the unpalatable truth that he had got clean away. With enemy commandos fanning out across the veld, Bobs' hope of an early end to the war was doomed.

The remainder of Bobs' war conformed to what was to become a depressingly familiar pattern of frustration, with the Boers staging lightning raids and withdrawals, and the slower but remorseless British following doggedly in pursuit. Though many of the Imperial blows fell on thin air, with a mobile and dexterous enemy evading the sweating column, Boer commandos—ill-equipped and numerically inferior as they were —could get no rest. Soon the British were sweeping through the eastern regions, hunting the elusive de Wet. De la Rey had to raise the siege of Brakfontein, and Botha, fearful now of his men's shaky morale, found his line broken on 26 August by, of all men, Buller, who had quite accidentally assailed the weakest point in his enemy's defence. Victory seemed in the air, and by early September Bobs was advising the home government that the real war was over. This, in the orthodox sense was true, since the days of set-piece battles were past. Nonetheless, a drawn-out war of attrition against obstinate irregulars was a grim affair, requiring resource, energy and courage. Though, to that extent, Bobs was wrong in his estimate, the decision that he should relinquish command was correct, for the campaign which followed was an ordeal to which, with his age and health, he would probably have succumbed. Kitchener, at the peak of his ability and strength, inherited the supreme command, and in December the old man landed in England once more.

In retrospect, Bobs' service in South Africa, splendid as it was, seems oddly out of context, for he was essentially a Frontier captain, to be associated with that legendary horizon of peaks and forlorn hopes that had intermittently burst upon the headlines of Victorian journals from 1840 onwards. In the same way, Kitchener, for all his vaunted 'Method', was equipped neither by experience nor training for the responsibilities of the South African War; his triumphs had been achieved in the more shadowy background of the desert in which 'Chinese Gordon' had died. Both Roberts and Kitchener highlighted the achievements and the difficulties under which the truly professional officers of the British Army laboured. Both were men tried and proved in courage and capacity as junior leaders in a way in which the officers of non-colonial powers could never be proved. But both were equally men who, due to the very nature of Imperial commitment, had rarely had the opportunity to command large bodies of men, even on manœuvre.

Here was a problem that had bedevilled British commanders from 1815 on, and which was to be at the root of many of the disasters of the First World War. As Bobs found, to lead a small and streamlined force of professionals, as he had done from Kabul to Kandahar, was a vastly different matter to controlling huge armies comprised of regular and amateur alike. It was hardly surprising that British generals in 1914 should have found themselves in unfamiliar circumstances, for many of them had never led more than a brigade on manœuvres. In contrast, senior French and German officers were accustomed to elaborate exercises.

That both Bobs and Kitchener should have been able to adapt themselves so swiftly to an unfamiliar terrain and a mode of warfare different to any they had previously known was in itself a magnificent achievement. Accustomed to Asiatic warfare,* they had perforce to build anew an army whose morale was badly sapped by reverses, to remedy its defects in equipment and organization, and to lead it against a brave and knowledgeable European foe. In the field of tactics and orthodox warfare, Bobs was given the greater chance to shine, since by the time Kitchener acceded to supreme command, the time for conventional generalship was past. Even this was fortunate, since Bobs was by far the greater field commander. A general excelling in speedy decision, fluid tactics, and appreciation of terrain he was the man to combat the main Boer forces before defeat had splintered them into small itinerant raiding parties. In his strategic concepts, his avoidance of frontal assault, and his penchant for the unexpected, he had shown once again that he possessed that magic appreciative power which distinguishes the great commander.

Bobs was on less sure ground concerning the system of command adopted by Kitchener and himself, for he tended to use Kitchener far more as a Second-in-Command and less as the Chief of Staff he was supposed to be. Even here, however, Bobs had his reasons, for both he and Kitchener had come upon an army disrupted by defeat, disorganized by reverse, and in generally low morale. Far worse, through political manœuvre at home, for which the soldiers could not be held responsible, the General Staff system, so widely used on the Continent, had been denied to the British Army. The result was that, lacking any firm and efficient framework on which to build, Bobs and Kitchener had

* The inspiration of the Khalifa in the Sudan was Islamic and Asiatic rather than African.

been obliged to improvise, relying more upon the opportunity of the moment than upon orthodox routines which presupposed the existence of a trained staff.

Fortunately they were both masters of improvisation after their long years of experience at the perimeter, but whilst Bobs preferred a definite system and improvised only where necessary, Kitchener was fundamentally an enemy of organization inasmuch as he disliked delegating and preferred all matters of moment to come to him. It was no mere chance that he should have been nicknamed 'Kitchener of Chaos', yet the more one investigates the less one can resist the conclusion that it was a nickname bestowed more out of envy than fact. The changes of structure imposed by Bobs and Kitchener in partnership and often carried through by Kitchener alone, were necessary changes, and the results vindicated them.

Back in England, a great resurgence of national feeling was still taking place. For a brief moment men had felt the chill of disaster, as news of first one then another defeat had made headlines. Now, however, all this seemed of the past as newsboys in Piccadilly and the Strand shouted daily of fresh triumphs. The 'Khaki Election' had returned the Tories, their majority unimpaired. Lloyd George was still decisively rejected and there was a general feeling that, after a brief and fearful nightmare, all was well again. There was a good deal of justification for such a view, on the surface at least, for even the Kaiser became suddenly cautious in the face of British victories. But as we now know, appearances were deceptive, for nothing would ever be the same again. The high-tide of Imperialism had passed, and henceforth the national path would lead ever further from the green meadows of Victorian prosperity. The British of 1900, however, knew only that Britain was once more triumphant and that the man more than any other individual responsible for this change in fortune was Lord Roberts of Kandahar.

The magnificence of the reception which met Bobs on his return to England was on a scale rarely enjoyed in Britain by a military commander. With an earldom and the Garter conferred on him by the ancient Queen at Osborne, he was met at Paddington Station by Edward, Prince of Wales, whilst outside the streets were lined with cheering crowds and a divisional strength of troops. It was a homecoming of which emperors might dream, yet it could not change the character of the old soldier who had climbed the gang-plank of the *Dunottar Castle* only a year before, for there was a fundamental simplicity about him which nothing and no one could alter. Even his more studied gestures, such as announcing the annexation of the Orange Free State on the Queen's birthday, were always inseparably connected with the three great objects of his loyalty—the Crown, the Nation and the Army. If he lacked the majestic physical stature of Kitchener, there yet seemed something infinitely more British in his kindliness, modesty and courage, and his countrymen took him instantly to their hearts. If they venerated Kitchener, they loved Bobs, and he was saluted significantly as 'The kindest of the kind' as well as 'The bravest of the brave'.

Kitchener, for all his ardent patriotism and lonely grandeur, was a detached, almost Wagnerian symbol, a giant of sweeping moustaches and commanding presence who lacked the common touch. Though the masses worshipped him in his lonely solitude, and a small band of chosen friends followed his star faithfully to the end, it must be admitted that the impact of Kitchener's personality on chance acquaintances was sometimes profoundly repellent. Thus Kipling's reaction after a chance meeting at Cairo in 1913—'A fatted Pharaoh in spurs'. Such a description of Bobs, even by the most virulent anti-militarist, would have been impossible for he was the epitome of modest sincerity. Sir Winston Churchill wrote of him during the Boer War, 'The face remains motionless but the eyes convey the strongest emotion.' No one could doubt the quality of that emotion or the magnetic quality of his character.

In many ways, it is by his record in South Africa that Bobs' true mettle must be judged. An elderly man, he had emerged from relative obscurity, wholly to reverse the disasters of Buller's brief command. His achievements indeed become greater when one compares the wholly different character of the South African War with his earlier Burmese and Afghan expeditions. While some commentators, incorrectly, have tended to underestimate the difficulties of campaigns on the North-West Frontier, it is certainly true that in South Africa he had to deal with a vaster sphere of operations, incomparably greater forces and, above all, an infinitely more wily and courageous foe. It is on these principles that he must be judged, and on them he emerges with startling credit.

It would be incorrect to regard all Bobs' decisions during this war as uniformly successful. At Paardeburg, for example, a desire to spare his soldiers' lives gave Boer groups elsewhere the breathing space they so desperately needed. At other times he preferred to drive the enemy before him rather than to use annihilation as a means of victory. To a military purist, trained in the precepts of von Clausewitz, this is indisputably wrong and yet, in such measures, Bobs was undoubtedly acceding to the quasi-fraternal nature of the South African War. Though in the end 'Dutch' national resistance and illicit support for the guerrillas forced him to sterner measures, it is hard to blame him—morally, politically or militarily—for trying the gentler means first.

Above all, it was not weakness that made him chivalrous and human, but an outlook at once honourable and realistic. Twenty years before, the political Left in Britain had stridently denounced his vigorous and equally realistic measures against the Afghan assassins who had murdered Cavagnari. What critics of Bobs' gentlemanly policy in South Africa often fail to appreciate is that the campaign, though garbed in the grim trappings of war, was essentially a vast police action against an allied though rebellious race, rather than a European war of survival in which the sterner principles of von Clausewitz would seem more apt. Where he differed from his fellow officers was in the perception, genius and personality that enabled him to escape the persecution to which they were increasingly subjected by propagandists and political personalities in the years after his death.

In short, though both Bobs and Kitchener made mistakes during the Boer War, they were tactical mistakes which could often be defended on other grounds, since there is rarely the one perfect solution in battle. Bobs has been criticized for being too gentle, yet Kitchener was attacked—with equal disregard of realities—for being too severe. They had both come late in the day to put right what Kitchener had described as 'a big business badly begun', and events justified the famous partnership to the full. Roberts' flair for manoeuvre and his many other qualities had restored the faith of Britain, and of the army in itself. Bobs was to perform one last service to the British cause in the Boer War soon after his return to England, and that was to put the principal blame squarely where it belonged. As the Royal Commission on the war stated bluntly, 'No plan of campaign ever existed for operations in South Africa.' Roberts was even more explicit: 'When Sir George White arrived in Natal, he had no instructions in regard to the wishes of the Government—nor was he aware of any general plan of operations in South Africa.' A great deal of more detailed information followed with Bobs submitting to heavy cross-examination over a number of days on all aspects of the army's efficiency. He was by then already nominal head of the British Army, as Commander-in-Chief based on London, and his already existent appreciation of the need for reform was sharpened by a visit to German military manœuvres as the Kaiser's guest. Though the British Army had the edge on its imperial adversary in most respects save size, there could be no room for false complacency, as Bobs was well aware.

CHAPTER XIII

War Lord

WHEN Bobs landed in England once more, the laurels of his last and greatest victory fresh upon him, it must have been obvious that there was no longer any question of his being again placed on half-pay. Yet until the very moment of his appointment as Commander-in-Chief, there was doubt as to how he should be employed. In experience and ability there was no serving officer, not even Kitchener, to measure against him, but the influence of the court remained as strong as ever, and the old Queen was determined to secure the highest military office in the land for her son, the Duke of Connaught. Serious soldiers, with memories of the damage done by the last royal incumbent still fresh in their minds, might look askance at the prospect but there was no doubt that the Queen and the Prince of Wales (for once of the same mind) were a formidable alliance to defeat. In the end it was Salisbury who won the day, for the Prime Minister was immovable in his opinion that by right, title and ability the vacancy could be filled by only one man, and that was Bobs.

It was a decade when military reform was more than ever vital, if Britain was to survive the challenge of a new and fearsome age. Since 1880 the army had, under Wolseley's tutelage, been emerging from the shadows of a long neglect, but the pace had been too slow as first Cambridge and then political intrigue had thwarted the *avant-garde*. Bobs, more favourably placed in India, had watched the struggle from afar, but though the subcontinental situation was entrancing, he was well aware that the seat of military power lay in Britain. The soldiers of the Raj were a fine sight in their blue and green uniforms, but when it came down to the serious business of battle few thinking officers, even of the Indian Service, doubted that in the last resort it was upon the solid uncomplaining privates of the British line regiments that the Empire would stand or fall.

Now, with the Supreme Command of all British Land Forces confirmed in his hand, Bobs had good reason to expect that he would be able to set to rights half a century of neglect. It was an opinion also shared by the public. Unfortunately, as the last years of Wolseley's service showed, nothing was farther from the truth than the belief that the Commander-in-Chief was in control. His powers had, since Cambridge's retirement, been grievously shorn and in a most unsatisfactory fashion. In theory this had been to facilitate the introduction of a General Staff, but practice had worked out differently under a spicing of political intrigue introduced by such experts as Campbell-Bannerman.* Now, six years and a major war after that unsatisfactory compromise, matters were at last changing though still in a typically haphazard fashion.

In consequence, military organization continued to suffer, as the Government groped its way reluctantly towards the General Staff system, with its vital corollary of abolishing the Commandership-in-Chief, for the present structure was as yet neither the one nor the other. There was no military justification for the delay, since all the service antagonists of the scheme, once so powerful, were either dead or in their dotage. Wolseley had for years pressed the advisability of a General Staff upon successions of disinterested British politicians, and Bobs himself was well disposed towards the change. It was a problem that had been searchingly considered as early as 1890 in one of the most profound books to be published since Clausewitz's *Vom Krieg*— Spencer Wilkinson's *The Brain of an Army*. Had logic had its way, there would have been a clean sweep in 1895, but political interests, fearing the influence of a powerful and efficient army control, had insisted instead on the retention of an emasculated figurehead in the person of the Commander-in-Chief.

Such a position was incapable of inspiring any soldier of worth, least of all a man of Bobs' temperament, though he characteristically made the best of it. It was almost entirely

* Campbell-Bannerman refused to implement the Hartington Report's recommendation of the General Staff system, claiming it would make the enemy too powerful.

through his efforts that, pending a change to the General Staff
system, an interim reorganization was effected which made the
existing and cumbersome routine at least workable. That in
itself was a minor victory, won in spite of the then Secretary of
State for War. Brodrick* was one of those luckless and un-
attractive figures who flit through the pages of British political
history to the country's undoubted detriment. As Curzon was
soon to find, Brodrick could prove perilous even to those whom
he had once been pleased to call friends whilst, to less exalted
figures (such as Francis Younghusband) who had the misfortune
to cross his path, he could display a vindictive spleen at once
graceless in form and unjust in detail.

Brodrick now intruded into the purely military sphere of
discipline, contradicting Bobs and opining from the wealth of
his (parliamentary) experience that the old soldier was unduly
lenient. Bobs in his turn reacted vigorously, challenging him in
addition for consulting secretly and behind his back with Milner
and Kitchener on a matter within the Commander-in-Chief's
competence. In all this Bobs was right, and Brodrick hopelessly
wrong, yet in the main the Secretary of State undoubtedly had
his way. Brodrick appears to have been an arrogant spirit, of
unbounded self-confidence, who availed himself of every opportunity to use his political powers in spheres normally reserved
for those expert in them. The contest was inevitably unequal,
since the very terms of Bobs' appointment put him at a disadvantage. He was also never at his best when defending
himself against personal slights. The man to have duelled with
Brodrick was undoubtedly Kitchener but even he, in his turn,
was destined to be destroyed by Lloyd George.

It would be quite erroneous to represent Bobs as perpetually
occupied in feuding with his political overlord during this period,
even though their relations became distinctly cold, for much of
his time was taken up with technical and training innovations.
He had always been a confirmed exponent of the need for
individual marksmanship to replace the old massed volleys of
Waterloo, and his views had been strengthened and confirmed
by what he had seen in South Africa. A great military innovator,
he used his time in the War Office to good effect, standardizing

* William St John Fremantle Brodrick, ninth Viscount Midleton and first Earl
of Midleton.

and improving small arms, artillery, uniform, and a number of undramatic but essential items.

Like Cromwell and Moore, Bobs stood in the great tradition of military training, and both among the cadets at Sandhurst and throughout the Army, the syllabus of education and instruction was improved. He had always sought, by means of competition and colour, to inject something of his own vital enthusiasm into the troops under his command (as his revolutionary musketry programmes in India had shown) and in this he was far ahead of his day, for the hoarse voice of the sergeant-major, repeating the manuals in metallic tones, was still the yardstick of tuition. The essence of his approach remained, as ever, humane, with understanding of and compassion for the soldier the focal point of all his efforts. It was this which had angered Brodrick, a man who preferred Kitchener's tough and arbitrary methods in an age which still believed in treating its troops harshly.

Intelligence services and mobilization were two subjects which also engaged Roberts' attention, as in the past they had engaged Wolseley's. Until recently the despised Cinderella of the Army, Intelligence had been remoulded and improved by Brackenbury, but it remained a relatively untouched field, crying out for further reform which Bobs was quick to essay. Dull and unspectacular as all this appeared, it was the stuff nevertheless from which victories were to be forged in after-years. Though the contemporary press delighted to call his administration inefficient, the editor of the *Spectator* had to admit that the Commander-in-Chief had wrought profound reforms in the spheres of organization, training and equipment.

One of the fields that offered the greatest scope for improvement was tactical doctrine and training, and Bobs, with his wide battle experience, did not hesitate to make his opinions known. Amongst the infantry there was little disposition to argue, for heavy casualties amongst massed assault formations in South Africa had, for the time being at least, swept away any British support for the views now being expounded in extreme form by Ferdinand Foch and Grandmaison.* Matters were, however, very different with the cavalry, for they had always

* The French exponents of *'offensive à outrance'*—the doctrine of the irresistible offensive.

considered themselves several cuts above their opposite numbers of the line, and virtually immune from criticism. In recent years, moreover, the *Arme Blanche* had developed a singular mystique at variance with all tenets of warfare and common sense. The 'Cavalry Spirit' (they claimed) in effect was sufficient to tide them over any emergency, and the lance and sabre were held out as fit weapons with which to ride into modern battle. It was even hinted that machine-guns were not proof against charging cavalry.

Today, with nearly three-quarters of a century of bloodstained history to intervene, it seems incredible that mature and experienced officers should have been led into such fallacies, yet the facts are indisputable. Against them were ranged a smaller but more incisive school of coldly analytical soldiers, of whom Bobs and Kitchener were only the greatest. The struggle had long been waged behind closed doors in army circles, but with the publication of Erskine Childers' *War and the Arme Blanche*, the feud came out into the open and took on a new intensity, with professionals and amateurs alike separating into opposing groups. Though there were those, such as Allenby, who frankly faced reality and accepted horsed warfare as outdated, the majority of support for the continued use of the *Arme Blanche* undoubtedly came from its own commissioned ranks.

Nothing could be more natural than for the officers of a particular arm to claim special virtues for it—there would have been something wrong with men such as Gough and Haig had they not done so—but it was unfortunate that by 1914 cavalry officers should still have been in a position of supremacy in British military circles. Not only had they—in common with cavalry officers in other European armies—clung to their own arm long after it was seen by other discerning observers to be outmoded, but when the First World War broke out, the cavalry generals moved in at the gallop to take a quite disproportionate share of command over higher infantry formations. So great was the favour shown to regular cavalry officers in matters of promotion that even the Foot Guards became restive.

Such attitudes were anathema to the cool and scientific military philosophy of Bobs. He had in his time shared the excitement and delight of horsed action to the full, but he realized that, for better or for worse, the charger's place on the battlefield was over. At best its use was now limited to transporting infantry from one point to another over terrain unsuited to motor vehicles, but that was to turn the cavalry themselves into mounted infantry, and though British tactical training laid stress on such requirements, they were not always popular. To the high priests of the *Arme Blanche* mystique, sabre and lance remained the ultimate weapons and 'Mounted Infantry' was an ugly and a dirty phrase.

Nonetheless, it is a matter of record generally speaking that, of all the horsed troops who took the field between 1914 and 1918, the British Cavalry were outstandingly the best prepared in equipment, uniform, weapon training and tactics. No human agency could turn the horse into a fighting vehicle, but within its inescapable limits, the British leaders had done their best. Their tragedy lay in a refusal to accept the fact of obsolescence and in a misguided loyalty to a romantic past. Only one decade was to pass before a more suitable steed was found, but even that was to be wasted at the outset in penny packets. By the time that armoured warfare had evolved into its present form, treasury parsimony had done its worst, and the tanks that thundered across the Low Countries in 1940 bore the Iron Cross.

In the campaign to cut the cavalry extravaganza down to size, Bobs played a leading and invaluable role. It was not before time, for already the sands were running out.

Other and pressing engagements meanwhile remained to be fought and won, if Britain was not to enter European Continental warfare with both hands tied behind her back. One of the most important of these remained reform of the War Office system in face of Cabinet hostility or, at least, inertia. In this at least, Bobs could claim an ally of immense prestige, for the Royal Commission on the war in South Africa had already probed straight to the heart of the matter. As Lord Esher commented temperately to the King, 'It would appear strange that, upon a question of purely military organization, within the Army, involving no expense, the most experienced and eminent soldier of Your Majesty's Empire should have to yield to civilian authority.'

In all these disputes, Bobs' position, like that of Wolseley before him, was most unenviable for whilst the public believed him to be the fountain-head of military power, and the press treated him as the officer responsible on all occasions, the truth was quite otherwise, and the Commander-in-Chief was subject to political interference and control even in quite mundane administrative details. The fact that such control was hidden had also undoubted advantages for the Cabinet, since any deficiency could be conveniently ascribed to the Commander-in-Chief, whilst power continued to reside in the Minister.

It was in fact the very War Office system which Bobs so wished to alter that the Radical press selected as a ground for criticizing him. Bobs was also accused of favouritism, an allegation not merely unfounded but which his critics only made when under the cover of Parliamentary privilege. It was a return to an old charge, though when such charges had been levelled against him in India, the suggestion was that he had been too inclined towards those whose operational experience had been under him. Now, on a national scale in England, the criticism went further, but it was unfounded, for there was nothing in any phase of his career to suggest that Bobs would have appointed officers on any criterion except his belief in their fitness for the job. Everything—his character, record, and transcendent sense of patriotic duty—point indeed in entirely the opposite direction, as his earliest critic in India, Rudyard Kipling, would have been the first to accept.

Slowly and hesitantly, the staff changes of which Bobs had been a persistent advocate were now coming into being, and though they included innovations of which he was somewhat doubtful, he accepted the general scheme without hesitation. Though the proposals involved abolition of the post of Commander-in-Chief, Lord Esher was still able to proclaim him as the only officer of the old school who accepted the new system with the enthusiasm shown by the younger cadres. All this was quite consistent with Bobs' outlook since, basically, the changes were only a variation of the structure he had sought for years. No officer of intelligence or perception could in the middle period of the Edwardian reign have questioned a system as completely vindicated as the General Staff organization had proved to be on the Continent.

From the start of his term of office, it had been understood that Bobs would be the last Commander-in-Chief of the British Army, and it was also clear that at his age he no longer had the right to expect nomination as the first Chief of the Imperial General Staff. The business of preparing for a European war, by now recognized as almost inevitable, required younger hands at the helm. They were hands unlikely to prove as skilful, for none of the younger generals, French or British (with the possible exceptions of Allenby and Franchet d'Esperey) were destined to show anything approaching Bobs' skill and imagination in the ensuing years. It was essential, however, that the new CIGS should be capable of retaining control over the next fateful decade, a consideration manifestly excluding Bobs.

The question of his retirement therefore became one of timing, and in this he was not free from blame, for he tended to temporize over the final stages of the change-over. Like most men who have achieved the heights in a profession they love, he was reluctant to retire and even flirted a little, at Balfour's instigation, with filling the proposed new post of Inspector-General. However, there could never have been any doubt in the minds of those who knew him that, when the time came, he would retire on request, with the minimum of fuss. To have clung to office, once the Government had set a date for constitution of the General Staff, would have been wholly in conflict with his character and tenets.

In the circumstances it was a national scandal when Britain's premier soldier, arriving at his office one morning, found that his staff had without prior notice been evicted, bag and baggage, to make way for the personnel of the new General Staff. It has never been clearly established whether this *coup de grâce* derived from a genuine muddle or whether, as seems the more probable, it was a pointed and disgraceful snub. Whatever its origin, this action made it very clear that in the eyes of the Government Bobs was dispensable. Younger generals, ambitious and energetic, were waiting in the wings for their turn, and the task of modernizing the whole Army before 1914 was enough to tax the endurance of any man to his limits. With the portents plain to read, Bobs hesitated no longer as to the course he should take, and resigned. With his retirement as the last Commander-in-Chief that the British Army was ever to know, Bobs passed finally from the theatre of active soldiering.

CHAPTER XIV

Nocturne

THE Edwardian age was an era of health and promise, of
captivating fashions and gracious women. The drab coat and
Dundreary whiskers of Victorian industry were yielding to the
straw boater, blazer and flannels of a youth still privileged
beyond those of any other nation. Young Britons moved abroad,
secure in the knowledge that they belonged to the greatest
power on earth. Yet, in many ways, it was in retrospect a tragic
age for the generation that came to maturity in the years
between 1905 and 1914 was destined to die horribly upon the
battlefields of the Western Front. Such knowledge, however,
was mercifully hidden from its victims, for in 1905 they were
young and the world seemed at their feet.

In Imperial affairs there seemed equal promise, for if the
fiercely acquisitive instincts of the Victorians had given way to a
sentiment a shade more paternalist and liberal, it was still
fashionable to speak in terms of an Empire on which the sun
never set. These were opinions, moreover, with which the vast
bulk of the colonial peoples had no argument. A doctor, visiting
what then were called the Straits Settlements was surprised and
not a little flattered to find the Straits Chinese speaking of
themselves as British.* The disasters of the South African War
had shaken the image, but they were only minor tremors;
victory had come without real catastrophe, and the national
wealth was great enough to sustain the expense without
austerity. Ambitious soldiers also discerned that the results had
given the army a chance to put its own house in order. As
Kipling wrote,

* *The Surgeon's Log*, J. J. Abraham.

We have had an Imperial lesson. It may make us an
Empire yet.[21]

Unfortunately, complacency and self-satisfaction bred lethargy
at the top and among the professional classes. Technical prowess
in the senior ranks of the Army was as lacking as imagination.
Men such as Haig were honest, worthy, industrious—but
military genius seemed to have missed a generation after Bobs
and Wolseley. Bobs was not alone in noticing such trends, for
Kipling, who allied a reporter's powers of observation to a
poet's intuition was, within a year of the South African War's
end, writing bitterly of a Britain,

[. . .] Saved by a remnant (and your land's long-suffering
    star),
When your strong men cheered in their millions while your
    striplings went to the war.

Still more savagely he wrote of how,

Ye pushed them raw to the battle as ye picked them raw
    from the street.
And what did ye look they should compass? Warcraft
    learned in a breath [. . .]?[22]

Britain's state of mind was a challenge to men of Bobs'
temperament and discernment. He had lived hard all his days
and now, in his old age, he saw the dangers mounting about a
country still great, rich as never before, but sunk in com-
mercialism and comfort, lacking the will to improve. Across the
Channel, Frenchmen could assess the peril clearly enough, but
of the whole British Army only one officer could spare time to
study the problems of Franco-British co-operation—and that
was in the teeth of his countrymen's disdain. Henry Wilson was
neither the greatest nor the finest of British soldiers, and the
defects in his military capacity were equalled by his unreliability
of character, but there could be no doubting the service he gave
his country in laying the foundations of military liaison with the
French. Wilson knew only too well the nature of the menace
rising in the east. The difficulty was to convince the politicians
of the fact, for at the very time when the officers of the Kaiser's
Imperial Army were drinking in their messes to *'Der Tag'*, men

such as Lloyd George were denouncing all who sought to rearm Britain.

These were pressing perils which acted as a spur to Bobs, for though well over seventy, his mercurial spirit could not bear to rest in face of the dangers crowding in upon his country. Though the first few months of his retirement were spent in hunting and in a visit to South Africa, by June 1905 he had become involved in the opening rounds of what was to prove one of the bravest, though not the most successful of his campaigns.

The battle for conscription, which had been threatening for some time, opened in earnest with his call for the formation of rifle clubs on a national scale. By July, he had returned to the charge with an attack on the state of Britain's military preparations. Speech followed speech as Bobs expanded the theme of national service as the only means of meeting the threat from the military juggernaut on the Continent, and his ultimate resignation from the Imperial Defence Committee became in consequence only a matter of time. The bridge was crossed on 9 November, when, failing to carry his colleagues with him for a variety of reasons largely unconnected with the national interest, he withdrew in exasperation and, a few days later, accepted the presidency of the National Service League.

For the next few years the old soldier, cast in the unfamiliar role of agitator (though in a familiar cause), spoke endlessly throughout the country of the need to prepare, and in retrospect it is impossible to doubt that he was correct. For the army he had served so well was quite inadequate, numerically and in terms of equipment, to meet the challenge. Nor was his tactical prescience his least remarkable feature for at a time when cavalry soldiers were still fiercely advancing the claims of their service and 'Spirit' as decisive, Bobs was to sharply dispose of them in a penetrating foreword to Erskine Childers' classic. One of the main opponents of his efforts to place army planning on a sound footing was a man destined, during the First World War, to regard himself as strategically beyond reproach. Yet one of Lloyd George's biographers admits that he 'As Chancellor of the Exchequer, had always expressed his dislike of heavy expenditure in armaments'. Indeed, he pointed out that 'our relations with Germany were, in spite of rumours, increasingly friendly'.[23] A more sublime disregard for realities it would be hard to imagine, especially from a man who during the Great War constituted himself the chief critic of the general officers of an army which, until the outbreak of war, he had done his best to starve of the equipment essential to victory. It was hardly surprising therefore that, during that war, as the same author remarks, 'There was unfortunately among the military chiefs a resentment at interference in strategy by men whom they considered incapable of grasping the military situation.' In Lloyd George, who regarded himself as a master of every subject, such attitudes aroused immediate hostility.

Though the First World War still lay over the horizon, the trend was already manifest during the early years of Roberts' retirement, and every fibre of his being revolted at the thought of silence in face of such a peril. Dangers once manifest from France and Russia were now wholly overshadowed by the German challenge, and Roberts' references to the Hohenzollern threat became so marked that the King himself, at Cabinet request, sought unavailingly to stifle his words. Others too, far removed from the councils of orthodoxy, took their chance to attack him, for he had long been a favourite target of the Left Wing press. A prominent Liberal politician suggested that his army pension should be terminated because of his campaign, but *John Bull* outdid them all when it described him (20 February, 1909) as 'a dangerous dolt'.

The campaign was fierce and fluid and, though Bobs and his supporters spoke with dignity, the blows were far from being one-sided. In the main retired officers supported him, whilst those still serving tacitly approved. There were abstentions, of course, such as French (who had always disliked 'The Chief' since South African days) and Ian Hamilton who quite unaccountably burst into print against conscription after a period as one of its more prominent military supporters. Though no one today can doubt that a period of conscription between 1910 and 1914 would have been of the greatest value when war broke out, the Government had set its face against the project, and Roberts' efforts were doomed to failure. A hundred years free of national emergency had taken the edge off the British sense of international reality, and it required more than the efforts of the National Service League to rouse a purblind Parliament to the need for prompt action. The time was soon to come when they would recognize the wisdom of Roberts' words, but by then he would be dead.

There was one more battle for Roberts to fight on behalf of his country, this time in the position virtually of a rebel. Of this struggle, Brigadier-General Gough was the hero, but Roberts holds a high and honourable place in the wider canvas of resistance to the British Government's attempt to coerce Northern Ireland into union with the South. The need to reach a settlement with Ulster cannot be doubted, and Roberts was amongst those agreeable to a fair Federal solution, but the attempt by Westminster to force Ulster against her will into what amounted to subjugation by the South was a grievous betrayal. To the British, and in particular the Ulster and Anglo-Irish patriots in the age before August 1914, such tactics came as an appalling revelation of dishonour in high places. The fact was that for years Britain had relied upon the unshakeable loyalty of the Ulstermen in the North, and of both the Anglo-Irish and of a section of Imperialist Catholics in the South, but now it seemed as if their affections had become inconvenient. Gladstone had already spent a couple of decades trying to whittle away the foundations of Imperial rule, and in the process he had been quite prepared to sacrifice the lives and prosperity of those who had served Britain well, Catholic and Protestant alike.

In 1914 there were salient reasons why the Liberals should have sought a settlement over the Irish question. In the first place, it seemed the only way in which their Parliamentary majority could be maintained, and supremacy in Westminster in 1914 loomed larger on their horizon than the continued possession of a contiguous island that was strategically vital to the Kingdom. It was left to the British sailors in the Battle of the Atlantic from 1940 on to pay the price of their efforts. There was another immediate reason; and this lay in the person of the politician who currently headed the Irish Nationalist movement. John Redmond, leader of the Southern Catholics, ranked as a moderate and, individually, he was a wise and reasonable man. He was also, however, the principal of a party deeply rooted in terrorism, a party moreover which, though it paid lip service to democracy, was unwilling to allow the Protestant North the right to decide its own destiny. Though Redmond had no chance of vanquishing an industrialized and militant Ulster, he and his followers pinned their faith upon British military intervention. English bayonets would, they reckoned, be able to crush all Northern opposition, and to hand them over what remained.

In all these calculations, three vital factors had been omitted. First was the temper of the British people who, as a whole, were unwilling to coerce Ulster, and they made their sentiments unmistakably plain. The second factor was undoubtedly the temper and quality of the Protestant Irish as led, politically, by men such as Lord Carson and supported by a wide variety of eminent patriots of whom Bobs, Rudyard Kipling and Professor Dicey were the most famous. The most important element of all was probably the homogeneous nature of the officer corps of the British Army, for an extraordinarily high proportion of them was drawn from the ranks of the Protestant Irish gentry—the descendants of the officers of Cromwell's New Model Army.

It was against this background therefore of a Liberal administration in Westminster relying on nationalist support for its majority, a terrorist movement in Southern Ireland, and the outright hostility of Anglo-Irish, Ulstermen, and English Tories, that the crisis developed. By early 1914, the political cards were squarely on the table. In all this Bobs was deeply implicated, for as Ulster volunteers drilled, and huge numbers of rifles were secretly imported, he was in the inner councils of those who planned to resist the excesses of the British Government and of the Southern nationalists with military force.

The Liberals in the meantime, though they found it convenient to stand upon legality, were infinitely unscrupulous in the tactics they employed, and the history of their campaign of subterfuge and evasion as employed against Carson and his men makes sorry reading. They were also determined to disregard the racial, religious and political differences that separated the North from the South of Ireland, and to use the army to coerce Ulster. Here they erred profoundly, since in the British and Indian Armies of the day, as stated, an immense proportion of the officer corps came of Anglo-Irish and Ulster stock, and of these Bobs was doyen.

Secret Liberal intrigue now burgeoned swiftly into public scandal as the 'Curragh Incident' (for it was never a 'mutiny') hit the headlines first of the *Morning Post*, and thus an astonished world. It was a situation which had long been developing behind the scenes, for even Henry Wilson, an adept at protecting his own interests, when pressed to the point by French, had been unable to forswear his ancestry, admitting that he would feel unable to open fire 'at the behest of Redmond'. Lord Stamfordham, the King's Private Secretary, was probably very accurate when he estimated that two-fifths of the officers and men would leave the army if ordered to march against Ulster.

The first round of the conflict that brought astonished army officers straight into the political arena came when the Secretary of State, Seeley, told assembled generals that they need not obey orders which were not 'reasonable in the circumstances', adding the qualification that 'they must not pick and choose'. Then, since nobody seemed to know what he meant, he followed it up hastily with the comment that all the soldiers would be required to do in Ulster would be to support the civil power in protecting life and property, should the police prove unable to cope. By now, all the assembled Brass Hats were confused, but this was hardly surprising, for, as one jester remarked, if Seeley had had a few more brains he would have been half-witted. Nonetheless, Seeley's final remarks had been reassuring, and the assembly dispersed in a slightly easier frame of mind.

Upon a stage already tense with emotion, Winston Churchill in one of the less happy phases of his career, chose to electrify everyone on behalf of the Government with the blunt announcement that they 'would fight it out'. 'Priscilla' Morley,* who loathed the military, increased the tension by declaring that the Army would be used against Ulster. Even so, the point of no return had, for the soldiers at least, not yet been reached, since a clash between civil and military authorities had still not occurred. Bobs and the retired general he had nominated to command the Ulster volunteers were active enough, but they and the officers of that body had no longer any practical connection with the British Regular Army. Individual officers in many regiments were searching their consciences and deciding their attitudes, but nothing in the shape of a co-ordinated stand had been canvassed, much less agreed, among the commissioned ranks of the professional force.

* Lord Morley, a veteran and recently ennobled Liberal politician, renowned for his anti-military attitudes.

239

Matters moved swiftly to a head when on 19 March, 1914, orders went out for the issue of ball ammunition to the troops at the Curragh. A new figure, till then hidden in the wings, now intervened with devastating effect. A man of the old 'Court Circle', General Paget had little claim to military immortality, but he did have the misfortune to occupy a position from which he could fan the flames of crisis with remarkable effect—and few men have done so with less intention or more efficiency. Conceited, pompous, and devoid of the imagination needed to see the disasters which his behaviour could create, Paget, as Commander-in-Chief, Ireland, arrived back from London and treated his senior officers to an insufferable lecture. Using the King's name freely and without permission, he declared that operations against Ulster were imminent and that he expected the whole 'place to be in a blaze by next day'. Officers of Ulster domicile could, he stated, contract out but this concession did not extend to Anglo-Irishmen of the South who, in common with all other officers, must bind themselves, in advance and on pain of dismissal, to obey orders as yet undisclosed. Looking pointedly at Hubert Gough (who had as yet kept silent) General Paget declared in tones of gratuitous insult before the assembled officers that Gough need expect no mercy from Sir John French.

The challenge was plain, and the answer immediate. The officers had been offered the choice of obedience or dismissal, and by evening the result was clear. Hubert Gough and fifty-seven out of seventy of the officers of his 3rd Cavalry Brigade preferred dismissal.

The effect was immediate, as Britain digested the shock, for the rot had spread far beyond the cavalry. Many infantry units were themselves affected, and there seemed no reason to doubt that, if it came to the point, a sizeable proportion of the non-commissioned ranks would follow their officers' lead. With Carson heading the Ulster Political Front, British Tories supporting them, and the man in the street aghast at the spectre of civil war so suddenly apparent, the Government's chances of coercing Ulster into acceptance of Southern Catholic domination shrank fast.

Meanwhile Liberal dialectic filled the air, more fevered (if less pugnacious) now that their chances had shrunk. Though the Constitution was inevitably advanced by those who sought justification to dismember the Kingdom, Roberts' reply was pithy and to the point. The officers, he remarked, were well aware that 'No matter under what legal guise the order may be given to them, they may be asked to shoot down fellow-countrymen who, like themselves, would be fighting under the Union Jack [. . .] and please remember, as our soldiers will remember, that all this will seem to them to be done at the bidding of men who have never missed an opportunity of slandering and vilifying the Army in the grossest manner.' As usual, Bobs' summing up of the situation had been accurate. The Liberals had not been merely anti-militarist but, as a party, anti-military for years, and there were many soldiers to echo the old field-marshal's sentiments. Much later, Sir William Robertson* was to write much the same in his memoirs. Meanwhile, the Government was in full retreat after unsuccessfully trying to bully Hubert Gough into submission, for, with the nation by now thoroughly roused, there was little chance of being able to effect a sudden *coup-de-main*. Haldane recognized as much when he rose to tell the House of Lords that, 'No order will be issued for the coercion of Ulster'; the fact that he was later caught red-handed in the alteration of Hansard's account to read 'for the *immediate* coercion of Ulster'† served only to emphasize the Liberals' deviousness. With that denouement, it could be said that the Government's part in the Ulster crisis was over.

There were many men to share the credit for victory, from household names like Milner to humble artisans in Belfast, whose identities would never be known. Nonetheless it had been a shattering experience for Britain. Never since the days of the Regency had the cracks in unity opened so wide. Many wild words had been uttered, often in exalted places, and a Labour MP had gone so far as to warn the Tories 'in ringing tones [. . .] that if they wanted civil war they could have it'.

In all this, Bobs had played a prominent and honourable part, for he had never stooped to ambiguity. From first to last his stand had been crystal-clear, his pronouncements blunt and unequivocal. He stood for the sanctity of the Imperial connection and for loyalty to those who had themselves shown loyalty to

* Later CIGS during the middle years of the First World War.
† Author's Italics.

the throne. By his speeches, his committee work, and his assistance to the military leaders of the Ulster cause, he risked not merely his pension but his decorations, rank and title— everything in fact that soldiers are supposed to hold dear. As President of the Covenanters (they included Kipling, Dicey, Milner, and Amery), he was throwing down a gage that not even as old a campaigner as Lloyd George dared pick up. It was his tragedy and that of Britain that, after 28 June, it hardly seemed to matter any more, for on that date the Arch-Duke Ferdinand was assassinated at Sarajevo.

CHAPTER XV

The Last Cannonade

THE build-up in national rivalries which had convulsed Europe for more than a decade and which reached its tragic climax in mid-1914 has no part in the story of Frederick Sleigh Roberts' life. Yet, in retrospect it proved his wisdom as surely as it showed his rivals' lack of sagacity, for almost every development he had prophesied, occurred. The cavalry, on which certain senior officers had built such extravagant hopes, proved useless in every theatre except Palestine. The Germans, whom Lloyd George and other Liberals had claimed as increasingly friendly, were immediately discovered to be the painstaking and inveterate foes that Bobs had predicted them to be. The small, mobile, highly trained professional force that Britain had formed was rapidly swamped by the war of the masses which Bobs had foreseen, and the conscript armies for which he had vainly called were desperately improvised and thrown, half-trained, into the battle, long after the best of the nation's youth had died in the equally ill-trained volunteer divisions of the early years.

In most other ways, his foresight was proved time and again, though never acknowledged, for had his blunt attitudes been adopted with diplomatic variations, Germany would have been left in no doubt of where Britain stood, and the conflict might have been averted. In tactics and in the wider field of strategy the lead which Bobs had given was also disregarded, with fearful effects upon Britain's future, for he was, above all, the exponent of the flank attack, whilst those who led the nation into this most terrible of wars chose instead, perhaps in an excess of cavalry 'spirit', the unimaginative and costly manœuvre of frontal assault. As Churchill was to write in after years, 'No war is so sanguinary as the war of exhaustion. No plan could be more unpromising than the plan of frontal attack. Yet on these two brutal expedients the military authorities of France and Britain consumed, during three successive years, the flower of their national manhood.'[24] Such appalling slaughter was unnecessary, for as the same author remarked, 'There were regions where flanks could have been turned; there were devices by which fronts could have been pierced. And these could have been discovered [. . .] not by any departure from the principles of military art, but simply by the true comprehension of those principles [. . .]'[24]

Few who have studied Bobs' career and the tactical development of his campaigns could doubt that his own recipe for success would have been very different to those of French, Haig or Robertson. It is impossible to imagine the commander who flinched at unnecessary slaughter before Paardeburg leading his men into the holocausts of the Somme and Third Ypres, for economy of British lives was the unvarying keynote of his campaigns. Allenby was the British Commander who came nearest to him in strategic and tactical concept during the First World War, and the reason is not far to seek, for Allenby never forgot the lessons of Bobs' South African campaign. As Wavell, in a now famous telegram, advised the British Prime Minister after the Italian attack on British Somaliland, 'Heavy butcher's bill not necessarily indication of good tactics.' The similarity of viewpoint is no mere chance, for if Allenby was admiring of Bobs' tactics, Wavell was Allenby's disciple.

Bobs was destined to play no vital part in this greatest and most dismal of wars though, Suvarov-like, he was one of the first to offer his services, when well over eighty. No one could have been more cast down than he when Kitchener courteously but firmly refused him an active appointment, for despite his years the sword still rang true in its scabbard, and his mental acumen was unimpaired. To Bobs, schooled in half a century of battle, it seemed unthinkable that the great struggle which he had so long foreseen was upon his country—and he was too old. Sadly, the little field-marshal watched the regiments march out to war and, more sadly still, the news of casualties flow in. Though he worked hard and willingly at schemes for military welfare, his heart lay in the front line, and it was with delight that on

11 November, 1914, he sailed for France to visit the Indian Division.

It was a historic and appealing spectacle, with the old field-marshal, still straight as a die, again visiting the army of his youth—an army soon, like him, to pass away. *Sowars* and sepoys, tall and dignified in their *puggarees*, stood strangely out of place against the tragic background of the Western Front, and not many miles away the guns were contending fiercely. Once, many years before, Roberts had written of that Anglo-Indian contingent, long vanished into the shadows of the past, which he had overtaken, after the most spectacular victory of his career, marching triumphantly through the Bolan Pass, with its pipes playing *Auld Lang Syne*. Now, for the very last time in this world, he saw and spoke to the sons and grandsons, perhaps even the great-grandsons of the men he had served and led across half a century of hardship and glory. Historic regiments and names were there, British and Indian alike, sealed now in the melancholy fastnesses of a dead Imperial decade, but then still resurgent with the pride of a great tradition.

It was a time of memories for Bobs, but he had lost none of his magnetism for those who lived in the present. The old touch had not deserted him, and the soldiers surrendered at once to the little white-haired man, so plainly delighted to be with the army once more, as he toured from unit to unit. Among Indian troops in particular reaction was immediate and emotional for, traditionalists to a man, they had heard the great tales of Bobs, and along the regimental lines his name was legend yet. Theirs was an army in which, above all else, the ties of family tradition were strong, and they were of the blood that had marched to Kandahar. Those were three sublime days in France before, as Kipling wrote:

> He passed to the very sound of the guns;
> But before his eyes grew dim,
> He had seen the faces of the sons
> Whose sire had served with him.[25]

From Nicholson and Delhi, the road swept on through fields of glory, with never a murky recess. Abyssinia [. . .] Lushai [. . .] Kurram [. . .] his minor campaigns were no less part of him than his great victories. Already the figures of the past were stretching out their arms to embrace him—Donald Stewart, Hills-Johnes, Harry Tombs, and above all Freddy, his own son, killed at Colenso. Lesser ghosts watched too from the wings, unimportant in terms of history, yet milestones in his life—Vonolel, the old grey stallion, and the little greyhound bitch which had followed him so faithfully in Mutiny days. There was not long to wait. On the evening of 13 November, 1914, he developed a chill; on the 14th pneumonia set in, and by half-past eight in the evening, he was dead.

There was now one last business to be attended to, and on 17 November the journey back to England began under grey skies, with the Rajput Prince, Sir Pertab Singh, defying his caste to act as escort for the body, and French cavalry trumpets to speed their passage. The loss to his friends was immediate and profound, and throughout the Empire old soldiers still survived to remember and to grieve. Amongst the new generation rising up, there was less remembrance and less time, for they were fighting as few had before, and Armageddon could not halt for a little old soldier riding home. Lord Rawlinson in his diary could write of him as 'the greatest and most lovable man I have ever known', and Lansdowne, the former Viceroy, was equally laudatory, but it was left to Kipling to add the final touch.

> Three hundred mile of cannon spoke
> When the Master-Gunner died.

In that valediction he set a seal upon Roberts' character in verses as clear-cut and dignified as the man himself had been.

> Clean, simple, valiant, well-beloved,
> Flawless in faith and fame,
> Whom neither ease nor honours moved
> An hair's breadth from his aim.

There was, too, no more than the truth in his ending:

> And glory is the least of things
> That follow this man home.[26]

The manner of Roberts' passing was everything he could have wished and vested as it was with a gentle, if military, dignity was intensely symbolic of the man himself.

As a public figure, Bobs stands in a class alone for, in terms of integrity, personal character and purity of purpose, there has probably never been a personality on the British national stage to compare with him. However one searches his private or public life, it is impossible to fault his sincerity or to point to mean or ungenerous actions. Ambition was there, but it was controlled and strictly honourable in its expression. His military abilities were likewise of the great tradition, for as a regimental officer he was fatherly to his men and, in battle, swift and fearless to an extraordinary degree. As a field commander, he had a flair for instant decision and, like all great soldiers, an eye for ground and an instinct for tactical manœuvre. A military innovator ahead of his time, he was brave in opinion and unafraid of the press, and to him must go the credit for the amazing improvement in British marksmanship between 1900 and 1915 which so disconcerted the Germans. It was perhaps his tragedy that, with these great gifts, he was never destined to cross swords with an enemy equal in all other respects to himself. The Afghans, who always greatly outnumbered his men, were deplorable soldiers, whilst the Boers, who were good, lacked weight and numbers. Nevertheless, his brilliant qualities are discernible in even the slightest study of his campaigns.

In ability he stood far above the supreme commanders of 1914–18, although he was fortunate in always having a war of movement in which to display his gifts. He would certainly have been more at home in the Western Desert than upon the Somme, but this is probably true of most generals who were not experts in siege. Between Wellington and Napoleon on the one hand, and a handful of British and German commanders in the 1939–45 war, few names rise supreme, and Roberts' is among that number.

Despite his inspiration in the field, it is still as a man that Bobs most deserves to be remembered, and it was as a man, still more than as a successful commander, that his troops loved him. Care for his soldiers and chivalry to a beaten foe who had observed the rules were traits inalienable from his character, though when the need arose he could be as remorseless as he judged the situation to require. In the magnetism of leadership he was certainly supreme, as in his inimitable personality, for he never lost his unerring sense of modesty and good taste, and to his dying day adults and children of all ages loved him.

Perhaps his magic also lay in the fact that in brain and spirit he never grew old, and the simple virtues of honesty, patriotism and courage were his guiding principles.

Among the giants of the world's past, his is a puny wraith, for he toppled no dynasties in pursuit of ambition, and wrought no Brumaire for personal gain. Roberts would certainly have had it no other way for, almost alone of the world's great military machines, the British Army has remained virtually unsullied by the scramble for political power. In the perpetuation of such a tradition, Bobs and the other great Victorian commanders have played an honourable part. Theirs was a perilous profession, as old General Abercrombie remarked, for the risks —political as well as physical—were great and the rewards, save for the fortunate few, only modest. But it was an honourable and an interesting life, not least to Roberts since, like all the great military officers, in an age of Empire his theatre was the world.

Delhi [. . .] Abyssinia [. . .] Lushai [. . .] Pretoria [. . .] and the arid veld—the names are endless. But it was upon the Frontier that he made his name, at Kurram and among the gaunt mountains which run north-west from tribal territory to the Hindu Kush. For it is with the Frontier and with Afghanistan that the legend of Bobs is inextricably entwined, and it is upon those far frontiers that his claim to immortality must rest. There is a romance in it all which will never come again, least of all to the grey industrial people of the Britain that he loved. But in years to come, among those who care for the telling of a tale, among those who care for honour, courage, and glory, the name 'Kandahar' will always evoke the trumpets of the past with the phantom of Kipling's General riding by.

REFERENCES TO WORKS QUOTED

The quotations from the poems of Rudyard Kipling are reprinted by kind permission of Mrs George Bambridge, Methuen and Co Ltd, and the Macmillan Company of Canada.

1 'Bobs', Rudyard Kipling.
2 *Journal of the Siege of Lucknow*, Maria Germon.
3 'Route Marchin'', Rudyard Kipling.
4 'Route Marchin'', Rudyard Kipling.
5 'The Young British Soldier', Rudyard Kipling.
6 'Back to the Army Again', Rudyard Kipling.
7 *Bengal Lancer*, F. Yeats-Brown.
8 'Screw Guns', Rudyard Kipling.
9 'Screw Guns', Rudyard Kipling.
10 'Ford o' Kabul River', Rudyard Kipling.
11 'That Day', Rudyard Kipling.
12 'Mandalay', Rudyard Kipling.
13 'Bobs', Rudyard Kipling.
14 *Wavell, Portrait of a Soldier*, Bernard Fergusson.
15 'Bobs', Rudyard Kipling.
16 *English Saga*, Arthur Bryant.
17 'Shillin' a Day', Rudyard Kipling.
18 The song *Goodbye, Dolly Gray*.
19 *The Last of the Gentlemen's Wars*, Major-General J. F. C. Fuller.
20 *Goodbye, Dolly Gray*, Rayne Kruger.
21 'The Lesson', Rudyard Kipling.
22 'The Islanders', Rudyard Kipling.
23 *L.G.*, Basil Murray.
24 *The World Crisis*, Winston S. Churchill.
25 'Lord Roberts', Rudyard Kipling.
26 'Lord Roberts', Rudyard Kipling.

BIBLIOGRAPHY

Among the many works referred to are the following:

A Guardsman's Memories, Major-General Lord Gleichen.

A History of Europe, H. A. L. Fisher, Ed. Arnold (1941).

A History of South Africa, C. W. Kiewiet, Oxford (1941).

A History of Southern Africa, Eric A. Walker, Longmans (1957).

A History of the English-Speaking Peoples, Winston S. Churchill, Cassell.

A History of the Regiments and Uniforms of The British Army, Major R. M. Barnes, Seeley Service and Co. (1954).

A Short History of British Colonial Policy, H. E. Egerton, Methuen (1897).

Allenby, Brian Gardner, Cassell (1965).

August 1914, Barbara Tuchman, Constable (1962).

Battles of the Indian Mutiny, Michael Edwardes, Batsford (1963).

Bayonets to Lhasa, Peter Fleming, Rupert Hart-Davis (1961).

Bengal Lancer, Francis Yeats-Brown, Gollancz (1930).

Brass Hat, Basil Collier, Secker & Warburg (1961).

Bugles and a Tiger, John Masters, Michael Joseph (1956).

Cambridge History of The British Empire, Cambridge University Press.

Clive of India, R. J. Minney, Hutchinson (1931).

Commando, Deneys Reitz, Faber and Faber (1929).

Dictionary of National Biography.

Disraeli, André Maurois, The Bodley Head (1927).

Douglas Haig, the Educated Soldier, John Terraine, Hutchinson (1963).

Eminent Victorians, Lytton Strachey (1918).

England 1870–1914, R. K. Ensor, Oxford (1936).

England Since Waterloo, Sir J. A. R. Marriott, Methuen (1913).

English Saga, Arthur Bryant, Collins.

Forty-One Years In India, F.-M. Lord Roberts, Macmillan and Co. (1897).

Francis Younghusband, George Seaver, John Murray (1952).

Gladstone, Philip Magnus, John Murray (1954).

Goodbye Dolly Gray, Rayne Kruger, Cassell (1959).

Haig, Duff Cooper, Faber and Faber (1935).

Haldane of Cloany, Dudley Sommer, George Allen & Unwin (1960).

Havelock, Leonard Cooper, The Bodley Head (1957).

Ian Hamilton's March, Winston S. Churchill (1920).

Jan Christian Smuts, J. C. Smuts, Cassell (1952).

King Edward VII, Sir Sidney Lee, Macmillan (1925).

Kitchener, Philip Magnus, John Murray (1958).

Lady Lytton's Court Diary, Mary Luytens, Rupert Hart-Davis (1961).

L. G., Basil Murray, Sampson Low Marston & Co. Ltd. (1932).

Letters of Queen Victoria (1861–1901), Ed. G. Buckle (1926–32).

Life of Disraeli, vol. vi, G. E. Buckle and W. F. Monypenny.

Life of Kitchener, Sir George Arthur, Macmillan (1920).

Life of Lord Rawlinson, by F. Maurice, Cassell (1928).

Lloyd George's Expedients (part 2), John Terraine, History Today (May, 1963).

Lord Roberts, David James, Hollis and Carter (1954).

Mandalay The Golden, E. C. V. Fougar, Dennis Dobson (1963).

Memoirs of the Mogul Court, Niccolao Manucci, Folio Society.

Memory Hold-The-Door, John Buchan, Hodder & Stoughton (1940).

Men and Power 1917–1918, Lord Beaverbrook, Hutchinson (1956).

My Early Life, Winston S. Churchill, Thornton Butterworth (1930).

Paul Kruger, Manfred Nathan, The Knox Publishing Co., Durban (1941).

Proconsul in Politics, A. M. Gollin, Anthony Blond Ltd. (1964).

Queen Victoria, Lytton Strachey, Chatto and Windus (1921).

Rudyard Kipling—His Life and Work, Charles Carrington, Macmillan (1955).

Rudyard Kipling's Verse—The Definitive Edition, Hodder and Stoughton (1940).

Soldier True, Victor Bonham Carter, Frederick Muller Ltd. (1963).

The Age of Elegance, Arthur Bryant, Collins (1950).

The Age of Improvement, Asa Briggs, Longmans (1959).

The Boer War, Edgar Holt, Putnam (1958).

The Brain of An Army, Spenser Wilkinson, Constable and Co.

The Curragh Incident, Sir James Ferguson, Faber & Faber (1964).

The Duke, Philip Guedalla, Hodder & Stoughton (1931).

The Fall of Kruger's Republic, J. S. Marais, Oxford (1961).

The Fifth Army, General Sir Hubert Gough, Hodder & Stoughton (1931).

The First World War, Cyril Falls, Longmans (1960).

The Last of the Gentlemen's Wars, Major-General J. F. C. Fuller, Faber & Faber (1936).

The Letters of Lord and Lady Wolseley, Ed. by Sir Geo. Arthur, Heinemann (1922).

The Letters of Private Wheeler, Ed. by B. H. Liddell-Hart, Michael Joseph (1951).

The Life of Lord Curzon, the Earl of Ronaldshay, Ernest Benn (1928).

The Making of Burma, Dorothy Woodman, Cresset Press (1962).

The Memoirs of the Aga Khan, The Aga Khan, Cassell (1954).

The Men Who Ruled India, The Founders, Philip Woodruff, Cape (1953 and 1954).

The Men Who Ruled India, The Guardians, Philip Woodruff, Cape (1953 and 1954).

The Mystery of Lord Kitchener's Death, Donal McCormick (1959).

The New Cambridge Modern History, Cambridge University Press.

The Queen and Mr. Gladstone, Philip Guedalla (1933).

The Reason Why, Cecil Woodham-Smith (1953).

The Science of War, Col. G. F. R. Henderson, Longmans Green (1905).

The Siege of Lucknow, Maria Germon, Constable and Co.

The Sound of Fury, Richard Collier, Collins.

The Story of a Soldier's Life, Field-Marshal Viscount Wolseley, Constable (1903).

The Story of the Victoria Cross, Brig. Sir John Smythe, Muller (1963).

The Subaltern, G. R. Gleig, J. M. Dent and Sons (1845).

The White Nile, Alan Moorhead, Hamish Hamilton (1960).

The World Crisis, Winston S. Churchill, Thornton & Butterworth (1931).

The Yellow Scarf, Sir Francis Tuker.

War And The Arme Blanche, Erskine Childers (1910).

War Memoirs, David Lloyd George, Nicholson and Watson (1934).

Wavell—Portrait of a Soldier, Bernard Fergusson, Collins (1961).

Wellington's Officers, Douglas Bell, Collins (1938).

Who's Who, Published by Adam and Charles Black.

Who Was Who, Published by Adam and Charles Black.

Wingate of the Sudan, Ronald Wingate, John Murray (1952).

INDEX

Numbers in italic figures refer to the *page* on which a map will be found.

28–30; accepted into Horse Artillery, 30–1; becomes Deputy Assistant Quartermaster General 32; appointed staff officer, 40; in action in Indian Mutiny, 40–1, 42; to Delhi with mobile column, 46–7; receives first serious wound, 47–8; at storming of Delhi, 52–7; goes to Cawnpore, 59–62; at siege of Lucknow, 66–75; in battle at approach to Cawnpore, 76–8; in assault of Khudaganj, 78–9; awarded Victoria Cross, 79; at Lucknow when reconquered, 82–5; hands over as DAQMG to Wolseley, 85; on leave in Ireland 1858–9, 87–8; marries Nora Bews, 88; sails for India 1859, 88–9; organizes Viceroy's triumphal march, 89–93, 95–7; promoted to captain and brevet-major, 94; takes part in Umbeyla Expedition 97–105; suffers ill-health, 85, 106, 170, 174, 176; on leave in England 1865, 106–7; returns to India 1866, 107; takes part in Abyssinian Expedition, 110–12; gazetted brevet lieutenant-colonel, 112; in action in Lushai Hills, 117–18; appointed Deputy Quartermaster-General, 119; appointed Quartermaster-General, 119; appointed Chief Commissioner, 123; appointed commander of Punjab Frontier Force, 123; commands Kurram Field Force, 125–40; created KCB, 140, 142; commands Kabul Field Force, 143–64; at Kabul, 150–64; commands Kabul-Kandahar Field Force, 167–75; on leave in England 1880, 176–8; Commander-in-Chief of Madras Army, 178–182; appointed Commander-in-Chief, India, 184; Chairman of Defence and Mobilization Committeees, 190; meets Rudyard Kipling, 191; receives peerage, 194; leaves India and retires to England, 195; replaces Wolseley in Irish Command, 198–201; in South African War, 201, 207–24;

Queen Victoria confers earldom and the Garter upon, 221; appointed Commander-in-Chief, 225–32; retires, 232; attacks state of Britain's military preparedness before World War I, 235–6; resists proposed union of Northern and Southern Ireland, 237–42; visits Western Front, 244–6; death of, 246

Roberts, Freddie, 119, 211, 246
Roberts, Nora, 88, 89, 93–4, 96, 97, 105, 107–8, 113, 114, 117, 119, 177, 178, 179, 187, 188, 189, 193, 195, 211, 217
Robertson, Sir William, 241, 244
Rorke's Drift, 19, 176
Rose, Sir Hugh, 95, 96, 97, 98, 100, 105, 110
Ross, Major-General, 172
Ross, Tyrrell, 79
'Route Marchin' ' (Kipling), 97
Russian activity on North-West Frontier, 121, 122, 124, 125, 126, 182, 183, 186, 192

Salisbury, Marquess of, 204, 210, 211, 225
Sapari, 135
Sarajevo, 242
Sati-Choura Ghat, 65
Savha Khan, 64
Scarlet Flamingoes, 50, 58
Schleswig-Holstein, 178
'Screw Guns' (Kipling), 124, 135
Sealey, John, 189
Second World War, see World War, Second
Seeley, John, 239
Senafé, 111
Shah Najaf Mosque, 71–2
Sher Ali, 121, 122, 123, 125, 127, 137, 163, 165
Sherpur, 126, 153, 158–9
'Shillin' a Day' (Kipling), 197
Showers, Brigadier, 47
Shutargardan Pass, 126, 140, 144–5, 147, 152
Sialkot, 41, 97
Sikandarbagh, 69
Sikhs, 59, 65, 70, 82, 99, 101, 128, 132, 153, 157, 172, 175